The Houghton Mifflin Guide to Reading Textbooks

The Houghton Mifflin Guide to Reading Textbooks

Houghton Mifflin Company   Boston   New York

Senior Sponsoring Editor: Mary Jo Southern
Development Editor: Ann Marie Radaskiewicz
Associate Editor: Kellie Cardone
Editorial Associate: Danielle Richardson
Manufacturing Manager: Florence Cadran

Acknowledgments

Alan Sherman et al., *Basic Concepts of Chemistry,* Sixth Edition. Copyright © 1996 by Houghton Mifflin Company. Reprinted by permission.

Robert Kreitner, *Management,* Eighth Edition. Copyright © 2001 by Houghton Mifflin Company. Reprinted with permission.

Douglas Bernstein et al., *Psychology,* Fifth Edition. Copyright © 2000 by Houghton Mifflin Company. Reprinted with permission.

Mary Ann Witt et al., *The Humanities, Volume II,* Fifth Edition. Copyright © 1997 by Houghton Mifflin Company. Reprinted with permission.

Study Guide to accompany Mary Ann Witt et al., *The Humanities, Volume II,* Fifth Edition. Copyright © 1997 by Houghton Mifflin Company. Reprinted with permission.

Mary Beth Norton et al., *A People and a Nation,* Fifth Edition. Copyright © 1998 by Houghton Mifflin Company. Reprinted with permission.

Printed in the U.S.A.

ISBN: 0-618-131159

123456789-EB-05 04 03 02 01

Contents

Introduction

Now that you're attending college, you'll be reading many textbooks. In most of your classes, you'll be tested on how well you understand and remember the information in those books. So, it's important to learn how to read them effectively.

Textbook Characteristics

Textbooks are different than other types of publications. First, their main purpose is always to inform or to explain. Other types of publications—such as magazine articles or novels—seek to entertain readers, while still other types—such as editorials and essays—aim to persuade readers to change beliefs or behaviors. The informative purpose of textbooks affects their length and their scope; textbooks are usually longer and cover topics in more detail than other publications do. They are also based on research and scientific evidence rather than on opinions or speculation. As a result, their tone and style is serious, scholarly, and sophisticated. All of these characteristics can make reading them more difficult.

The Importance of Attitude

You may not enjoy reading, and you may not be looking forward to the challenge of reading textbooks. So, the first step in becoming a more effective reader is to create a positive attitude. Your attitude includes your feelings about reading, about *what* you read, and about your own abilities. If these feelings are negative, your reading experiences will be negative. If these feelings are positive, your experiences will be more enjoyable.

If you are determined to dislike reading, it will always be a tedious chore for you. Instead, think of reading as a valuable tool for acquiring new knowledge and ideas. Also, think of reading as an important component of your own academic success. This more positive attitude will make the reading process easier and more pleasant.

Try to resist the urge to pronounce a particular subject "boring" or "irrelevant." If you tell yourself a book is dull and worthless, reading it will always be a struggle for you. Instead, cultivate an attitude of intellectual curiosity. Tell yourself you're interested in learning all you can about the world around you, and expect to find valuable information in everything you read. Try to apply the information to your other courses, to your career, and to your personal life.

Finally, improve your attitude by thinking more positively about your own abilities. If you expect to fail, then you probably will. If you believe you can improve, you'll be able to strengthen your reading skills. Many of these skills require a confident, "can-do" attitude. For example, good concentration and memory both begin with the reader's conscious decision to pay attention and to remember. A positive attitude will provide the foundation for learning to read more effectively.

The Purpose, Organization, and Features of This Text

The purpose of this text is to help you strengthen your textbook reading skills by giving you practice with actual chapters from various academic disciplines. The book is divided into five parts, one for each of five different textbook chapters. Following each chapter are two sections of instruction and exercises designed to help you better understand and remember what you read. The first section, "Textbook Features," explains and shows you how to use important features that appear in textbooks. The second section, "Tips and Techniques," explains proven methods for improving your reading skills. Both of these sections include activities that offer opportunities to practice your new skills before you actually use them in your courses.

Upon completing the activities in this book, you will better understand the characteristics and features of textbooks, and you will have learned a wide range of strategies you can use to get more out of what you read. I wish you success on your journey toward better reading skills.

PART 1

"Matter and Energy, Atoms and Molecules" from *Basic Concepts of Chemistry*

MATTER AND ENERGY, ATOMS AND MOLECULES

We all learn the scientific method when we take a chemistry course, yet few of us think that we'll ever have to use it in our personal lives. This is the story of Joan Penn, who used the training and knowledge she received in a chemistry course to help her 11-year-old son Mike over a serious illness.

Our story begins on a Sunday afternoon in late September. Mike returned home from playing soccer complaining that he had a headache. By morning he felt better, so Mike went off to school. When he came home, he was coughing and running a low-grade fever. Two days later his mother took him to the doctor who diagnosed a viral infection. The doctor recommended that Mike rest until the virus passed.

After two days, his conditioned worsened. He was coughing and running a high fever. In addition, a rash appeared on his arms. A strep test proved positive and Mike was placed on an antibiotic. After two days on the medication, his condition continued to worsen, and he was now coughing severely and having bronchial spasms.

Joan was quite concerned. After all, the antibiotic Mike was on should have certainly wiped out any strep infection, yet Mike was still getting worse. She thought that perhaps her son was actually not suffering from a virus, but rather that he was having an allergic reaction to something environmental—for instance, something in the park, where he played every day. She decided to retrace Mike's schedule over the past two weeks to look for something—anything—that stood out from his regular schedule.

Joan checked Mike's school for any unusual incidents. Nothing. She checked the parks where he had played; she called the township to see if pesticides were being sprayed in the parks. All results proved negative. Joan decided to ask Mike if there was anything he had done over the past two weeks that he usually didn't do. One event stood out as slightly unusual.

49

50   **CHAPTER 3**   *Matter and Energy, Atoms and Molecules*

On the day his initial symptoms appeared, Mike was at a friend's house. He and his friend had decided to build a tree house in the backyard, and they worked several hours cutting branches and putting the tree house together. Upon its completion, his friend's Mom bought them pizza to celebrate their fine work, which the boys gobbled down without having washed up.

Joan decided to find out more about the tree house and discovered that the boys built it using juniper branches. Joan called the county health department to find out if junipers could cause allergic reactions. The health officer stated that sticky sap from the pines *could* cause allergic reactions in humans, and he recited a list of symptoms that were identical to Mike's. The puzzle was solved! Mike was allergic to the juniper sap. When Joan later told her son about her findings, Mike recalled getting the sticky sap on his arms, where his rash had formed. He also said that he may have ingested some of the sap when he ate the pizza, which would explain his breathing problems.

Joan called Mike's doctor and told her about the information she had uncovered. Mike was immediately placed on Ventolin to relieve the bronchial spasms. He was also given a nebulizer to help him breathe more easily. Two weeks later Mike's fever was down, the rash had disappeared, and his breathing had returned to normal. Thanks to some good detective work by his mother, Mike was once again healthy.

■■■ LEARNING GOALS

After you've studied this chapter, you should be able to:
1. Explain what is meant by the scientific method.
2. Explain the Law of Conservation of Mass and Energy.
3. Explain the difference between physical and chemical properties.
4. Describe the difference between homogeneous and heterogeneous matter, between mixtures and compounds, and between compounds and elements.
5. Describe the difference between an atom and a molecule.
6. Explain the Law of Definite Composition (or Definite Proportions).
7. Explain the terms *atomic mass*, *formula mass*, and *molecular mass*.
8. Determine the formula or molecular mass of a compound when you are given the formula for the compound.

▌▌▌ INTRODUCTION

This chapter is really the beginning of your study of chemistry. We start with discussions of the most elementary concepts, those of matter and energy. Then, in this chapter and later chapters, we build on and extend these concepts. As we do this, we shall be discussing the results of centuries of scientific research—the theories and laws of modern chemistry. These theories and laws are sometimes presented to students as though each resulted from a quick flash of insight on the part of some scientist. Actually they are the fruit of years—and sometimes decades or centuries—of hard work by many people.

3.1 The Scientific Method

Chemistry is an experimental science that is concerned with the behavior of matter. Much of the body of chemical knowledge consists of abstract concepts and ideas. Without application, these concepts and ideas would have little impact on society. Chemical principles are applied for the benefit of society through technology. Useful products are developed by the union of basic science and applied technology.

■ LEARNING GOAL 1

The scientific method

Over the past 200 years, science and technology have moved forward at a rapid pace. Ideas and applications of these ideas are developed through carefully planned experimentation, in which researchers adhere to what is called the **scientific method.** The scientific method is composed of a series of logical steps that allow researchers to approach a problem and try to come up with solutions in the most effective way possible. It is generally thought of as having four parts:

1. *Observation and classification.* Scientists begin their research by carefully observing natural phenomena. They carry out experiments, which are observations of natural events in a controlled setting. This allows results to be duplicated and rational conclusions to be reached. The data the scientists collect are analyzed, and the facts that emerge are classified.
2. *Generalization.* Once observations are made and experiments carried out, the researcher seeks regularities or patterns in the results that can lead to a generalization. If this generalization is basic and can be communicated in a concise statement or a mathematical equation, the statement or equation is called a *law*.
3. *Hypothesis.* Researchers try to find reasons and explanations for the generalizations, patterns, and regularities they discover. A hypothesis expresses a tentative explanation of a generalization that has been stated. Further experiments then test the validity of the hypothesis.
4. *Theory.* The new experiments are carried out to test the hypothesis. If they support it without exception, the hypothesis becomes a theory. A

theory is a tested model that explains some basic phenomenon of nature. It cannot be proven to be absolutely correct. As further research is performed to test the theory, it may be modified or a better theory may be developed.

The scientific method represents a systematic means of doing research. There are times when discoveries are made by accident, but most knowledge has been gained via careful, planned experimentation. In your study of chemistry you will examine the knowledge and understanding that researchers using the scientific method have uncovered.

3.2   Matter and Energy

We begin with the two things that describe the entire universe: *matter* and *energy*. **Matter** is *anything that occupies space and has mass*. That includes trees, clothing, water, air, people, minerals, and many other things. Matter shows up in a wide variety of forms.

Energy is the *ability to perform work*. Like matter, energy is found in a number of forms. Heat is one form of energy, and light is another. There are also chemical, electrical, and mechanical forms of energy. And energy can change from one form to another. In fact, matter can also change form or change into energy, and energy can change into matter, but not easily.

3.3   Law of Conservation of Mass and Energy

■ LEARNING GOAL 2
Law of Conservation of Mass and Energy

The **Law of Conservation of Mass** tells us that when a chemical change takes place, no detectable difference in the mass of the substances is observed. In other words, mass is neither created nor destroyed in an ordinary chemical reaction. This law has been tested by extensive experimentation in the laboratory, and the work of the brilliant French chemist-physicist Antoine Lavoisier provides evidence for this conclusion. Lavoisier performed many experiments involving matter. In one instance he heated a measured amount of tin and found that part of it changed to a powder. He also found that the *product* (powder plus tin) weighed *more* than the original piece of tin. To find out more about the added weight, he heated metals in sealed jars, which, of course, contained air. He measured the mass of his starting materials (*reactants*), and when the reaction concluded and the metal no longer changed to powder, he measured the mass of the products. In every such reaction, the mass of the reactants (oxygen from the air in the jar plus the original metal) equaled the mass of the products (the remaining metal plus the powder). Today we know that the reaction actually stopped when all of

3.3   Law of Conservation of Mass and Energy   **53**

■ **FIGURE 3.1**

An experiment like Lavoisier's. An experimenter puts a test tube containing a lead nitrate solution into a flask containing a potassium chromate solution. The experimenter weighs the flask and contents, then turns the flask upside down to mix the two solutions. A chemical reaction takes place, producing a yellow solid. The experimenter weighs the flask and contents again and finds no change in mass.

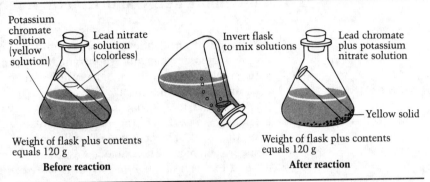

the oxygen in the sealed jar combined with the metal to form the powder. Lavoisier concluded that when a chemical change occurs, *matter is neither created nor destroyed, it just changes from one form to another* (Figure 3.1), which is a statement of the Law of Conservation of Mass.

Whenever a chemical change occurs, it is accompanied by an energy transformation. In the 1840s, more than half a century after Lavoisier, three scientists—the Englishman James Joule and the Germans Julius von Mayer and Hermann von Helmholtz—performed a number of experiments in which energy transformations were studied. They provided experimental evidence that led to the discovery of the **Law of Conservation of Energy.** The law tells us that *in any chemical or physical change, energy is neither created nor destroyed, it is simply converted from one form to another.*

An auto engine provides a good example of how one form of energy is converted to a different form. *Electrical* energy from the battery generates a spark that contains *heat* energy. The heat ignites the gasoline–air mixture, which explodes, transforming chemical energy into heat and *mechanical* energy. The mechanical energy causes the pistons to rise and fall, rotating the engine crankshaft and moving the car.

At the same time, in the same engine, matter is changing from one form to another. When the gasoline explodes and burns, it combines with oxygen in the cylinders to form carbon dioxide and water vapor. (Unfortunately, carbon monoxide and other dangerous gases may also be formed. This is one of the major causes of air pollution, as you will see in Chapter 18.)

To appreciate the significance of these facts, think of the universe as a giant chemical reactor or system. At any given time there are certain amounts of matter and energy present, and the matter has a certain mass. Matter is always changing from one form to another, and so is energy. Besides that, matter is changing to energy and energy to matter. But *the sum of all the matter (or mass) and energy in the universe always remains the same.* This repeated observation is called the **Law of Conservation of Mass and Energy.**

54 CHAPTER 3 *Matter and Energy, Atoms and Molecules*

3.4 Potential Energy and Kinetic Energy

Which do you think has more energy, a metal cylinder held 1 foot above the ground or an identical cylinder held 5 feet above the ground? If you dropped them on your foot, you would know immediately that the cylinder with more energy was the one that was 5 feet above the ground. But where does this energy come from?

Work had to be done to raise the two cylinders to their respective heights—to draw them up against the pull of gravity. And energy was needed to do that work. The energy used to lift each cylinder was "stored" in each cylinder. The higher the cylinder was lifted, the more energy was stored in it—due to its position. *Energy that is stored in an object by virtue of its position* is called **potential energy.**

If we drop the cylinders, they fall toward the ground. As they do so, they lose potential energy because they lose height. But now they are moving; their potential energy is converted to "energy of motion." The more potential energy they lose, the more energy of motion they acquire. *The energy that an object possesses by virtue of its motion* is called **kinetic energy.** The conversion of potential energy to kinetic energy is a very common phenomenon. It is observed in a wide variety of processes, from downhill skiing to the generation of hydroelectric power.

3.5 The States of Matter

Matter may exist in any of the three physical states: solid, liquid, and gas.

A **solid** has a definite shape and volume that it tends to maintain under normal conditions. The particles composing a solid stick rigidly to one another. Solids most commonly occur in the **crystalline** form, which means they have a fixed, regularly repeating, symmetrical internal structure. Diamonds, salt, and quartz are examples of crystalline solids. A few solids, such as glass and paraffin, do not have a well-defined crystalline structure, although they do have a definite shape and volume. Such solids are called **amorphous solids,** which means they have no definite internal structure or form.

A **liquid** has a definite volume but does not have its own shape since it takes the shape of the container in which it is placed. Its particles cohere firmly, but not rigidly, so the particles of a liquid have a great deal of mobility while maintaining close contact with one another.

A **gas** has no fixed shape or volume and eventually spreads out to fill its container. As the gas particles move about they collide with the walls of their container causing *pressure,* which is a force exerted over an area. Gas particles move independently of one another. Compared with those of a liquid or solid, gas particles are quite far apart. Unlike solids and liquids, which cannot be compressed very much at all, gases can be both compressed and expanded.

Often referred to as the fourth state of matter, **plasma** is *a form of matter composed of electrically charged atomic particles*. Many objects found in the earth's outer atmosphere, as well as many celestial bodies found in space (such as the sun and stars), consist of plasma. A plasma can be created by heating a gas to extremely high temperatures or by passing a current through it. A plasma responds to a magnetic field and conducts electricity well.

3.6   Physical and Chemical Properties

> **LEARNING GOAL 3**
> **Physical and chemical properties**

Matter—whether it is solid, liquid, or gas—possesses two kinds of properties: physical and chemical. These unique properties separate one substance from another and ensure that no two substances are alike in every way. The **physical properties** are those that can be observed or measured without changing the chemical composition of the substance. These properties include state, color, odor, taste, hardness, boiling point, and melting point. A **physical change** is one that alters at least one of the physical properties of the substance without changing its chemical composition. Some examples of physical change are (1) altering the physical state of matter, such as what occurs when an ice cube is melted; (2) dissolving or mixing substances together, such as what happens when we make coffee or hot cocoa; and (3) altering the size or shape of matter, such as what happens when we grind or chop something.

Chemical properties stem from the ability of a substance to react or change to a new substance that has different properties. This often occurs in the presence of another substance. For example, iron reacts with oxygen to produce iron(III) oxide (rust). This is an example of a **chemical change.** The chemical properties can be observed or measured when a substance undergoes chemical change. The rusting of iron is an example of a chemical property of iron. When we pass an electric current through water, it decomposes to form hydrogen gas and oxygen gas. This reaction is an example of a chemical property of water.

Sometimes it is difficult to differentiate a chemical change from a physical change. In fact, physical changes almost always accompany chemical changes. Some of the signs of physical change that tell us that a chemical change has occurred include the presence of a large amount of heat or light, the presence of a flame, the formation of gas bubbles, a change in color or odor, or the formation of a solid material that settles out of a solution.

3.7   Mixtures and Pure Substances

Since matter consists of all the material things that compose the universe, many distinctly different types of matter are known. Matter that has a definite and *fixed composition* is called a **pure substance,** which is a substance that

56 CHAPTER 3 *Matter and Energy, Atoms and Molecules*

cannot be separated into any other form of matter by physical change. Some of the pure substances that you are familiar with are helium, oxygen, table salt, water, gold, and silver. Two or more pure substances can be combined to form a **mixture,** whose *composition can be varied.* The substances in a mixture can be separated by physical means; we can separate the substances without chemical change.

Matter can also be classified as heterogeneous or homogeneous (Figure 3.2). **Homogeneous matter** has the same parts with the same properties throughout, and **heterogeneous matter** is made up of different parts with different properties. A combination of salt and pepper is an example of heterogeneous matter, whereas a teaspoonful of sugar is an example of homogeneous matter. Another example of homogeneous matter is a teaspoonful of salt dissolved in a glass of water. We call this a **homogeneous mixture** because it is a uniform blend of two or more substances, and its proportion can be varied. In a homogeneous mixture every part is exactly like every other part. The salt can be separated from the water by physical means. Seawater and air are also examples of homogeneous mixtures.

We know that there are two types of homogeneous matter: pure substances and homogeneous mixtures. According to this classification scheme, matter can be broken down even further. Let's look at both homogeneous mixtures and heterogeneous mixtures. In a **heterogeneous mixture** different parts have different properties. A salt-sand mixture is heterogeneous because it is composed of two substances, *each of which retains its own unique properties.* It does not have the same composition or properties throughout, and its composition can be varied. A salt-sand mixture can be separated by physical means. If the mixture is placed in water, the salt will dissolve. The sand can be filtered out, and the salt can be recovered by heating the saltwater until the water evaporates (Figure 3.3).

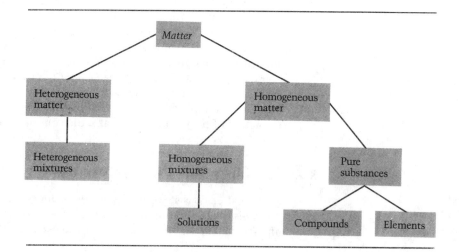

■ FIGURE 3.2

Classification of matter

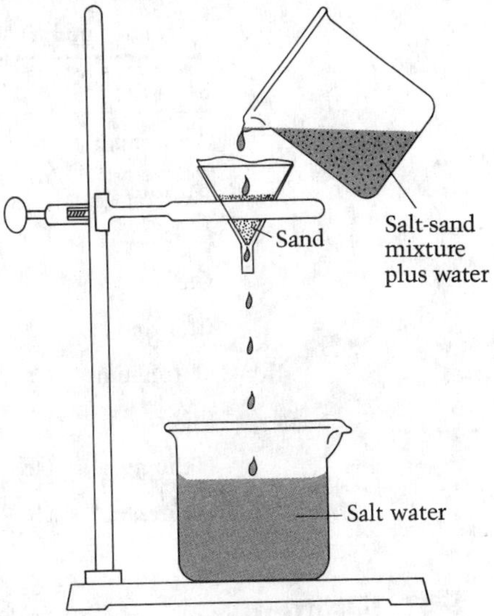

■ FIGURE 3.3

Separating sand from saltwater

We call any part of a system with uniform composition and properties a **phase**. A **system** is the body of matter being studied. A heterogeneous mixture is composed of two or more phases separated by physical boundaries. Additional examples of heterogeneous mixtures are oil and water (two liquids) and a tossed salad (several solids). It is important to note that although a pure substance is always homogeneous in composition, it may actually exist in more than one phase in a heterogeneous system. Think of a glass of ice water. This is a two-phase system composed of water in the solid phase and water in the liquid phase. In each phase the water is homogeneous in composition, but since two phases are present, the system is heterogeneous.

3.8   Solutions

Solutions are homogeneous mixtures. That is, they are uniform in composition. Every part of a solution is exactly like every other part. The salt-and-water mixture described in Section 3.7 is a solution. Even if we add more water to the solution, it will still be homogeneous, because the salt particles will continue to be distributed evenly throughout the solution. We would get the same result if we added more salt to the solution. However, we couldn't do this indefinitely. Homogeneity would end when the solution reached *saturation* (the point at which no more salt could dissolve in the limited amount of water). We will discuss this further in Chapter 15.

TABLE 3.1

Names and Symbols of Some Common Elements

ELEMENT	SYMBOL	ELEMENT	SYMBOL
Aluminum	Al	Iodine	I
Bromine	Br	Magnesium	Mg
Calcium	Ca	Nickel	Ni
Carbon	C	Nitrogen	N
Chlorine	Cl	Oxygen	O
Chromium	Cr	Phosphorus	P
Fluorine	F	Silicon	Si
Helium	He	Sulfur	S
Hydrogen	H	Zinc	Zn

3.9 Elements

An **element** is *a pure substance that cannot be broken down into simpler substances, with different properties, by physical or chemical means.* The elements are the basic building blocks of all matter. There are now 109 known elements.* Each has its own unique set of physical and chemical properties. (The elements are tabulated on the inside front cover of this book, along with their *chemical symbols*—a shorthand notation for their names. Some common elements are listed in Table 3.1.) The elements can be classified into three types: **metals, nonmetals,** and **metalloids.**

Examples of metallic elements are sodium (which has the symbol Na), calcium (Ca), iron (Fe), cobalt (Co), and silver (Ag). These elements are all classified as metals because they have certain properties in common. They have luster (in other words, they are shiny), they conduct electricity well, they conduct heat well, and they are malleable (can be pounded into sheets) and ductile (can be drawn into wires).

Some examples of nonmetals are chlorine, which has the symbol Cl (note that the second letter of this symbol is a lower-case "el" and not the numeral *one*), oxygen (O), carbon (C), and sulfur (S). These elements are classified as nonmetals because they have certain properties in common. They don't shine, they don't conduct electricity well, they don't conduct heat well, and they are neither malleable nor ductile.

The metalloids have some properties like those of metals and other properties like those of nonmetals. Some examples are arsenic (As), germanium (Ge), and silicon (Si). These particular metalloids are used in manufacturing transistors and other semiconductor devices (Table 3.1).

*In early 1995 a team of German and Russian scientists reported the synthesis of elements 110 and 111.

3.10   Atoms

Suppose we had a chunk of some element, say gold, and were able to divide it again and again, into smaller and smaller chunks. Eventually we could get a particle that could not be divided any further without losing its identity. This particle would be an atom of gold. An **atom** is *the smallest particle of an element that enters into chemical reactions.*

The atom is the ultimate particle that makes up the elements. Gold is composed of gold atoms, iron of iron atoms, and neon of neon atoms. These atoms are so small that billions of them are needed to make a speck large enough to be seen with a microscope. In 1970, Albert Crewe and his staff at the University of Chicago's Enrico Fermi Institute took the first black-and-white pictures of single atoms, using a special type of electron microscope. In late 1978, Crewe and his staff took the first time-lapse moving pictures of individual uranium atoms.

3.11   Compounds

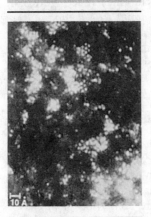

Uranium single atoms and microcrystals obtained from a solution of uranyl acetate (Courtesy Albert V. Crewe)

A **compound** is *a pure substance that is made up of two or more elements chemically combined in a definite proportion by mass.* Unlike mixtures, compounds have a definite composition. Water, for instance, is made up of hydrogen and oxygen in the ratio of 11.1% hydrogen to 88.9% oxygen by mass. No matter what the source of the water, it is always composed of hydrogen and oxygen in this ratio. This idea, that *every compound is composed of elements in a certain fixed proportion,* is called the **Law of Definite Composition** (or the Law of Definite Proportions). It was first proposed by the French chemist Joseph Proust in about 1800.

The properties of a compound need not be similar to the properties of the elements that compose it. For example, water is a liquid, whereas hydrogen and oxygen are both gases. When two or more elements form a compound, they truly form a new substance.

Compounds can be broken apart into elements only by chemical means—unlike mixtures, which can be separated by physical means. More than thirteen million compounds have been reported to date, and millions more may be discovered. Some compounds we are all familiar with are sodium chloride (table salt), which is composed of the elements sodium and chlorine, and sucrose (cane sugar), which is composed of the elements carbon, hydrogen, and oxygen.

3.12   Molecules

We have discussed what happens when a chunk of an element is continually divided: We eventually get down to a single atom. What happens when we

60   CHAPTER 3   *Matter and Energy, Atoms and Molecules*

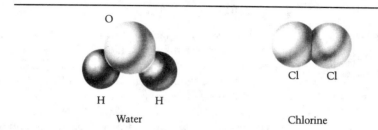

■ **FIGURE 3.4**

Molecules of water and chlorine

keep dividing a chunk of a compound? Suppose we do so with the compound sugar. As we continue to divide a sugar grain, we eventually reach a small particle that can't be divided any further without losing the physical and chemical properties of sugar. This ultimate particle of a compound, *the smallest particle that retains the properties of the compound,* is called a **molecule.** Like atoms, molecules are extremely small, but with the aid of an electron microscope we can observe some of the very large and more complex molecules. Molecules are uncharged particles. That is, they carry neither a positive nor a negative electrical charge.

Molecules, as you might have guessed, are made up of two or more atoms. They may be composed of different kinds of atoms (for instance, water contains hydrogen and oxygen) or the same kind of atoms (for instance, a molecule of chlorine gas contains two atoms of chlorine). (See Figure 3.4.) *The Law of Definite Composition states that the atoms in a compound are combined in definite proportions by mass.* We can see in Figure 3.4 that they are also combined in definite proportions by number. For example, water molecules always contain two hydrogen atoms for every oxygen atom.

3.13   Molecular Versus Ionic Compounds

As we just learned, a molecule is the smallest *uncharged* part of a compound formed by the chemical combination of two or more atoms. Such compounds are known as *molecular compounds,* and we usually say that such compounds are composed of molecules. Water is a molecular compound composed of water molecules. Many molecular compounds are composed of atoms of nonmetallic elements that are chemically combined.

However, there are many compounds composed of oppositely charged *ions.* An ion is *a positively or negatively charged atom or group of atoms.* Compounds composed of ions are known as *ionic compounds.* These compounds are held together by attractive forces between the positive and negative ions that compose the compound. Ordinary table salt, sodium chloride, is such a compound. For these compounds, it is more proper to talk about a **formula unit** of the compound, rather than a molecule, as being *the smallest part of an ionic compound that retains the properties of the compound.* Ionic compounds are composed of metallic and nonmetallic elements. (We'll have much more to say about ions and ionic compounds when we discuss chemical bonding in Chapter 7.)

3.14   Symbols and Formulas of Elements and Compounds

We have already mentioned the chemical symbols—the shorthand for the names of the elements. In some cases, as in the symbol O (capital "oh") for oxygen, the chemical symbol is the first letter of the element's name, capitalized. Often, though, the symbol for an element contains two letters. In these cases only the first letter is capitalized; the second letter is never capitalized. For instance, the symbol for neon is Ne and the symbol for cobalt is Co. (Be careful of this: CO does not represent cobalt, but a combination of the elements carbon and oxygen, which is a compound.) Some symbols come from the Latin names of the elements: iron is Fe, from the Latin *ferrum,* and lead is Pb, from the Latin *plumbum.* (See Table 3.2.)

Because compounds are composed of elements, we can use the chemical symbols as a shorthand for compounds too. We use the symbols to write the **chemical formula,** which shows the elements that compose the compound. For example, sodium chloride (table salt), an ionic compound, contains one atom of sodium (Na) and one atom of chlorine (Cl). The formula unit for sodium chloride is NaCl. Water, a molecular compound, is another example. The water molecule contains two atoms of hydrogen (H) and one atom of oxygen, so we write it as H_2O. The number 2 in the formula indicates that there are two atoms of hydrogen in the molecule; note that it is written as a *subscript.* A molecule of ethyl alcohol contains two atoms of carbon, six

TABLE 3.2

Elements with Symbols Derived from Latin Names

ELEMENT	SYMBOL	LATIN NAME
Copper	Cu	Cuprum
Gold	Au	Aurum
Iron	Fe	Ferrum
Lead	Pb	Plumbum
Mercury	Hg	Hydrargentum
Potassium	K	Kalium
Silver	Ag	Argentum
Sodium	Na	Natrium
Tin	Sn	Stannum

62   **CHAPTER 3**   *Matter and Energy, Atoms and Molecules*

of hydrogen, and one of oxygen. It is written as follows:

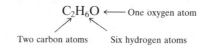

C_2H_6O ←—— One oxygen atom

Two carbon atoms   Six hydrogen atoms

EXAMPLE 3.1

State the number of atoms of each element in a molecule or formula unit of the following compounds: (a) $C_6H_{12}O_6$ (b) $Ca(OH)_2$ (c) $C_3H_6O_2$ (d) $Al_2(SO_4)_3$

Solution

UNDERSTAND THE PROBLEM

We ask, "What does the subscript mean?" Subscripts tell us the number of atoms in a molecule or formula unit of the substance.

DEVISE A PLAN

Our plan will be to look at the subscripts noted in each case. We can then determine the number of atoms of each element in a molecule or formula unit of the compound.

CARRY OUT THE PLAN

(a) There are 6 atoms of C, 12 atoms of H, and 6 atoms of O.
(b) There is 1 atom of Ca, 2 atoms of O, and 2 atoms of H. (In this case, the subscript 2 means multiply everything inside the parentheses by 2.)
(c) There are 3 atoms of C, 6 atoms of H, and 2 atoms of O.
(d) There are 2 atoms of Al, 3 atoms of S, and 12 atoms of O. (In this case, the subscript 3 means multiply everything inside the parentheses by 3.)

LOOK BACK

Recheck to be sure that you have followed the steps correctly.

Practice Exercise 3.1   State the number of atoms of each element in a molecule or formula unit of the following compounds: (a) C_2H_7N (b) $(NH_4)_2SO_4$

3.15 Atomic Mass

LEARNING GOAL 7

Atomic mass, formula mass, and molecular mass

Suppose we want to find the relative masses of the atoms of the various elements. Suppose also that we have a double-pan balance that can weigh a single atom. We begin by assigning an arbitrary mass to one of the elements. Let's say we decide to assign a mass of 1 unit to hydrogen. (This is what chemists did originally, because hydrogen was known to be the lightest element even before the relative atomic masses were determined.)

Then, to find the relative mass of, say, carbon, we place an atom of carbon on one pan. We place hydrogen atoms on the other pan, one by one, until the pans are exactly balanced. We find that it takes 12 hydrogen atoms to balance 1 carbon atom, so we assign a relative atomic mass of 12 to carbon. In the same way for an oxygen atom, we find that it takes 16 hydrogen atoms to balance 1 oxygen atom. So we assign a relative mass of 16 to oxygen. By doing this experiment for all the other elements, we can determine all the masses relative to hydrogen (which is assigned mass 1).

Unfortunately this kind of balance has never existed, and more elaborate means had to be developed to find the relative atomic masses of the elements. But the logic we used here is the same as that used by the many scientists who determined the relative masses. (The atomic mass scale has been revised. The present scale is based on a particular type of carbon atom, called carbon-12. This carbon is assigned the value of 12 atomic mass units, amu.) The periodic table (inside the front cover) lists the relative atomic masses of the elements below their symbols. From now on, instead of referring to "relative atomic mass," we will use the simpler term **atomic mass.**

EXAMPLE 3.2

Using the periodic table (inside the front cover), look up the atomic masses of the following elements. (For this exercise, round all atomic masses to one decimal place.)   (a) I   (b) Ba   (c) As   (d) S

Solution

Look up the atomic mass of each element in the periodic table. Remember, the atomic mass is the number below the symbol of the element.

(a) I is 126.9

(b) Ba is 137.3

(c) As is 74.9

(d) S is 32.1

Practice Exercise 3.2   Using the periodic table (inside the front cover), look up the atomic masses of the following elements. (For this exercise, round all atomic masses to one decimal place.)   (a) La   (b) Fe   (c) Ar   (d) Sn

3.16   Formula Mass and Molecular Mass

LEARNING GOAL 8
Formula or molecular mass of a compound from the formula

The **molecular mass** of a compound is *the sum of the atomic masses of all the atoms that make up a molecule of the compound.* The term *molecular mass* is applied to compounds that exist as molecules. For example, the molecule P_2O_5 has two phosphorus atoms and five oxygen atoms. The atomic mass of each P (to one decimal place) is 31.0, and the atomic mass of each O (to one decimal place) is 16.0. Therefore the molecular mass of the

64   CHAPTER 3   *Matter and Energy, Atoms and Molecules*

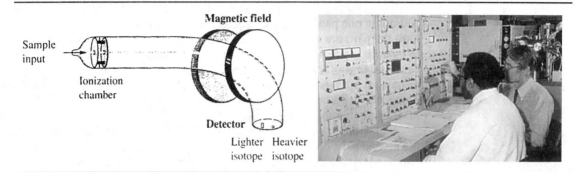

The masses of individual atoms are determined with a mass spectrometer. Electrons are removed from atoms (or molecules), and the resultant ions are accelerated through a magnetic field. The amount of bending in the path of the ions is related to the mass and the charge of the ions. (Photo: Ed Degginger)

compound is

$$(2 \times 31.0) + (5 \times 16.0) = 62.0 + 80.0 = 142.0$$

(Check this calculation and see whether you get the same answer. If not, you may have forgotten that in an equation like this, multiplication and division are done *before* addition and subtraction.)

The **formula mass** of a compound is *the sum of the atomic masses of all the ions that make up a formula unit of the compound.* The term *formula mass* is applied to compounds that are written as formula units and exist mostly as ions (charged atoms or groups of atoms). For example, the formula unit of aluminum oxide is Al_2O_3. This means that a formula unit of aluminum oxide has two aluminum atoms (actually aluminum ions) and three oxygen atoms (actually oxide ions). The atomic mass of aluminum (to one decimal place) is 27.0, and the atomic mass of oxygen (to one decimal place) is 16.0. Therefore the formula mass of Al_2O_3 is

$$(2 \times 27.0) + (3 \times 16.0) = 54.0 + 48.0 = 102.0$$

Now let's try to determine the formula and molecular masses of some additional compounds.

EXAMPLE 3.3

Find the molecular or formula masses (to one decimal place) of the following compounds: (a) H_2O (b) NaCl   (c) $Ca(OH)_2$ (d) $Zn_3(PO_4)_2$
Note: In a chemical formula, parentheses followed by a subscript mean that everything inside the parentheses is multiplied by the subscript. For example, in one formula unit of $Ca(OH)_2$, there is one Ca atom plus two O atoms and two H atoms.

Solution

We must find the atomic mass of each element in the periodic table and then add the masses of all the atoms in each compound.

Summary   **65**

(a) The atomic mass of H is 1.0, and the atomic mass of O is 16.0.

$$\text{Molecular mass of } H_2O = (2 \times 1.0) + (1 \times 16.0)$$

$$= 2.0 + 16.0 = 18.0$$

(b) The atomic mass of Na is 23.0, and the atomic mass of Cl is 35.5.

$$\text{Formula mass of } NaCl = (1 \times 23.0) + (1 \times 35.5)$$

$$= 23.0 + 35.5 = 58.5$$

(c) The atomic mass of Ca is 40.1, the atomic mass of O is 16.0, and the atomic mass of H is 1.0.

$$\text{Formula mass of } Ca(OH)_2 = (1 \times 40.1) + (2 \times 16.0) + (2 \times 1.0)$$

$$= 40.1 + 32.0 + 2.0 = 74.1$$

(d) The atomic mass of Zn is 65.4, the atomic mass of P is 31.0, and the atomic mass of O is 16.0.

$$\text{Formula mass of } Zn_3(PO_4)_2 = (3 \times 65.4) + (2 \times 31.0) + (8 \times 16.0)$$

$$= 196.2 + 62.0 + 128.0 = 386.2$$

Practice Exercise 3.3   Find the molecular or formula masses (to one decimal place) of the following compounds: (a) Na_2CO_3 (b) $CoCl_2$ (c) Cl_2O (d) N_2O_4 ■

SUMMARY

The body of knowledge called science has been developed through the scientific method: observation and classification of data, generalization of observations, and testing of generalizations. Of importance in all the sciences is the idea that the universe is made up of only matter and energy. Matter and energy can be neither created nor destroyed, but they can be changed to other forms. And matter can be transformed into energy, and vice versa. Potential energy is energy that is stored in a body because of its position. Kinetic energy is energy that is due to motion.

Matter may exist in any of three states—solid, liquid, or gas—and may be either heterogeneous (nonuniform) or homogeneous (uniform). Mixtures are combinations of two or more kinds of matter, each retaining its own chemical and physical properties. Mixtures too may be either homogeneous or heterogeneous, and solutions are homogeneous mixtures. Elements are the basic building blocks of matter. The 109 known elements are, in turn, made up of atoms. A compound is a substance that is made up of two or more elements chemically combined in definite proportions by mass. Molecules are the smallest particles that retain the properties of a compound, and atoms are the smallest particles that enter into chemical reactions.

66   **CHAPTER 3**   *Matter and Energy, Atoms and Molecules*

Each element has its own symbol, and every compound has its own chemical formula. Each element has a unique atomic mass. The atomic mass of an element is found in the periodic table. The formula mass or molecular mass of a compound is the sum of the atomic masses in a formula unit or molecule of the compound.

KEY TERMS

amorphous solid **(3.5)**

atom **(3.10)**

atomic mass **(3.15)**

chemical change **(3.6)**

chemical formula **(3.14)**

chemical property **(3.6)**

chemical symbols **(3.9)**

compound **(3.11)**

crystalline **(3.5)**

element **(3.9)**

energy **(3.2)**

formula mass **(3.16)**

formula unit **(3.13)**

gas **(3.5)**

heterogeneous matter **(3.7)**

heterogeneous mixture **(3.7)**

homogeneous matter **(3.7)**

homogeneous mixture **(3.7)**

kinetic energy **(3.4)**

Law of Conservation of
Energy **(3.3)**

Law of Conservation of Mass **(3.3)**

Law of Conservation of Mass and
Energy **(3.3)**

Law of Definite
Composition **(3.11)**

liquid **(3.5)**

matter **(3.2)**

metal **(3.9)**

metalloid **(3.9)**

mixture **(3.7)**

molecular mass **(3.16)**

molecule **(3.12)**

nonmetal **(3.9)**

phase **(3.7)**

physical change **(3.6)**

physical property **(3.6)**

plasma **(3.5)**

potential energy **(3.4)**

pure substance **(3.7)**

scientific method **(3.1)**

solid **(3.5)**

solution **(3.8)**

system **(3.7)**

CHEMICAL FRONTIERS

New Ceramic Material for Automobile Engines of the Future

When people think of ceramic materials, typically they think of dinnerware and pottery. Conventional ceramic materials are brittle, and they crack and break easily. Recently, however, Fumihiro Wakai

Self-Test Exercises **67**

and his coworkers at the Government Industrial Research Institute in Nagoya, Japan, announced that they had developed a new type of stretchable ceramic. This new ceramic was made from the compounds silicon nitride, silicon carbide, zirconium oxide, and yttrium oxide.

The scientists prepared strips of these materials and heated them to a temperature of 1,600°C. During the heating step, the strips were pulled in opposite directions. The strips stretched like taffy to more than 2.5 times their original length. Wakai and his colleagues think that this behavior is due to the formation of liquid regions within the crystalline structure of the ceramic.

This new ceramic material has the potential to revolutionize the design of automobile engines. Automobile manufacturers would like to make certain engine parts out of ceramics rather than metals, since ceramics can handle heat stress better than metals. In addition, ceramic engines could be run at higher temperatures than metal engines, which means better fuel efficiency—an important consideration for automobiles of the future. The properties of conventional ceramics do not allow them to be molded into shapes precise enough for engine parts, but this new ceramic material can be molded into shapes with little or no machining. Perhaps your next new car will have a ceramic engine.

SELF-TEST EXERCISES

LEARNING GOAL 1: *The Scientific Method*

1. (a) Explain the difference between a theory and a hypothesis.
(b) Explain the difference between a theory and a scientific law.
2. Suppose that you are a researcher and you believe that you have found a vaccine that can prevent AIDS. How would you use the scientific method to determine whether the vaccine is effective?

LEARNING GOAL 2: *Law of Conservation of Mass and Energy*

◄ 3. According to the Law of Conservation of Energy, in any chemical or physical change, energy is neither created nor destroyed. Then why are we always worried about running out of energy in the future?
4. What is the significance of the Law of Conservation of Mass and Energy in terms of your study of chemistry?

LEARNING GOALS 3 & 4: *Physical and Chemical Changes/Types of Matter*

5. Match each word on the left with its definition on the right.
(a) Homogeneous — 1. The basic building block of matter
(b) Heterogeneous — 2. The word used to describe matter that is uniform throughout
(c) Mixture — 3. A type of matter in which each part retains its own properties
(d) Compound — 4. A chemical combination of two or more elements
(e) Element — 5. The word used to describe matter that is not uniform throughout
◄ 6. (a) Distinguish among an element, a compound, and a mixture.
(b) What type of matter is uniform throughout?
(c) What type of matter is not uniform throughout?

68   CHAPTER 3   *Matter and Energy, Atoms and Molecules*

◀ 7. State whether each of the following processes involves physical or chemical changes: (a) Shredding paper (b) Burning paper (c) Cooking an egg (d) Mixing egg whites with egg yolk (e) Digesting food (f) Toasting bread

8. Determine whether each of the following processes involves chemical or physical processes:
   (a) Ice melts.
   (b) Sugar dissolves in water.
   (c) Milk sours.
   (d) Eggs become rotten.
   (e) Water boils.
   (f) An egg is hard-cooked.

LEARNING GOAL 5: *Difference Between Atom and Molecule*

9. Describe the difference between an atom and a molecule.

◀ 10. (a) What is the smallest particle of matter that can enter into a chemical combination?
   (b) What is the smallest uncharged individual unit of a compound that is composed of two or more atoms?

11. Classify each of the following elements as metal, metalloid, or nonmetal: (a) Ba (b) Si (c) O (d) Hg (e) Ge (f) In (g) U

12. Classify each of the following elements as metal, metalloid, or nonmetal: (a) Mn (b) Nd (c) Al (d) At (e) Pt (f) Cl (g) Ra

13. Explain the difference between Co and CO.
14. Explain the difference between Si and SI.

LEARNING GOAL 6: *Law of Definite Composition*

◀ 15. How does the following information obtained from several experiments confirm the Law of Definite Composition?
   Experiment 1: $\overline{100}$ g of water are decomposed by electrolysis into its elements: 88.9 g of oxygen gas and 11.1 g of hydrogen gas are obtained.
   Experiment 2: 25.0 g of water are decomposed by electrolysis into its elements: 22.2 g of oxygen gas and 2.8 g of hydrogen are obtained.
   Experiment 3: $\overline{500}$ g of water are decomposed by electrolysis into its elements: 444.5 g of oxygen gas and 55.5 g of hydrogen are obtained.

16. Give an example of the Law of Definite Composition (Proportions).

17. State the number of atoms of each element in a molecule or formula unit of the following compounds: (a) $C_{12}H_{22}O_{11}$ (b) K_2CrO_4 (c) $H_8N_2O_3S_2$ (d) $Zn(NO_3)_2$

◀ 18. State the number of atoms of each element in a molecule or formula unit of the following compounds: (a) H_2SeO_4 (b) $C_{21}H_{27}FO_6$ (c) $(NH_4)_3PO_4$ (d) $Fe_3(AsO_4)_2$

LEARNING GOAL 7: *Atomic Mass, Formula Mass, and Molecular Mass*

19. Using examples, explain the difference among atomic mass, formula mass, and molecular mass.

20. State which term—atomic mass, formula mass, or molecular mass—is best suited to describe each of the following substances. (a) $C_6H_{12}O_6$ (b) NaCl (c) Fe (d) CO_2 (e) H_2O (f) Al_2O_3 (g) Ca (h) $Ca(OH)_2$

◀ *21. If in the periodic table oxygen were assigned an atomic mass of 1, what would be the atomic mass of sulfur?

*22. If in the periodic table neon were assigned an atomic mass of 1, what would be the atomic mass of bromine?

23. Using the periodic table (inside front cover), look up the atomic masses of the following elements. (For this exercise, round all atomic masses to one decimal place.) (a) Rb (b) Cr (c) U (d) Se (e) As

24. Using the periodic table (inside front cover), look up the atomic masses of the following elements. (For this exercise, round all atomic masses to one decimal place.) (a) S (b) N (c) Li (d) Cs (e) Au

LEARNING GOAL 8: *Formula or Molecular Mass of a Compound from the Formula*

◀ 25. Determine the molecular or formula mass of each of the following compounds. (For this exercise, round all atomic masses to one decimal place.) (a) FeO (b) Fe_2O_3 (c) CuI_2 (d) Na_3PO_4 (e) $Mg(OH)_2$ (f) $NiBr_2$ (g) $Hg_3(PO_4)_2$ (h) $(NH_4)_2CO_3$

26. Determine the molecular or formula mass of each of the following compounds. (For this exercise, round all atomic masses to one decimal place.) (a) H_2O (b) H_2SO_4 (c) NaCl (d) $Ca_3(PO_4)_2$ (e) P_2O_5 (f) $SrSO_4$ (g) C_2H_6O (h) SO_2

27. Determine the molecular or formula mass of each of the following compounds. (For this exercise, round all atomic masses to one decimal place.) (a) SiO_2 (b) H_2SO_3 (c) $Sr(OH)_2$ (d) RbF (e) $Cu(NO_3)_2$ (f) $CoBr_2$ (g) $(NH_4)_3PO_4$ (h) $HC_2H_3O_2$

◄ 28. Determine the molecular or formula mass of each of the following compounds. (For this exercise, round all atomic masses to one decimal place.) (a) $LiOH$ (b) Na_2CO_3 (c) $CoCl_2$ (d) $NaBr$ (e) SO_3 (f) C_2H_6 (g) OF_2 (h) $(NH_4)_2SO_3$

EXTRA EXERCISES

29. State what each of the symbols and subscripts mean in the chemical formulas for (a) H_2O (b) $C_6H_{12}O_6$ (c) $Ca(OH)_2$ (d) H_2

◄ 30. Make a list of heterogeneous mixtures and homogeneous mixtures that you encounter in everyday life. Do the same for elements and compounds.

31. Write the names and symbols for the fourteen elements that have a one-letter symbol.

32. Write the names and symbols of all the metalloids.

◄ 33. How many metals are there in the periodic table? How many nonmetals? How many metalloids?

34. Write the names of the eleven elements whose symbols are not derived from their English names.

35. Name the elements present in each of the following compounds: (a) $MgCl_2$ (b) N_2O (c) $(NH_4)_2SO_4$ (d) H_3PO_4

36. Write the chemical formula of each of the following, given the number of atoms in a molecule or formula unit of the compound: (a) one nitrogen atom, two oxygen atoms (nitrogen dioxide) (b) two sodium atoms, one sulfur atom (sodium sulfide) (c) three potassium atoms, one arsenic atom, four oxygen atoms (potassium arsenate) (d) two phosphorus atoms, five oxygen atoms (diphosphorus pentoxide)

37. Classify each of the following as an element, a compound, or a mixture:
    (a) gold
    (b) air
    (c) carbon dioxide
    (d) wine
    (e) table salt

38. State whether each of the following involves a physical or chemical change:
    (a) toasting bread
    (b) water freezing
    (c) tearing paper
    (d) burning wood

39. Determine the molecular or formula mass of each of the following compounds. (For this exercise, round all atomic masses to one decimal place.) (a) OsO_4 (b) HNO_3 (c) $Fe(OH)_2$ (d) $Ba_3(PO_4)_2$

40. Explain the difference between Hf and HF.

Textbook Features

Learning Goals

Some textbooks will include lists of **learning goals,** statements about what you should know or be able to do after reading a chapter. These learning goals help you focus on the important concepts in each chapter.

The learning goals may appear at the beginning of a chapter. Or, they might be inserted into the margins throughout the chapter. For example, this chapter from the chemistry textbook labels paragraphs where you can find information related to each goal.

Use learning goals to check your understanding of what you read. Try to perform the action stated in each goal, either by talking aloud or by writing it down. For example, the first learning goal in the chapter about matter and energy is: *Explain what is meant by the scientific method.* You might respond with this answer:

> The scientific method is a series of four logical steps researchers follow to find solutions to problems. The first step involves observing a natural phenomenon, collecting data, and analyzing that data. In the second step, scientists look for patterns in the data and form generalizations. In the third step, they form a *hypothesis,* a tentative explanation of the generalizations. The fourth step involves testing the hypothesis through further experimentation so they can create a *theory,* a tested model that explains the natural phenomenon.

Always go back and reread the sections of the chapter that correspond to learning goals you have not yet mastered.

EXERCISE 1

Practice using the remaining seven learning goals in the "Matter and Energy" chapter. After reading, write down your answer for each of these learning goals identified at the beginning of the chapter. (You might need to use a separate sheet of paper for all of your answers.)

Key Terms

Textbooks often include lists of *key terms,* words you should know after you finish reading. Key terms may also be called *vocabulary* or *key words.* Many texts emphasize these terms with boldface print to make them stand out within the sentences of the chapter.

Use key terms to check your understanding of what you read. Make sure you can define or explain each term. For example, in the chapter about matter and energy, the first key term in the list is *amorphous solid.* You might begin a list of terms and definitions as follows:

> **amorphous solid:** matter with definite shape and volume but no definite internal structure or form (examples: glass and paraffin)

Always go back and reread sections that include the words you do not yet understand.

EXERCISE 2

Practice using key terms by writing a brief definition for the rest of the key terms in the list at the end of the "Matter and Energy" chapter. (You might need to use a separate sheet of paper for your definitions.)

Study Questions and Exercises

Many textbooks will offer you **study questions** or **exercises** to help you focus on important information or concepts in a chapter. Even if your instructor does not assign these questions, use them as a tool to verify your understanding of the reading selection. Complete the exercises, and then ask the instructor for an answer key so that you can check your work.

EXERCISE 3

Practice using this tool by completing the Self-Test Exercises at the end of the "Matter and Energy" chapter. Compare your answers to those in the Answer Key section at the end of this book.

Tips and Techniques

Your Physical Reading Environment

Your reading will be more productive if you do it in the right place at the right time. You'll probably be able to concentrate best in a quiet location with few distractions. Reading in a soft, comfortable chair may make you sleepy, so sit upright in a firm chair.

EXERCISE 4

Describe the place where you read the "Matter and Energy" chapter. Did the physical environment of this place interfere with your concentration as you were reading?

EXERCISE 5

Name two or three locations where you believe you could read most effectively.

The best time to read is the time of day or night when you are most mentally alert. If you're a night owl, read at night. If you're a morning person, try to fit in your reading time at the beginning of your day.

EXERCISE 6

At what time of day are you most mentally alert?

Dealing with Distractions

Finding a completely distraction-free environment is difficult, so you will need to learn to concentrate in spite of the other things that will compete for your attention as you read. You'll encounter external and internal distractions, but you can develop strategies for dealing with both kinds.

External distractions are the sights, sounds, and other sensations that will tempt you away from your reading. These distractions include ringing phones, people talking or walking nearby, the sound of a stereo, or a friend who stops by to chat. Obviously, the best strategy for handling this type of distraction is prevention. Try to choose a location for reading—such as an individual study carrel in your library—where these kinds of distractions are minimal. Notify your friends and family that you'll be unavailable for conversation and socializing. If you must read in places with more activity, try wearing earplugs and/or sitting with your back to the action so you're not tempted to watch the comings and goings of others.

EXERCISE 7

What external distractions most often pull your attention away from your reading? Based on the advice above, what can you do to reduce these distractions?

Internal distractions are often even more challenging for readers. They are the thoughts, worries, plans, daydreams, and other types of mental "noise" inside your own head. They will inhibit you from concentrating on what you are reading and from absorbing the information you need to learn.

You can try to ignore these thoughts, but they will usually continue trying to intrude. So, how do you temporarily silence them so you can devote your full attention to your reading? Instead of fighting them, try focusing completely on these thoughts for a short period of time. For 5 or 10 minutes, allow yourself to sit and think about your job, your finances, your car problems, your boyfriend or girlfriend, the paper you need to write, or whatever is on your mind. Better yet, write these thoughts down. Do a freewriting* exercise to empty your mind onto a piece of paper. If you can't stop thinking about all of the other things you need to do, devote 10 minutes to writing a detailed "To Do" list. Giving all of your attention to distracting thoughts will often clear your mind so you can focus on your reading.

EXERCISE 8

Before beginning your next textbook reading assignment, freewrite or create lists in the space below to clear your mind of distracting thoughts. After reading, evaluate the effectiveness of the technique you used. Were you able to concentrate better?

Time Management

How often should you read? How long should you try to read in one sitting? How many times should you read a chapter? Is it better to read the whole chapter at once or just a section at a time?

There are no right or wrong answers to these questions. The most effective length, amount, and frequency of reading time will differ from student to student and class to class. You will have to experiment to discover what works best for you, and you will probably need to make adjustments for each different course you take.

However, be aware of the following general principles of effective time management:

CHAPTER

14

GROUP DYNAMICS and TEAMWORK

CHAPTER OBJECTIVES

When you finish studying this chapter, you should be able to

1 Define the term *group*.

2 Explain the significance of cohesiveness, roles, norms, and ostracism in regard to the behavior of group members.

3 Identify and briefly describe the six stages of group development.

4 Define organizational politics and summarize relevant research insights.

5 Explain how groupthink can lead to blind conformity.

6 Define and discuss the management of virtual teams.

7 Discuss the criteria and determinants of team effectiveness.

8 Explain why trust is a key ingredient of teamwork and discuss what management can do to build trust.

"IT TAKES TIME, EFFORT, AND CONSIDERABLE RESOURCES TO BUILD AND MAINTAIN UNCONDITIONAL TRUST."

gareth r. jones
& jennifer m. george

428

Lear Team Takes Quality Problems Personally

A chance conversation over lunch launched one of the biggest cost-saving accomplishments at Lear's auto supplier plant . . . [in Strasburg, Virginia].

A nine-member team of workers, the Eliminators, had been looking for ways to reduce the number of parts rejected for poor paint quality.

The plant builds interior parts for General Motors, Ford Motor, Chrysler, and Nissan vehicles. Specifically, the Eliminators sought to improve the performance of the No. 2 paint line, where workers paint about 3.5 million door-pulls a year.

The problem: how to keep water that catches paint-gun overspray from leaving spots on parts.

Too many spots and the part must be repainted or rejected. Lear was repainting more than 35,000 parts a year.

Different paint nozzles, brighter lights, employee training, and other potential solutions helped, but none solved the problem.

To visualize the problem, imagine a worker standing in front of a moving rack of parts that looks similar to the overhead clothes rack found in most dry cleaners. The worker uses a paint gun to blast each part with paint.

Behind the rack is a waterfall. The water catches the overspray from the paint gun, keeping potentially harmful fumes from entering the atmosphere. But after months of research, meetings, and frustration, the team was hitting a dead end. Then one day during a lunch break, team members asked paint technician Rick Edge, who worked on another paint line, whether he had similar problems.

"I said no," Edge says. "I don't have a waterfall."

Edge's paint line, which handles armrests in a building across the street from the No. 2 paint line—uses vacuum air to suck the overspray onto a cardboardlike filter that is burned. Nancy Lloyd, the former continuous improvement coordinator for Lear, says it's common in a high-output, just-in-time production plant for workers not to communicate with others outside their work areas. "That's where the cross-functional team really helped us to bring people from different departments together."

The Eliminators began calling vendors, visiting other paint plants, and analyzing costs, savings, potential benefits, and the environmental impact of eliminating the waterfall.

After a few glitches (initially, the air filters clogged every hour), the team came up with a plan that lowered the plant's scrap rate by 16 percent and defects by 25 percent while improving productivity by 33 percent and saving Lear $112,000 this year.

The successful solution won the team the 1999 RIT/*USA Today* Quality Cup for manufacturing.

"What I thought was unusual, (Lear) allowed the team players to call up suppliers to get price quotes," says Chuck Blevins, a quality cup judge and CEO of his own company.

"And the team players were determined not to waste any of the company's money, like it was their personal company."

Source: Earl Eldridge, "After Spotting Paint Glitch, Lear Workers Eliminate It," *USA Today,* (May 7,1999): 6B. Copyright 1999, USA Today. Reprinted with permission.

A s in daily life itself, relationships rule in modern organizations. The more managers know about building and sustaining good working relationships, the better. A management consultant recently put it this way:

> *At the end of the day, a company's only sustainable competitive advantage is its relation-ships with customers, business partners, and employees. After all, we provide products and services to people, not to companies. A commitment to developing effective relationships strengthens the fabric of the organization in the long run.*[1]

Chapter 14   Group Dynamics and Teamwork   429

At Lear, effective working relationships both within the Eliminators team and between teams created a winning formula for the company, its employees, and its customers. The purpose of this chapter is to build a foundation of understanding in regard to how groups and teams function in today's organizations.

Fundamental Group Dynamics

According to one organization theorist, "All groups may be collections of individuals, but all collections of individuals are not groups."[2] This observation is more than a play on words; mere togetherness does not automatically create a group. Consider, for example, this situation. A half-dozen people who worked for different companies in the same building often shared the same elevator in the morning. As time passed, they introduced themselves and exchanged pleasantries. Eventually, four of the elevator riders discovered that they all lived in the same suburb. Arrangements for a car pool were made, and they began to take turns picking up and delivering one another. A group technically came into existence only when the car pool was formed. To understand why this is so, we must examine the definition of the term *group*.

What Is a Group?

From a sociological perspective, a **group** can be defined as two or more freely interacting individuals who share a common identity and purpose.[3] Careful analysis of this definition reveals four important dimensions (see Figure 14.1). First, a group must be made up of two or more people if it is to be considered a social unit. Second, the individuals must freely interact in some manner. An organization may qualify as a sociological group if it is small and personal enough to permit all its members to interact regularly with each other. Generally, however, larger organizations with bureaucratic tendencies are made up of many overlapping groups. Third, the interacting individuals must share a common identity. Each must recognize himself or herself as a member of the group. Fourth, interacting individuals who have a common identity must also have a common purpose. That is, there must be at least a rough consensus on why the group exists.

1 Define the term
group.

group *two or more freely interacting individuals with a common identity and purpose*

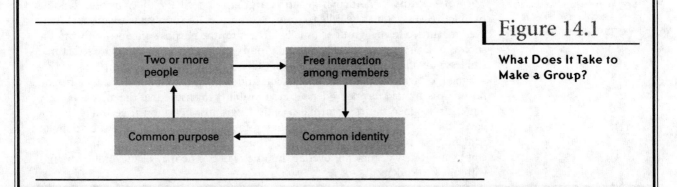

Figure 14.1

What Does It Take to Make a Group?

An Uphill Battle?   14A

Max De Pree, former CEO of Herman Miller, the Michigan office furniture maker:

In our group activities, intimacy is betrayed by such things as politics, short-term measurements, arrogance, superficiality, and an orientation toward self rather than toward the good of the group.

Source: Max De Pree, *Leadership Is an Art* (New York: Dell, 1989), p. 56.

Questions: *Which of the various barriers to effective group action mentioned by De Pree is the most difficult for managers to overcome? Why? Is De Pree being too negative, or just being realistic? Explain.*

For further information about the interactive annotations in this chapter, visit our Web site (**www.hmco.com/college**).

informal group *collection of people seeking friendship*

formal group *collection of people created to do something productive*

Types of Groups

Human beings belong to groups for many different reasons. Some people join a group as an end in itself. For example, an accountant may enjoy the socializing that is part of belonging to a group at a local health club. That same accountant's membership in a work group is a means to a professional end. Both the exercise group and the work group satisfy the sociological definition of a group, but they fulfill very different needs. The former is an informal group, and the latter is a formal group.

Informal Groups.   As Abraham Maslow pointed out, a feeling of belonging is a powerful motivator. People generally have a great need to fit in, to be liked, to be one of the gang. Whether the group meets at work or during leisure time, it is still an **informal group** if the principal reason for belonging is friendship.[4] Informal groups usually evolve spontaneously. They serve to satisfy esteem needs because one develops a better self-image when accepted, recognized, and liked by others. Sometimes, as in the case of a group of friends forming a service club, an informal group may evolve into a formal one.

Managers cannot afford to ignore informal groups because grassroots social networks can either advance or threaten the organization's mission.[5] As experts on the subject explained:

> These informal networks can cut through formal reporting procedures to jump-start stalled initiatives and meet extraordinary deadlines. But informal networks can just as easily sabotage companies' best-laid plans by blocking communication and fomenting opposition to change unless managers know how to identify and direct them. . . .
>
> If the formal organization is the skeleton of a company, the informal is the central nervous system driving the collective thought processes, actions, and reactions of its business units. Designed to facilitate standard modes of production, the formal organization is set up to handle easily anticipated problems. But when unexpected problems arise, the informal organization kicks in. Its complex web of social ties form[s] every time colleagues communicate and solidif[ies] over time into surprisingly stable networks. Highly adaptive, informal networks move diagonally and elliptically, skipping entire functions to get work done.[6]

Formal Groups.   A **formal group** is a group created for the purpose of doing productive work. It may be called a team, a committee, or simply a work group. Whatever its name, a formal group is usually formed for the purpose of contributing to the success of a larger organization. Formal groups tend to be more rationally structured and less fluid than informal groups. Rather than joining formal task groups, people are assigned to them according to their talents and the organization's needs. One person normally is granted formal leadership responsibility to ensure that the members carry out their assigned duties. Informal friendship groups, in contrast, generally do not have officially appointed leaders, although informal leaders often emerge by popular demand.[7] For the individual, the formal group and an informal group at the place of employment may or may not overlap. In other words, one may or may not be friends with one's coworkers.

The line between formal and informal groups can blur when you're working long hours on a project with a looming deadline. Here at a tropical camp in Peru—where the Andes Mountains give way to the Amazon River—botanist Bruce Holst, mammalogist Louise Emmons, and ornithologist Tom Schulenberg document their findings. With the help of their Peruvian colleagues, this team from the Rapid Assessment Program of Conservation International recently spent a month surveying the endangered rain forest.

Attraction to Groups

What attracts a person to one group but not to another? And why do some groups' members stay whereas others leave? Managers who can answer these questions can take steps to motivate others to join and remain members of a formal work group. Individual commitment to either an informal or formal group hinges on two factors. The first is *attractiveness*, the outside-looking-in view.[8] A nonmember will want to join a group that is attractive and will shy away from a group that is unattractive. The second factor is **cohesiveness,** the tendency of group members to follow the group and resist outside influences. This is the inside-looking-out view. In a highly cohesive group, individual members tend to see themselves as "we" rather than "I." Cohesive group members stick together.[9]

Factors that either enhance or destroy group attractiveness and cohesiveness are listed in Table 14.1. It is important to note that each factor is a matter of degree. For example, a group may offer the individual little, moderate, or great opportunity for prestige and status. Similarly, group demands on the individual may range from somewhat disagreeable to highly disagreeable. What all this means is that both the decision to join a group and the decision to continue being a member depend on a net balance of the factors in Table 14.1. Naturally, the resulting balance is colored by one's perception and frame of reference, as it was in the case of Richard Dale, a former manager of distribution at Commodore International, during his first meeting with the company's founder, Jack Tramiel:

> *Dale's first meeting with Tramiel began with a summons to appear at Tramiel's office. Dale flew from his office in Los Angeles to Santa Clara . . . , only to find that Tramiel had decided to visit him instead.*
>
> *Terrified, Dale caught a plane back to find his secretary shaking in her shoes and the burly Tramiel sitting at his desk. For an hour Tramiel grilled Dale on his philosophy of business, pronounced it all wrong, and suggested a tour of the warehouse. When they passed boxes of . . . [computers] waiting for shipment, recalls Dale, Tramiel seemed to "go crazy," pounding the boxes with his fists and yelling, "Do you think this is bourbon? Do you think it gets better with age?"[10]*

2 Explain the significance of cohesiveness, roles, norms, and ostracism in regard to the behavior of group members.

cohesiveness *tendency of group to stick together*

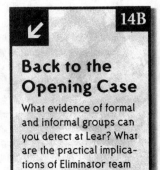

14B

Back to the Opening Case

What evidence of formal and informal groups can you detect at Lear? What are the practical implications of Eliminator team members being friends as well as coworkers?

Table 14.1

Factors That Enhance or Detract from Group Attractiveness and Cohesiveness

Factors that enhance	Factors that detract
1. Prestige and status	1. Unreasonable or disagreeable demands on the individual
2. Cooperative relationship	2. Disagreement over procedures, activities, rules, and the like
3. High degree of interaction	3. Unpleasant experience with the group
4. Relatively small size	4. Competition between the group's demands and preferred outside activities
5. Similarity of members	5. Unfavorable public image of the group
6. Superior public image of the group	6. Competition for membership by other groups
7. A common threat in the environment	

Source: Table adapted from *Group Dynamics: Research and Theory*, 2nd ed., by Dorwin Cartwright and Alvin Zander. New York: HarperCollins Publishers, Inc.

Dale's departure within a few months of this episode is not surprising in view of the fact that Tramiel's conduct destroyed work group attractiveness and cohesiveness.

Roles

role *socially determined way of behaving in a specific position*

According to Shakespeare, "All the world's a stage, and all the men and women merely players." In fact, Shakespeare's analogy between life and play-acting can be carried a step further—to organizations and their component formal work groups. Although employees do not have scripts, they do have formal positions in the organizational hierarchy, and they are expected to adhere to company policies and rules. Furthermore, job descriptions and procedure manuals spell out how jobs are to be done. In short, every employee has one or more organizational roles to play. An organization that is appropriately structured, in which everyone plays his or her role(s) effectively and efficiently, will have a greater chance for organizational success.

A social psychologist has described the concept of *role* as follows:

> The term role is used to refer to (1) a set of expectations concerning what a person in a given position must, must not, or may do, and (2) the actual behavior of the person who occupies the position. A central idea is that any person occupying a position and filling a role behaves similarly to anyone else who could be in that position.[11]

A **role,** then, is a socially determined prescription for behavior in a *specific* position. Roles evolve out of the tendency for social units to perpetuate themselves, and roles are socially enforced. Role models are a powerful influence. They are indispensable to those trying to resolve the inherent conflicts between work and family roles, for example.[12]

↙ **Toward a Sense of Community in the Workplace**   **14C**

Carolyn Schaffer and Kristin Anundsen, authors of the book, *Creating Community Anywhere: Finding Support and Connection in a Fragmented World:*

Community is a dynamic whole that emerges when a group of people:

- *Participate in common practices;*
- *Depend upon one another;*
- *Make decisions together;*
- *Identify themselves as part of something larger than the sum of their individual relationships; and*
- *Commit themselves for the long term to their own, one another's, and the group's well-being.*

Source: Quoted in Ron Zemke, "The Call of Community," *Training,* 33 (March 1996): 27.

Questions: *How important is it to build this sense of community in today's work groups and organizations? Explain. What is your personal experience with a genuine feeling of community? Are we naive to expect a sense of community in today's hurried and rapidly changing workplace? Explain.*

Norms

Norms define "degrees of acceptability and unacceptability."[13] More precisely, **norms** are general standards of conduct that help individuals judge what is right or wrong or good or bad in a given social setting (such as work, home, play, or religious organization). Because norms are culturally derived, they vary from one culture to another. For example, public disagreement and debate, which are normal in Western societies, are often considered rude in Eastern countries such as Japan.

Norms have a broader influence than do roles, which focus on a specific position. Although usually unwritten, norms influence behavior enormously.[14]

Every mature group, whether informal or formal, generates its own pattern of norms that constrains and directs the behavior of its members. Norms are enforced for at least four different reasons:

1. To facilitate survival of the group.
2. To simplify or clarify role expectations.
3. To help group members avoid embarrassing situations (protect self-images).
4. To express key group values and enhance the group's unique identity.[15]

As illustrated in Figure 14.2, norms tend to go above and beyond formal rules and written policies. Compliance is shaped with social reinforcement in the form of attention, recognition, and acceptance.[16] Those who fail to comply with the norm may be criticized or ridiculed. For example, consider the pressure Gwendolyn Kelly experienced in medical school:

> *The word among students is that if you've got any brains, "tertiary" medicine—which involves complex diagnostic procedures and comprehensive care—is where it's at. Instructors often*

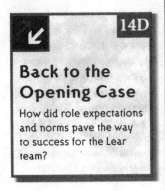

14D

Back to the Opening Case

How did role expectations and norms pave the way to success for the Lear team?

norms *general standards of conduct for various social settings*

Figure 14.2 | Norms Are Enforced for Different Reasons

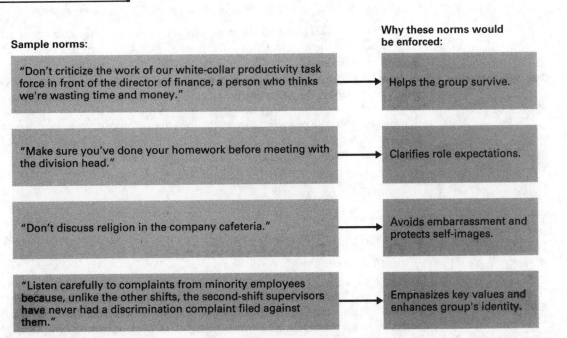

Sample norms:

"Don't criticize the work of our white-collar productivity task force in front of the director of finance, a person who thinks we're wasting time and money."

"Make sure you've done your homework before meeting with the division head."

"Don't discuss religion in the company cafeteria."

"Listen carefully to complaints from minority employees because, unlike the other shifts, the second-shift supervisors have never had a discrimination complaint filed against them."

Why these norms would be enforced:

Helps the group survive.

Clarifies role expectations.

Avoids embarrassment and protects self-images.

Emphasizes key values and enhances group's identity.

Team sports offer many instructive lessons in group dynamics. Pictured here are the Michigan State Spartans on their way to beating the defending national champion, the University of Connecticut Huskies, 85–66 toward the end of the 1999–2000 season. Referees made sure players on both basketball teams followed the rules. For example, UConn was called for charging on this play. But largely unseen by referees and fans are the subtle yet powerful pressures team members put on each other— to enforce norms about being a team player and always giving your best effort. Michigan State ultimately captured the national title.

refer to the best students as "future surgeons" and belittle the family-practice specialty. These attitudes trickle down. I've heard my peers say the reason so many women choose pediatrics is that "they want to be mommies." And students who take a family-practice residency may be maligned by colleagues who say the choice is a sign of subpar academic credentials.[17]

Reformers of the U.S. health care system, who want to increase the number of primary care (family practice) doctors from one-third to one-half, need to begin by altering medical school norms.

ostracism *rejection from a group*

Worse than ridicule is the threat of being ostracized. **Ostracism,** or rejection from the group, is figuratively the capital punishment of group dynamics. Informal groups derive much of their power over individuals through the ever-present threat of ostracism. Thus, informal norms play a pivotal role in on-the-job ethics.[18] Police officers, for example, who honor the traditional "code of silence" norm that demands *total* loyalty to one's fellow officers, face a tough moral dilemma (see Management Ethics).

Group Development

Like inept youngsters who mature into talented adults, groups undergo a maturation process before becoming effective. We have all experienced the uneasiness associated with the first meeting of a new group, be it a class, club, or committee. Initially, there is little mutual understanding, trust, and commitment among the new group

Management Ethics

A Cop-Turned-Professor Takes Aim at the Code of Silence

Several factors enable the code to infect even the most well-intentioned officers. The way a law enforcement organization describes its mission can influence how much misbehavior officers will tolerate from peers. Many police managers and politicians portray officers as a thin line of warriors standing between civilization and the barbarian hordes.

This unrealistic expectation that cops, rather than communities, control crime increases the zeal with which many officers approach their job. When one participates in a crusade, it is easy to rationalize extreme measures.

The patrol environment is also important. We often have unrealistic expectations of patrol officers in high-crime areas, who regularly handle several adrenaline-pumping incidents a shift. Moreover, they often do so while exhausted from overtime assignments, off-duty court appearances, and job-related activities such as attending college. This combination of environmental stressors and fatigue magnifies perceptions of threats, degrades decision-making, and increases the tendency to overreact. . . .

Combining institutionally fostered zealousness with unrealistic physical and emotional expectations is a recipe for misconduct.

Take the case of a normally diligent and professional officer who erupts and strikes that one person too many who screams in his face at the end of an arduous night. Acting out of anger rather than fear for his safety, he has committed a felony. If he is truthful, the career that defines him is over. He could go to prison. If he chooses to lie, he must obtain his partner's complicity. They both know he was wrong, but they also know that any person who repeatedly dealt with the same situation would blow it eventually. Recognizing that the system makes impossible demands and offers impossible choices, they choose to submit a false report and, if necessary, perjure themselves.

The code of silence is reborn each time this decision is made.

Later, when his partner uses excessive force, our officer reciprocates. Eventually, even the most idealistic officers can be infected by the code. As this erodes an officer's moral fiber, self-interest and continued stress make future compromises easier. Since police agencies promote mostly from within, many supervisors and managers are tainted by past misdeeds. This hardly leaves them in a position to control the behavior of subordinates.

The code of silence can undermine even determined attempts at police reform. If we want to control the conduct of our police and strengthen their ability to work with communities to control crime, we need to inhibit the code. How? First, we should debunk the demagoguery of the "thin blue line" myth. Our inner cities need calm professional officers, not exhausted crusaders.

More fundamentally, we must ensure that officers are emotionally and physically fit for duty each time they hit the streets, just as the military must ensure the reliability of those who control nuclear weapons. For decades, the military has accomplished this via personnel reliability programs combining cooperative self-regulation with active monitoring by health-care professionals.

Exhausted or otherwise debilitated cops should be encouraged to excuse themselves from duty. Good cops protect one another. Supervisors and peers need to learn that protection includes convincing unfit officers to stay off the streets. As a final safety check, a trained professional should have the authority to immediately remove unfit officers from duty. Personnel reliability program costs would be offset by fewer lawsuits and accidents.

Steps such as these would neither condone nor excuse police misbehavior. But they would attack the source of the awful silence that allows it to persist.

Source: Excerpted from Bryan Vila, "The Cops' Code of Silence," *The Christian Science Monitor* (August 31, 1992): 18. Reprinted by permission of the author.

members, and their uncertainty over objectives, roles, and leadership doesn't help. The prospect of cooperative action seems unlikely in view of defensive behavior and differences of opinion about who should do what. Someone steps forward to assume a leadership role, and the group is off and running toward eventual maturity (or perhaps premature demise). A working knowledge of the characteristics of a mature group can help managers envision a goal for the group development process.

Characteristics of a Mature Group

If and when a group takes on the following characteristics, it can be called a mature group:

1. Members are aware of their own and each other's assets and liabilities vis-à-vis the group's task.
2. These individual differences are accepted without being labeled as good or bad.
3. The group has developed authority and interpersonal relationships that are recognized and accepted by the members.
4. Group decisions are made through rational discussion. Minority opinions and dissension are recognized and encouraged. Attempts are not made to force decisions or a false unanimity.
5. Conflict is over substantive group issues such as group goals and the effectiveness and efficiency of various means for achieving those goals. Conflict over emotional issues regarding group structure, processes, or interpersonal relationships is at a minimum.
6. Members are aware of the group's processes and their own roles in them.[19]

Effectiveness and productivity should increase as the group matures. Recent research with groups of school teachers found positive evidence in this regard. The researchers concluded: "Faculty groups functioning at higher levels of development have students who perform better on standard achievement measures."[20] This finding could be fruitful for those seeking to reform and improve the American education system.

A hidden but nonetheless significant benefit of group maturity is that individuality is strengthened and not extinguished.[21] Protecting the individual's right to dissent is particularly important in regard to the problem of blind obedience, which we shall consider later in this chapter.

Six Stages of Group Development

3 Identify and briefly describe the six stages of group development.

Experts have identified six distinct stages in the group development process[22] (see Figure 14.3). During stages 1 through 3, attempts are made to overcome the obstacle of uncertainty over power and authority. Once this first obstacle has been surmounted, uncertainty over interpersonal relations becomes the challenge. This second obstacle must be cleared during stages 4 through 6 if the group is to achieve maturity. Each stage confronts the group's leader and contributing members with a unique combination of problems and opportunities.

Stage 1: Orientation.   Attempts are made to "break the ice." Uncertainty about goals, power, and interpersonal relationships is high. Members generally want and accept any leadership at this point. Emergent leaders often misinterpret this "honeymoon period" as a mandate for permanent control.

Stage 2: Conflict and Challenge.   As the emergent leader's philosophy, objectives, and policies become apparent, individuals or subgroups advocating alternative courses of action struggle for control. This second stage may be prolonged while members strive to clarify and reconcile their roles as part of a complete redistribution of power and authority. Many groups never continue past stage 2 because they get bogged down due to emotionalism and political infighting. Committees within the organization often bear the brunt of jokes because their frequent failure to mature beyond stage 2 prevents them from accomplishing their goals. (As one joke goes, a camel is a horse designed by a committee.)

Figure 14.3   Group Development from Formation to Maturity

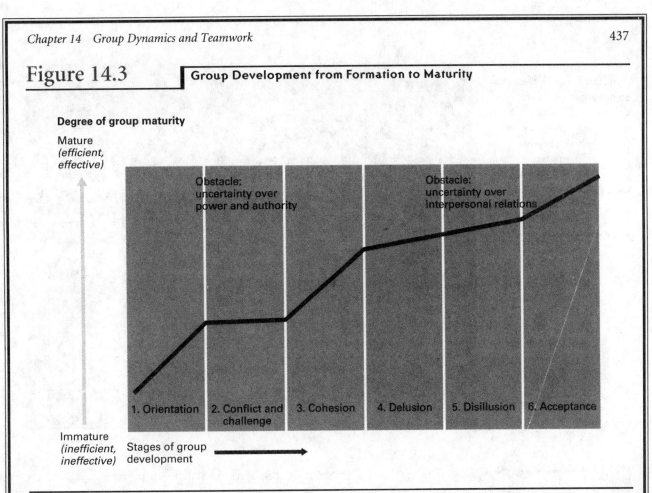

Source: Group Effectiveness in Organizations, by Linda N. Jewell and H. Joseph Reitz, p. 20. Used with permission of the authors.

Stage 3: Cohesion.   The shifts in power started in stage 2 are completed, under a new leader or the original leader, with a new consensus on authority, structure, and procedures. A "we" feeling becomes apparent as everyone becomes truly involved. Any lingering differences over power and authority are resolved quickly. Stage 3 is usually of relatively short duration. If not, the group is likely to stall.

Stage 4: Delusion.   A feeling of "having been through the worst of it" prevails after the rather rapid transition through stage 3. Issues and problems that threaten to break this spell of relief are dismissed or treated lightly. Members seem committed to fostering harmony at all costs. Participation and camaraderie run high as members believe that all the difficult emotional problems have been solved.

Stage 5: Disillusion.   Subgroups tend to form as the delusion of unlimited goodwill wears off, and there is a growing disenchantment with how things are turning out. Those with unrealized expectations challenge the group to perform better and are prepared to reveal their personal strengths and weaknesses if necessary. Others hold back. Tardiness and absenteeism are symptomatic of diminishing cohesiveness and commitment.

Stage 6: Acceptance.   It usually takes a trusted and influential group member who is concerned about the group to step forward and help the group move from conflict to cohesion. This individual, acting as the group catalyst, is usually someone

Developing a work group into an effective and efficient team sometimes can be a life-and-death matter. Following the devastating earthquakes in Turkey in 1999, search-and-rescue teams from around the world joined in a race against the clock. This nine-year-old girl, buried in rubble for 100 hours, was rescued by an Israeli military team.

Back to the Opening Case

Making reasonable assumptions, Lear's nine-member Eliminators team appears to be at which stage of group development? How can you tell?

other than the leader. Members are encouraged to test their self-perceptions against the reality of how others perceive them. Greater personal and mutual understanding helps members adapt to situations without causing problems. Members' expectations are more realistic than ever before. Since the authority structure is generally accepted, subgroups can pursue different matters without threatening group cohesiveness. Consequently, stage 6 groups tend to be highly effective and efficient.

Time-wasting problems and inefficiencies can be minimized if group members are consciously aware of this developmental process. Just as it is impossible for a child to skip being a teenager on the way to adulthood, committees and other work groups will find that there are no short cuts to group maturity. Some emotional stresses and strains are inevitable along the way.[23]

Organizational Politics

4 **Define organizational politics and summarize relevant research insights.**

Only in recent years has the topic of organizational politics (also known as impression management) begun to receive serious attention from management theorists and researchers.[24] But as we all know from practical experience, organizational life is often highly charged with political wheeling and dealing. A corporate executive has underscored this point by asking:

Have you ever done a very satisfactory piece of work only to have it lost in the organizational shuffle? Have you ever come up with a new idea only to have your boss take credit for it? Have you ever faced a situation where someone else made a serious mistake and somehow engineered it so you got the blame?[25]

Workplace surveys reveal that organizational politics can hinder effectiveness and be an irritant to employees. A recent three-year study of 46 companies attempting to establish themselves on the Internet "found that poor communication and political infighting were the No. 1 and No. 2 causes, respectively, for slowing down change."[26] Meanwhile, 44 percent of full-time employees and 60 percent of independent contractors listed "freedom from office politics" as extremely important to their job satisfaction.[27]

Whether politically motivated or not, managers need to be knowledgeable about organizational politics because their careers will be affected by it.[28] New managers, particularly, should be aware of the political situation in their organization. As "new kids on the job" they might be more easily taken advantage of than other more experienced managers.[29] Certain political maneuvers also have significant ethical implications[30] (see Table 14.2).

Table 14.2 — How Do You Feel About "Hard Ball" Organizational Politics?

Circle one number for each item, total your responses, and compare your score with the scale below:

	Unacceptable attitude/conduct			Acceptable attitude/conduct	
1. The boss is always right.	1	2	3	4	5
2. If I were aware that an executive in my company was stealing money, I would use that information against him or her in asking for favors.	1	2	3	4	5
3. I would invite my boss to a party in my home even if I didn't like that person.	1	2	3	4	5
4. Given a choice, take on only those assignments that will make you look good.	1	2	3	4	5
5. I like the idea of keeping a "blunder (error) file" about a company rival for future use.	1	2	3	4	5
6. If you don't know the correct answer to a question asked by your boss, bluff your way out of it.	1	2	3	4	5
7. Why go out of your way to be nice to any employee in the company who can't help you now or in the future?	1	2	3	4	5
8. It is necessary to lie once in a while in business in order to look good.	1	2	3	4	5
9. Past promises should be broken if they stand in the way of one's personal gain.	1	2	3	4	5
10. If someone compliments you for a task that is another's accomplishment, smile and say thank you.	1	2	3	4	5

Scale

10–20 = Straight arrow with solid ethics.
21–39 = Closet politician with elastic ethics.
40–50 = Hard ball politician with no ethics.

Total score = _____

Source: From *Winning Office Politics* by Andrew Dubrin. Copyright © 1990. Reprinted with permission of Prentice-Hall Direct.

What Does Organizational Politics Involve?

organizational politics
the pursuit of self-interest in response to real or imagined opposition

As the term implies, self-interest is central to organizational politics. In fact, **organizational politics** has been defined as "the pursuit of self-interest at work in the face of real or imagined opposition."[31] Political maneuvering is said to encompass all self-serving behavior above and beyond competence, hard work, and luck.[32] Although the term organizational politics has a negative connotation, researchers have identified both positive and negative aspects:

> *Political behaviors widely accepted as legitimate would certainly include exchanging favors, "touching bases," forming coalitions, and seeking sponsors at upper levels. Less legitimate behaviors would include whistle-blowing, revolutionary coalitions, threats, and sabotage.*[33]

Recall our discussion of whistle-blowing in Chapter 5.

Employees resort to political behavior when they are unwilling to trust their career solely to competence, hard work, or luck. One might say that organizational politicians help luck along by relying on political tactics. Whether employees will fall back on political tactics has a lot to do with an organization's climate or culture. A culture that presents employees with unreasonable barriers to individual and group success tends to foster political maneuvering. Consider this situation, for example: "A cadre of Corvette lovers inside General Motors lied, cheated, and stole to keep the legendary sports car from being eliminated during GM's management turmoil and near-bankruptcy in the late 1980s and early 1990s."[34] The redesigned Corvette finally made it to market in 1997, thanks in part to the Corvette team giving high-level GM executives thrilling unauthorized test rides in the hot new model.

Research on Organizational Politics

Researchers in one widely cited study of organizational politics conducted structured interviews with 87 managers employed by 30 electronics firms in southern California. Included in the sample were 30 chief executive officers, 28 middle managers, and 29 supervisors. Significant results included the following:

- The higher the level of management, the greater the perceived amount of political activity.
- The larger the organization, the greater the perceived amount of political activity.
- Personnel in staff positions were viewed as more political than those in line positions.
- People in marketing were the most political; those in production were the least political.
- "Reorganization changes" reportedly prompted more political activity than any other type of change.
- A majority (61 percent) of those interviewed believed organizational politics helps advance one's career.
- Forty-five percent believed that organizational politics distracts from organizational goals.[35]

Regarding the last two findings, it was clear that political activities were seen as helpful to the individual. On the other hand, the interviewed managers were split on the question of the value of politics to the organization. Managers who believed political behavior had a positive impact on the organization cited the following reasons: "gaining visibility for ideas, improving coordination and communication, developing teams and groups, and increasing *esprit de corps*. . . ."[36] As listed above, the most often cited negative effect of politics was its distraction of managers from organizational goals. Misuse of resources and conflict were also mentioned as typical problems.

Political Tactics

As defined earlier, organizational politics takes in a lot of behavioral territory. The following six political tactics are common expressions of politics in the workplace:

- *Posturing.* Those who use this tactic look for situations in which they can make a good impression. "One-upmanship" and taking credit for other people's work are included in this category.
- *Empire building.* Gaining and keeping control over human and material resources is the principal motivation behind this tactic. Those with large budgets usually feel more safely entrenched in their positions and believe they have more influence over peers and superiors.
- *Making the supervisor look good.* Traditionally referred to as "apple polishing," this political strategy is prompted by a desire to favorably influence those who control one's career ascent. Anyone with an oversized ego is an easy target for this tactic.
- *Collecting and using social IOUs.* Reciprocal exchange of political favors can be done in two ways: (1) by helping someone look good or (2) by preventing someone from looking bad by ignoring or covering up a mistake. Those who rely on this tactic feel that all favors are coins of exchange rather than expressions of altruism or unselfishness.

How Political Are You? 14F
Characteristics of Political Behaviors

Characteristics	Naive	Sensible	Sharks
Underlying Attitude	Politics is unpleasant	Politics is necessary	Politics is an opportunity
Intent	Avoid at all costs	Further departmental goals	Self-serving and predatory
Techniques	Tell it like it is	Network; expand connections; use system to give and receive favors	Manipulate; use fraud and deceit when necessary
Favorite Tactics	None—the truth will win out	Negotiate, bargain	Bully; misuse information; cultivate and use "friends" and other contacts

Source: Model from Jeffrey K. Pinto and Om P. Kharbanda, "Lessons for an Accidental Profession." Reprinted with permission from *Business Horizons*, 38 (March–April 1995): 45. Copyright © 1995 by the Board of Trustees at Indiana University, Kelley School of Business.

Questions: *Based on your responses to the quiz in Table 14.2 and your review of the above model, are you politically naive, politically sensible, or a political shark? Thinking of people you know who fit into the different categories, how well are their careers progressing? What are the personal and organizational implications of your political tendencies? What are the ethical implications of your orientation toward organizational politics?*

■ *Creating power and loyalty cliques.* Because there is power in numbers, the idea here is to face superiors and competitors as a cohesive group rather than alone.

■ *Destructive competition.* As a last-ditch effort, some people will resort to character assassination through suggestive remarks, vindictive gossip, or outright lies. This tactic also includes sabotaging the work of a competitor.[37]

Obvious illegalities notwithstanding, one's own values and ethics and organizational sanctions are the final arbiters of whether or not these tactics are acceptable. (See Table 14.3 for a practicing manager's advice on how to win at office politics.)

Antidotes to Political Behavior

Each of the foregoing political tactics varies in degree. The average person will probably acknowledge using at least one of these strategies. But excessive political maneuvering can become a serious threat to productivity when self-interests clearly override the interests of the group or organization. Organizational politics can be kept within reasonable bounds by applying the following five tips:

■ Strive for a climate of openness and trust.
■ Measure performance results rather than personalities.
■ Encourage top management to refrain from exhibiting political behavior that will be imitated by employees.
■ Strive to integrate individual and organizational goals through meaningful work and career planning.[38]
■ Practice job rotation to encourage broader perspectives and understanding of the problems of others.[39]

Table 14.3	
One Manager's Rules for Winning at Office Politics	1. Find out what the boss expects.
	2. Build an information network. Knowledge is power. Identify the people who have power and the extent and direction of it. Title doesn't necessarily reflect actual influence. Find out how the grapevine works. Develop good internal public relations for yourself.
	3. Find a mentor. This is a trusted counselor who can be honest with you and help train and guide you to improve your ability and effectiveness as a manager.
	4. Don't make enemies without a very good reason.
	5. Avoid cliques. Keep circulating in the office.
	6. If you must fight, fight over something that is really worth it. Don't lose ground over minor matters or petty differences.
	7. Gain power through allies. Build ties that bind. Create IOUs, obligations, and loyalties. Do not be afraid to enlist help from above.
	8. Maintain control. Don't misuse your cohorts. Maintain the status and integrity of your allies.
	9. Mobilize your forces when necessary. Don't commit your friends without their approval. Be a gracious winner when you do win.
	10. Never hire a family member or a close friend.

Source: Adapted from David E. Hall, "Winning at Office Politics," *Credit & Financial Management*, 86 (April 1984): 23. Reprinted with permission from *Credit & Financial Management*, copyright April 1984, published by the National Association of Credit Management, 475 Park Avenue South, New York, NY 10016.

Conformity and Groupthink

Conformity means complying with the role expectations and norms perceived by the majority to be appropriate in a particular situation. Conformity enhances predictability, generally thought to be good for rational planning and productive enterprise. How can anything be accomplished if people cannot be counted on to perform their assigned duties? On the other hand, why do so many employees actively participate in or passively condone illegal and unethical organizational practices involving discrimination, environmental degradation, and unfair competition? The answers to these questions lie along a continuum with anarchy at one end and blind conformity at the other. Socially responsible management is anchored to a point somewhere between them.

conformity *complying with prevailing role expectations and norms*

Research on Conformity

Social psychologists have discovered much about human behavior by studying individuals and groups in controlled laboratory settings. One classic laboratory study conducted by Solomon Asch was designed to answer the question, How often will an individual take a stand against a unanimous majority that is obviously wrong?[40] Asch's results were both intriguing and unsettling.

The Hot Seat.   Asch began his study by assembling groups of seven to nine college students, supposedly to work on a perceptual problem. Actually, though, Asch was studying conformity. All but one member of each group were Asch's confederates, and Asch told them exactly how to behave and what to say. The experiment was really concerned with the reactions of the remaining student—called the naive subject—who didn't know what was going on.

All the students in each group were shown cards with lines similar to those in Figure 14.4. They were instructed to match the line on the left with the one on the right that was closest to it in length. The differences in length among the lines on the right were obvious. Each group went through 12 rounds of the matching process, with a different set of lines for every round. The researcher asked one group member at a time to announce to the group his or her choice. Things proceeded normally for the first two rounds as each group member voiced an opinion. Agreement was unanimous. Suddenly, on the third round only one individual, the naive subject, chose the correct pair of lines.

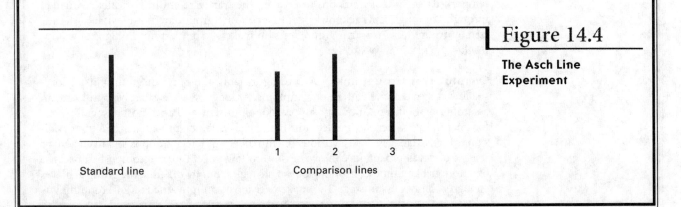

Figure 14.4

The Asch Line Experiment

Standard line   Comparison lines

All the other group members chose a different (and obviously wrong) pair. During the rounds in which there was disagreement, all of Asch's confederates conspired to select an incorrect pair of lines. It was the individual versus the rest of the group.

Following the Immoral Majority.   Each of the naive subjects was faced with a personal dilemma. Should he or she fight the group or give in to the obviously incorrect choice of the overwhelming majority? Among 31 naive subjects who made a total of 217 judgments, two-thirds of the judgments were correct. The other one-third were incorrect; that is, they were consistent with the majority opinion. Individual differences were great, with some subjects yielding to the incorrect majority opinion more readily than others. *Only 20 percent of the naive subjects remained entirely independent in their judgments.* All the rest turned their backs on their own perceptions and went along with the group at least once. In other words, 80 percent of Asch's subjects knuckled under to the pressure of group opinion at least once, even though they knew the majority was dead wrong.

Replications of Asch's study in the Middle East (Kuwait) and in Japan have demonstrated that this tendency toward conformity is not unique to American culture.[41] Indeed, a recent statistical analysis of 133 Asch conformity studies across 17 countries concluded that blind conformity is a greater problem in collectivist ("we") cultures than in individualist ("me") cultures. Japan is strongly collectivist, whereas the United States and Canada are highly individualistic cultures.[42] (You may find it instructive to ponder how you would act in such a situation.)

Because Asch's study was a contrived laboratory experiment, it failed to probe the relationship between cohesiveness and conformity. Asch's naive subjects were outsiders. But more recent research on "groupthink" has shown that a cohesive group of insiders can fall victim to blind conformity.

Groupthink

5 Explain how groupthink can lead to blind conformity.

groupthink *Janis's term for blind conformity in cohesive in-groups*

After studying the records of several successful and unsuccessful American foreign policy decisions, psychologist Irving Janis uncovered an undesirable byproduct of group cohesiveness. He labeled this problem **groupthink** and defined it as a "mode of thinking that people engage in when they are deeply involved in a cohesive in-group, when the members' strivings for unanimity override their motivation to realistically appraise alternative courses of action."[43] Groupthink helps explain how intelligent policymakers, in both government and business, can sometimes make incredibly unwise decisions.

One dramatic result of groupthink in action was the Vietnam War. Strategic advisors in three successive administrations unwittingly rubber-stamped battle plans laced with false assumptions. Critical thinking, reality testing, and moral judgment were temporarily shelved as decisions to escalate the war were enthusiastically railroaded through. Although Janis acknowledges that cohesive groups are not inevitably victimized by groupthink, he warns group decision makers to be alert for the signs of groupthink—the risk is always there.

Symptoms of Groupthink.   According to Janis, the onset of groupthink is foreshadowed by a definite pattern of symptoms. Among these are excessive optimism, an assumption of inherent morality, suppression of dissent, and an almost desperate quest for unanimity.[44] Given such a decision-making climate, the probability of a poor decision is high. Managers face a curious dilemma here. While a group is still in stage 1 or stage 2 of development, its cohesiveness is too low to get much accomplished because of emotional and time-consuming power struggles. But by the time the group achieves enough cohesiveness in stage 3 to make decisions promptly, the risk of groupthink is high. The trick is to achieve needed cohesiveness without going to the extreme of groupthink.

Preventing Groupthink. According to Janis, one of the group members should periodically ask, "Are we allowing ourselves to become victims of groupthink?"[45] More fundamental preventive measures include the following:

- Avoiding the use of groups to rubber-stamp decisions that have already been made by higher management.[46]
- Urging each group member to be a critical evaluator.
- Bringing in outside experts for fresh perspectives.
- Assigning to someone the role of devil's advocate to challenge assumptions and alternatives.[47]
- Taking time to consider possible side effects and consequences of alternative courses of action.[48]

> ### 14G Fighting Groupthink with Diversity
>
> *Because group cohesiveness is directly related to degree of homogeneity, and because groupthink only occurs in highly cohesive groups, the presence of cultural diversity in groups should reduce the probability of groupthink.*
>
> *Source:* Taylor Cox Jr., *Cultural Diversity in Organizations: Theory, Research, and Practice* (San Francisco: Berrett–Koehler, 1993), p. 34.
>
> **Questions:** *Is groupthink likely to be more or less of a problem in a group whose members are both women and men of varying ages from different cultures and with different backgrounds and life experiences? Explain.*

Ideally, decision quality will improve when these steps become second nature in cohesive groups. Dayton Hudson Corp. has structured its board of directors to avoid groupthink and effectively monitor the performance of its chief executive officer. Lots of outside advice keeps the Minneapolis-based owner of Marshall Field's and Target department stores on track:

> Twelve out of 14 directors are outsiders. A vice chairman chosen from among the outside directors serves as a special liaison between the board and the CEO. The result is a powerful, independent group of directors—a rare species in boardrooms today.[49]

Managers who cannot imagine themselves being victimized by blind conformity are prime candidates for groupthink. Dean Tjosvold of Canada's Simon Fraser University recommends "cooperative conflict" (see Skills & Tools at the end of this chapter). The constructive use of conflict is discussed further in Chapter 16.

Teams, Teamwork, and Trust

Ask Gordon Bethune, CEO of Continental Airlines, about the secret to success in his highly competitive industry today and he zeros in on *teamwork:*

> Running an airline is the biggest team sport there is. It's not an approach, it's not reorganization, and it's not a daily team plan. We are like a wristwatch—lots of different parts, but the whole has value only when we all work together. It has no value when any part fails. So we are not a cross-functional team, we're a company of multi functions that has value when we all work cooperatively—pilots, flight attendants, gate agents, airport agents, mechanics, reservation agents. And not to understand that about doing business means you're going to fail. Lots of people failed because they don't get it.[50]

Thus, teams and teamwork are vital group dynamics in the modern workplace.[51] Unfortunately, team skills in today's typical organization tend to lag far behind technical

You want the finest hand-tailored Italian suit? Ciro Paone, founder of Kiton in Naples, Italy, has the right formula. A team of master tailors + 24 hours of labor + lots of passion + love + the finest materials = one suit costing up to $5,000. World-class quality takes incredible talent, teamwork, and dedication to craft. And in this case, it doesn't come cheap!

skills.[52] It is one thing to be a creative software engineer, for example. It is quite another for that software specialist to be able to team up with other specialists in accounting, finance, and marketing to beat the competition to market with a profitable new product. In this final section, we explore teams and teamwork by discussing cross-functional teams, virtual teams, a model of team effectiveness, and the importance of trust.

Cross-Functional Teams

cross-functional team
task group staffed with a mix of specialists pursuing a common objective

A **cross-functional team** is a task group staffed with a mix of specialists focused on a common objective. This structural innovation deserves special attention here because cross-functional teams are becoming commonplace.[53] They may or may not be self-managed, although self-managed teams generally are cross-functional. Cross-functional teams are based on assigned rather than voluntary membership. Quality control (QC) circles made up of volunteers, discussed in Chapter 13, technically are in a different category. Cross-functional teams stand in sharp contrast to the tradition of lumping specialists into functional departments, thereby creating the problem of integrating and coordinating those departments. Boeing, for example, relies on cross-functional teams to integrate its various departments to achieve important strategic goals. The giant aircraft manufacturer thus accelerated its product development process for the Boeing 777 jetliner. Also, Boeing engineer Grace Robertson turned to cross-functional teams for faster delivery of a big order of customized jetliners to United Parcel Service:

> *When UPS ordered 30 aircraft, Boeing guaranteed that it could design and build a new, all-cargo version of the 767 jet in a mere 33 months—far faster than the usual cycle time of 42 months. The price it quoted meant slashing development costs dramatically.*
>
> *Robertson's strategy has been to gather all 400 employees working on the new freighter into one location and organize them into "cross-functional" teams. By combining people from the design, planning, manufacturing, and tooling sectors, the teams speed up development and cut costs by enhancing communication and avoiding rework.*[54]

This teamwork approach helped Robertson's group stay on schedule and within its budget, both vitally important achievements in Boeing's quest to remain the world's leading aircraft maker.

Cross-functional teams have exciting potential. But they present management with the immense challenge of getting technical specialists to be effective boundary spanners.

Virtual Teams

Along with the move toward virtual organizations, discussed in Chapter 10, have come virtual teams. A **virtual team** is a physically dispersed task group linked electronically.[55] Face-to-face contact usually is minimal or nonexistent. E-mail, voice mail, videoconferencing, and other forms of electronic interchange allow members of virtual teams from anywhere on the planet to accomplish a common goal. It is commonplace today for virtual teams to have members from different organizations, different time zones, and different cultures.[56] Because virtual organizations and teams are so new, paced as they are by emerging technologies, managers are having to learn from the school of hard knocks rather than from established practice.

As discussed in Chapter 10 relative to virtual organizations, one reality of managing virtual teams is clear. *Periodic face-to-face interaction, trust building, and team building are more important than ever when team members are widely dispersed in time and space.* While faceless interaction may work in Internet chat rooms, it can doom a virtual team

6 **Define and discuss the management of virtual teams.**

virtual team *task group members from dispersed locations who are electronically linked*

Call it new millennium motherhood. When Joanna Dapkevich got pregnant in 1997, her boss at IBM okayed her proposal to retain a part-time portion of her job as the manager of 50 software sales representatives. Here she steers her "virtual team" in Raleigh, North Carolina, from her home ten miles away. Dapkevich's long-distance management requires just the right combination of teamwork and trust. Her toddler seems to be very pleased with the arrangement.

with a crucial task and pressing deadline. Additionally, special steps need to be taken to clearly communicate role expectations, performance norms, goals, and deadlines (see Table 14.4). Virtual teamwork may be faster than the traditional face-to-face kind, but it is by no means easier (see Closing Case).

What Makes Workplace Teams Effective?

7 Discuss the criteria and determinants of team effectiveness.

Widespread use of team formats—including QC circles, self-managed teams, cross-functional teams, and virtual teams—necessitates greater knowledge of team effectiveness.[57] A model of team effectiveness criteria and determinants is presented in Figure 14.5. This model is the product of two field studies involving 360 new-product development managers employed by 52 high-tech companies.[58] Importantly, it is a generic model, applying equally well to all workplace teams.[59]

Table 14.4 | It Takes More than E-mail to Build a Virtual Team

Teams need a structure to work successfully across time and distance. In *Mastering Virtual Teams: Strategies, Tools, and Techniques That Succeed*, authors Deborah Duarte and Nancy Tennant Snyder list six steps for creating a virtual team, of which each acts as a support beam that helps uphold the structure.

   1. Identify the team's sponsors, stakeholders, and champions. These are the people who connect the team to the power brokers within the organizations involved.

   2. Develop a team charter that includes its purpose, mission, and goals. The authors say it's best to do this in a face-to-face meeting that includes the team's leader, management, and other stakeholders.

   3. Select team members. Most virtual teams have at least three types of members: *core* members who regularly work on the project; *extended* members who provide support and advice; and *ancillary* members who review and approve work.

   4. Contact team members and introduce them to each other. During this initial meeting, team leaders should make sure members understand why they've been selected, use computers that are compatible, and have a forum in which to ask and get answers to questions. Duarte says leaders should use this time to find out what other projects members are working on. "It's easy to put people on a team when you can't see them," she says. "People don't say 'no,' but then they find themselves on five or six teams and don't have time for any of them."

   5. Conduct a team-orientation session. This is one of the most important steps. Duarte says an eyeball-to-eyeball meeting is essential, unless team members are working on a very short task or have worked together in another capacity and know each other. "This forms the basis for more natural dialogue later if problems arise," she says. At this getting-to-know-you session, which often includes some type of team-building activity, the leader should provide an overview of the team's charter so members understand the task they are charged with and their roles in achieving it.

   Leaders also should provide guidance in developing team norms. This includes discussing telephone, audio- and video-conference etiquette; establishing guidelines for sending and replying to e-mail and returning phone calls; determining which meetings members must attend in person and which can be done by audio- or videoconference; outlining how work will be reviewed; and discussing how meetings will be scheduled.

   Team leaders also can use this session to decide which technologies the team will use and discuss how members will communicate with each other, with the leader, and with management.

   6. Develop a team process. Leaders should explain how the team's work will be managed, how information will be stored and shared, and who will review documents and how often.

   Duarte says teams that follow these steps often have a better sense of clarity about their goals, the roles of each member, how the work will get done, and how the team will communicate. "They don't feel as though they've been left floating."

Source: Kim Kiser, "Building a Virtual Team," *Training*, 36 (March 1999): 34. Reprinted with permission from the March 1999 issue of *Training* magazine. Copyright 1999, Bill Communications, Minneapolis, Minn. All rights reserved. Not for resale.

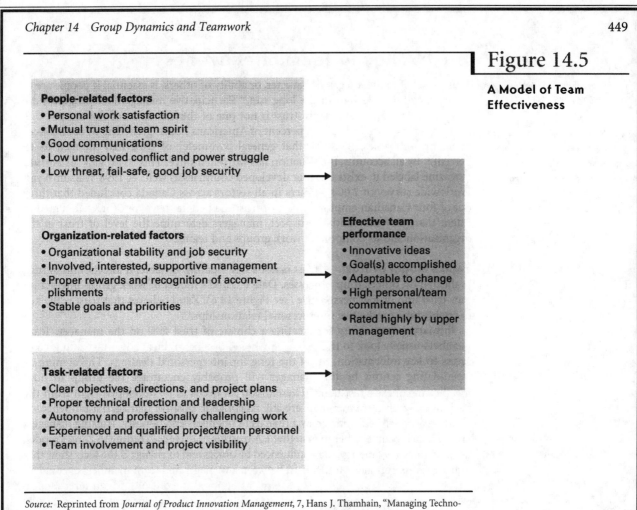

Figure 14.5

A Model of Team Effectiveness

People-related factors
- Personal work satisfaction
- Mutual trust and team spirit
- Good communications
- Low unresolved conflict and power struggle
- Low threat, fail-safe, good job security

Organization-related factors
- Organizational stability and job security
- Involved, interested, supportive management
- Proper rewards and recognition of accomplishments
- Stable goals and priorities

Task-related factors
- Clear objectives, directions, and project plans
- Proper technical direction and leadership
- Autonomy and professionally challenging work
- Experienced and qualified project/team personnel
- Team involvement and project visibility

Effective team performance
- Innovative ideas
- Goal(s) accomplished
- Adaptable to change
- High personal/team commitment
- Rated highly by upper management

Source: Reprinted from *Journal of Product Innovation Management*, 7, Hans J. Thamhain, "Managing Technologically Innovative Team Efforts Toward New Product Success," pp. 5–18. Copyright 1990, with permission from Elsevier Science, Inc.

The five criteria for effective team performance in the center of Figure 14.5 parallel the criteria for organizational effectiveness discussed in Chapter 9. Thus, team effectiveness feeds organizational effectiveness. For example, if the Boeing 777 product development teams had not been effective, the entire corporation could have stumbled.

Determinants of team effectiveness, shown in Figure 14.5, are grouped into people-, organization-, and task-related factors. Considered separately, these factors involve rather routine aspects of good management. But the collective picture reveals each factor to be part of a complex and interdependent whole. Managers cannot maximize just a few of them, ignore the rest, and hope to have an effective team. In the spirit of the Japanese concept of *kaizen*, managers and team leaders need to strive for "continuous improvement" on all fronts. Because gains on one front will inevitably be offset by losses in another, the pursuit of team effectiveness and teamwork is an endless battle with no guarantees of success.[60]

Let us focus on trust, one of the people-related factors in Figure 14.5 that can make or break work teams.

Trust: A Key to Team Effectiveness

trust *belief in the integrity, character, or ability of others*

8 Explain why trust is a key ingredient of teamwork and discuss what management can do to build trust.

Trust, a belief in the integrity, character, or ability of others, is essential if people are to achieve anything together in the long run.[61] Participative management programs are very dependent on trust.[62] Sadly, trust is not one of the hallmarks of the current U.S. business scene. Back in 1966, 55 percent of Americans had a "great deal of confidence" in major companies. By 1994, that general barometer of trust had plunged to 19 percent.[63] By all accounts, the situation has worsened since. This "trust gap," as *Fortune* magazine labeled it, exists in other developed countries as well. "A 1998 Watson Wyatt Worldwide survey of 2,004 workers in all sectors across Canada concluded that three out of four Canadian employees do not trust the people they work for."[64] To a greater extent than they may initially suspect, managers determine the level of trust in the organization and its component work groups and teams.

Zand's Model of Trust.   Trust is not a free-floating variable. It affects, and in turn is affected by, other group processes. Dale E. Zand's model of work group interaction puts trust into proper perspective (see Figure 14.6). Zand believes that trust is the key to establishing productive interpersonal relationships.[65]

Primary responsibility for creating a climate of trust falls on the manager. Team members usually look to the manager, who enjoys hierarchical advantage and greater access to key information, to set the tone for interpersonal dealings. Threatening or intimidating actions by the manager will probably encourage the group to bind together in cohesive resistance. Therefore, trust needs to be developed right from the beginning, when team members are still receptive to positive managerial influence.

Trust is initially encouraged by a manager's openness and honesty. Trusting managers talk *with* their people rather than *at* them. A trusting manager, according to Zand's model, demonstrates a willingness to be influenced by others and to change if the facts show that a change is appropriate. Mutual trust between a manager and team members encourages *self-control*, as opposed to control through direct supervision. Hewlett-Packard, for example, has carefully nurtured an organizational culture based on trust.

> *The faith that HP has in its people is conspicuously in evidence in the corporate "open lab stock" policy. . . . The lab stock area is where the electrical and mechanical components are kept. The open lab stock policy means that not only do the engineers have free access to this equipment, but they are actually encouraged to take it home for their personal use![66]*

HP's rationale for this trusting policy is that the company will reap innovative returns no matter how the engineers choose to work with the valuable lab equipment.

Paradoxically, managerial control actually expands when committed group or team members enjoy greater freedom in pursuing consensual goals. Those who trust each other generally avoid taking advantage of others' weaknesses or shortcomings.[67]

Six Ways to Build Trust.   Trust is a fragile thing. As most of us know from personal experience, trust grows at a painfully slow pace, yet can be destroyed in an

---

↙ **How to Be a Good Team Facilitator**   **14H**

The ability to facilitate comprises a collection of skills. Expert facilitators do the following tasks:

- manage meetings
- help teams agree on clear goals, roles, and procedures
- ensure that all team members contribute
- discourage disruptive behaviors
- manage conflict
- guide teams' decision-making processes
- communicate clearly with all team members
- observe and accurately interpret group dynamics.

Source: Greg Burns, "The Secrets of Team Facilitation," *Training & Development*, 49 (June 1995): 46.

Questions: *Is it better today to use the term* team facilitator *rather than* team manager *or* team leader? *Why or why not? Which of the above team facilitation skills are the most important to team success? Explain. Which of your team facilitation skills need development. How?*

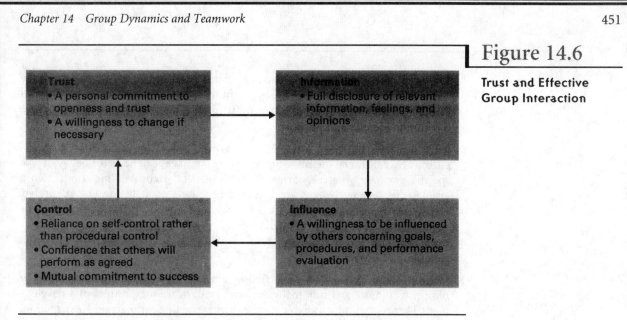

Figure 14.6

Trust and Effective Group Interaction

Source: Reprinted from "Trust and Managerial Problem Solving," by Dale E. Zand and published in *Administrative Science Quarterly*, 17, no. 2 (June 1972) by permission of *Administrative Science Quarterly*. © 1972 by Cornell University.

instant with a thoughtless remark. Mistrust can erode the long-term effectiveness of work teams and organizations. According to management professor and consultant Fernando Bartolomé, managers need to concentrate on six areas: communication, support, respect, fairness, predictability, and competence.

- *Communication:* Keep your people informed by providing accurate and timely feedback and explaining policies and decisions. Be open and honest about your own problems. Do not hoard information or use it as a political device or reward.
- *Support:* Be an approachable person who is available to help, encourage, and coach your people. Show an active interest in their lives and be willing to come to their defense.
- *Respect:* Delegating important duties is the sincerest form of respect, followed closely by being a good listener.
- *Fairness:* Evaluate your people fairly and objectively and be liberal in giving credit and praise.
- *Predictability:* Be dependable and consistent in your behavior and keep all your promises.
- *Competence:* Be a good role model by exercising good business judgment and being technically and professionally competent.[68]

Managers find that trust begets trust. In other words, those who feel they are trusted tend to trust others in return.[69]

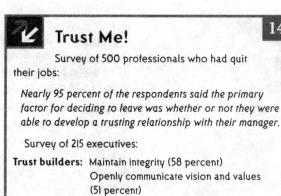

Trust Me!   14I

Survey of 500 professionals who had quit their jobs:

Nearly 95 percent of the respondents said the primary factor for deciding to leave was whether or not they were able to develop a trusting relationship with their manager.

Survey of 215 executives:

Trust builders: Maintain integrity (58 percent)
Openly communicate vision and values (51 percent)
Show respect for fellow employees as equal partners (47 percent)

Trust busters: Act inconsistently in what they say and do (69 percent)
Seek personal gain above shared gain (41 percent)
Withhold information (34 percent)

Sources: "Good Relationship with Boss a Key to Retention," *HRMagazine*, 44 (October 1999): 28; and Jenny C. McCune, "That Elusive Thing Called Trust," *Management Review*, 87 (July–August 1998): 13.

Questions: *How important is a trusting relationship with your boss? Explain. What makes you trust (or distrust) your manager? Your coworkers? Your family and friends?*

Summary

1. Managers need a working understanding of group dynamics because groups are the basic building blocks of organizations. Both informal (friendship) and formal (work) groups are made up of two or more freely interacting individuals who have a common identity and purpose.

2. After someone has been attracted to a group, cohesiveness—a "we" feeling—encourages continued membership. Roles are social expectations for behavior in a specific position, whereas norms are more general standards for conduct in a given social setting. Norms are enforced because they help the group survive, clarify role expectations, protect self-images, and enhance the group's identity by emphasizing key values. Compliance with role expectations and norms is rewarded with social reinforcement; noncompliance is punished by criticism, ridicule, and ostracism.

3. Mature groups that are characterized by mutual acceptance, encouragement of minority opinion, and minimal emotional conflict are the product of a developmental process with identifiable stages. During the first three stages—orientation, conflict and challenge, and cohesion—power and authority problems are resolved. Groups are faced with the obstacle of uncertainty over interpersonal relations during the last three stages—delusion, disillusion, and acceptance. Committees have a widespread reputation for inefficiency and ineffectiveness because they tend to get stalled in an early stage of group development.

4. Organizational politics centers on the pursuit of self-interest. Research shows greater political activity to be associated with higher levels of management, larger organizations, staff and marketing personnel, and reorganizations. Political tactics such as posturing, empire building, making the boss look good, collecting and using social IOUs, creating power and loyalty cliques, and destructive competition need to be kept in check if the organization is to be effective.

5. Although a fairly high degree of conformity is necessary if organizations and society in general are to function properly, blind conformity is ultimately dehumanizing and destructive. Research shows that individuals have a strong tendency to bend to the will of the majority, even if the majority is clearly wrong. Cohesive decision-making groups can be victimized by groupthink when unanimity becomes more important than critical evaluation of alternative courses of action.

6. Teams are becoming the structural format of choice. Today's employees generally have better technical skills than team skills. Cross-functional teams are particularly promising because they enable greater strategic speed. Although members of virtual teams by definition collaborate via electronic media, there is still a need for periodic face-to-face interaction and team building. Three sets of factors—relating to people, organization, and task—combine to determine the effectiveness of a work team.

7. Trust, a key ingredient of effective teamwork, is disturbingly low in the American workplace today. When work group members trust one another, there will be a more active exchange of information, more interpersonal influence, and hence greater self-control. Managers can build trust through communication, support, respect (primarily in the form of delegation), fairness, predictability, and competence.

Chapter 14   Group Dynamics and Teamwork 453

Terms to Understand

Group (p. 429)

Informal group (p. 430)

Formal group (p. 430)

Cohesiveness (p. 431)

Role (p. 432)

Norms (p. 433)

Ostracism (p. 434)

Organizational politics (p. 440)

Conformity (p. 443)

Groupthink (p. 444)

Cross-functional team (p. 446)

Virtual team (p. 447)

Trust (p. 450)

How to Use *Cooperative Conflict* to Avoid Groupthink

Skills & Tools

Guides for Action

- Elaborate positions and ideas.
- List facts, information, and theories.
- Ask for clarification.
- Clarify opposing ideas.
- Search for new information.
- Challenge opposing ideas and positions.
- Reaffirm your confidence in those who differ.
- Listen to all ideas.
- Restate opposing arguments that are unclear.
- Identify strengths in opposing arguments.
- Change your mind only when confronted with good evidence.
- Integrate various information and reasoning.
- Create alternative solutions.
- Agree to a solution responsive to several points of view.
- Use a new round of cooperative conflict to develop and refine the solution.

Pitfalls to Avoid

- Assume your position is superior.
- Prove your ideas are right and must be accepted.
- Interpret opposition to your ideas as a personal attack.
- Refuse to admit weaknesses in your position.
- Pretend to listen.
- Ridicule to weaken the others' resolve to disagree.
- Try to win over people to your position through charm and exaggeration.
- See accepting another's ideas as a sign of weakness.

Source: Reprinted from *Learning to Manage Conflict: Getting People to Work Together Productively* by Dean Tjosvold. Copyright © 1993 Dean Tjosvold. First published by Lexington Books. All rights reserved. All correspondence should be sent to Lexington Books, 4720 Boston Way, Lanham, Md., 20706.

454   *Part Four   Motivating and Leading*

Internet Exercises

1. **What's new with teams and teamwork?** Things are changing rapidly in this area because teams have become such an important part of organizational life. Lots of new ideas can be found on the Internet for those willing to search a bit. Here is a way to jump-start your Web search for updates on teams and teamwork. Go to *Fast Company* magazine's excellent Web site (**www.fastcompany.com**) and click on the main menu heading "Core Themes." At the themes and ideas page, select the category "Teamwork." Read at least two of the full-text articles, with the goal of picking up at least three good ideas about managing workplace teams. You may have to select and read additional articles if you don't find enough good ideas right away. *Note:* You may want to make hard copies of the articles you selected and notes of your good ideas for possible class discussion.

   Learning Points: 1. Why did you select those particular articles? 2. Among your "good ideas" about managing teams, which idea stands out as the best? Why? 3. Did other class members tend to focus on the same (or different) articles and ideas as you? 4. When comparing notes with your classmates, which of their "good ideas" are superior to the ones on your list?

2. **Getting "street smart" about organizational politics:** Ethical managers today play clean in the game of business but are street smart enough to avoid getting hurt by those who fight dirty. For good background reading, go back to *Fast Company* magazine's home page and click on the main menu heading "Archives." Select the heading "The Archives" and scroll down to the April–May 1998 issue (no. 14). From the table of contents for that issue, select and read the articles titled "The Bad Guy's (and Gal's) Guide to Office Politics" and "The Good Guy's (and Gal's) Guide to Office Politics." While you're in *Fast Company*'s online archives, you may want to search recent issues for articles relating to organizational and office politics.

   Learning Points: 1. Why is it fair to say organizational politics can be both good and bad? 2. What new ideas or useful tips did you learn about workplace politics? 3. Is political maneuvering an inescapable part of life on the job? Explain. 4. Is organizational politics a fun (or distasteful) aspect of organizational life for you? Explain. 5. Why is it important to know about political tactics in the workplace even if you don't enjoy engaging in them?

3. **Check it out:** The Briefings Publishing Group Web site (**www.briefings.com**) has a section titled "Team Management" containing a regularly updated collection of practical ideas about the exciting area of workplace teams. Be sure to explore the site's other management topics as well.

   For updates to these exercises, visit our Web site (**www.hmco.com/college**).

Closing Case · # Thirteen Time Zones Can't Keep Lucent's Virtual Team from Succeeding

Imagine designing the most complex product in your company's history. You need 500 engineers for the job. They will assemble the world's most delicate hardware and write more than a million lines of code. In communicating, the margin for error is minuscule.

Now, scatter those 500 engineers over 13 time zones. Over three continents. Over five states in the United States alone. The Germans schedule to perfection. The Americans work on the fly. In Massachusetts, they go to work early. In New Jersey, they stay late.

Now you have some idea of what Bill Klinger and Frank Polito have been through in the past 18 months. As

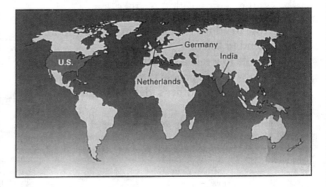

top software-development managers in Lucent Technologies' Bell Labs division, they played critical roles in creating a new fiber-optic phone switch called the Bandwidth Manager, which sells for about $1 million, the kind of global product behind the company's surging earnings. The high-stakes development was Lucent's most complex undertaking by far since its spin-off from AT&T in 1996.

Managing such a far-flung staff ("distributed development," it's called) is possible only because of technology. But as the two Lucent leaders painfully learned, distance still magnifies differences, even in a high-tech age. "You lose informal interaction—going to lunch, the water cooler," Mr. Klinger says. "You can never discount how many issues get solved that way."

The product grew as a hybrid of exotic, widely dispersed technologies: "lightwave" science from Lucent's Merrimack Valley plant, north of Boston, where Mr. Polito works; "cross-connect" products here in New Jersey, where Mr. Klinger works; timing devices from the Netherlands; and optics from Germany.

Development also demanded multiple locations because Lucent wanted a core model as a platform for special versions for foreign and other niche markets. Involving overseas engineers in the flagship product would speed the later development of spin-offs and impress foreign customers.

And rushing to market meant tapping software talent wherever it was available—ultimately at Lucent facilities in Colorado, Illinois, North Carolina, and India. "The scary thing, scary but exciting, was that no one had really pulled this off on this scale before," says Mr. Polito.

Communication technology was the easy part. Lashing together big computers in different cities assured everyone was working on the same up-to-date software version. New project data from one city were instantly available on Web pages everywhere else. Test engineers in India could tweak prototypes in New Jersey. The project never went to sleep.

Technology, however, couldn't conquer cultural problems, especially acute between Messrs. Klinger's and Polito's respective staffs in New Jersey and Massachusetts. Each had its own programming traditions and product histories. Such basic words as "test" could mean different things. A programming chore requiring days in one context might take weeks in another. Differing work schedules and physical distance made each location suspect the other of slacking off. "We had such clashes," says Mr. Klinger.

Personality tests revealed deep geographic differences. Supervisors from the sleek, glass-covered New Jersey office,

principally a research facility abounding in academics, scored as "thinking" people who used cause-and-effect analysis. Those from the old, brick facility in Massachusetts, mainly a manufacturing plant, scored as "feeling" types who based decisions on subjective, human values. Sheer awareness of the differences ("Now I know why you get on my nerves!") began to create common ground.

Amid much cynicism, the two directors hauled their technical managers into team exercises—working in small groups to scale a 14-foot wall and solve puzzles. It's corny, but such methods can accelerate trust building when time is short and the stakes are high. At one point Mr. Klinger asked managers to show up with the product manuals from their previous projects—then, in a ritualistic break from technical parochialism, instructed everyone to tear the covers to pieces.

More than anything else, it was sheer physical presence—face time—that began solidifying the group. Dozens of managers began meeting fortnightly in rotating cities, socializing as much time as their technical discussions permitted. (How better to grow familiar than over hot dogs, beer, and nine innings with the minor league Durham Bulls?) Foreign locations found the direct interaction especially valuable. "Going into the other culture is the only way to understand it," says Sigrid Hauenstein, a Lucent executive in Nuremberg, Germany. "If you don't have a common understanding, it's much more expensive to correct it later."

Eventually the project found its pace. People began wearing beepers to eliminate time wasted on voice-mail tag. Conference calls at varying levels kept everyone in the loop. Staffers posted their photos in the project's Web directory. Many created personal pages. "It's the ultimate democracy of the Web," Mr. Klinger says.

The product is now shipping—on schedule, within budget, and with more technical versatility than Lucent expected. Distributed development "paid off in spades," says Gerry Butters, Lucent optical-networking chief.

Even as it helps build the infrastructure of a digitally connected planet, Lucent is rediscovering the importance of face-to-face interaction. All the bandwidth in the world can convey only a fraction of what we are.

Source: Republished with permission of *The Wall Street Journal* from "With the Stakes High, a Lucent Duo Conquers Distance and Culture," by Thomas Petzinger Jr., *The Wall Street Journal* (April 23, 1999). Permission conveyed through Copyright Clearance Center, Inc.

FOR DISCUSSION

1. Which team effectiveness criteria in Figure 14.5 are apparent in this case?
2. How big a problem do you suppose organizational politics was during this project? Explain.
3. What practical lessons does this case teach managers about managing a virtual team?
4. Would you be comfortable working on this sort of global virtual team? Explain.

EXERCISE 5

Study the following excerpt from the table of contents of the *Management* textbook:

According to this excerpt of the table of contents, what are the five major topics discussed in the "Group Dynamics and Teamwork" chapter? How many topics are covered in the section called "Teams, Teamwork, and Trust"?

- **Think before you read.**   We digest new information more easily when we can relate it to what we already know. Therefore, before you read, take a little time to consider your prior knowledge about the topic. Also, think about your own personal experiences that relate to the chapter content you previewed. Writing will clarify your existing ideas and beliefs even more, so you may want to record your thoughts in a reading journal.

EXERCISE 6

In the space below, write at least one paragraph about your ideas, beliefs, and experiences related to group dynamics and teamwork. (You might want to continue writing your paragraph on a separate sheet of paper if there isn't enough space here.)

Step 2: Read

The second step of the reading process is to **read**. However, to read for increased comprehension and retention of information, you must do much more than just passively move your eyes over the words on the page. Instead, read actively. **Active reading** means marking the text with pens and/or highlighters.

What should you mark? First, turn all of the headings in the chapter into questions. In the "Group Dynamics and Teamwork" chapter, for example, you could change the first few headings in into these questions:

What Are the Fundamental Group Dynamics?
What Is a Group? (The authors did this one for you!)
What Are the Types of Groups?
Why Are People Attract[ed] to Groups?

EXERCISE 7

On a separate sheet of paper, transform the remaining headings in the "Group Dynamics and Teamwork" chapter into questions.

After you turn a heading into a question, read the section looking for the answer(s) to that question. When you encounter the answers, mark them by highlighting, underlining, or circling them. However, don't make the mistake of highlighting entire paragraphs. That won't help you quickly and easily see the main ideas when you review the chapter later.

EXERCISE 8

In the section entitled, "Organizational Politics," highlight or underline the answers to the questions you created from the headings.

You may want to add distinctive marking—such as boxes or another highlight color—to key terms within the chapter. This will make them stand out when you review later.

Finally, read with a dictionary close at hand, and always look up definitions of unfamiliar words. If you skip over words you don't know, you may lose important information or misinterpret the author's meaning. Circle each word that you do not know, look it up in your dictionary, and write its definition in the margin of the book's margin.

EXERCISE 9

Read the section entitled "Conformity and Groupthink" in the "Group Dynamics and Teamwork" chapter. Circle all of the words that are new to you, look them up, and write their definitions in the margins. If there is more than one definition for a word, use your understanding of the word's context within the sentence to determine the appropriate meaning.

Step 3: Review

The third and final step of the reading process is **review**. When you follow reading with review, you'll reinforce your understanding of the information. Your review should include some or all of the following activities:

- Reread as necessary.
- Answer the study questions or complete the exercises at the end of the chapter.
- Write a summary of the chapter.
- Discuss the chapter with your classmates and/or instructor in or outside of class.
- Outline the chapter.
- Reflect upon what you learned. Determine how you can use the information in your career, in your other courses, and in your personal life. Think about the content that surprised you, corrected your misconceptions, or reinforced information you already knew. Consider recording your reflections in a reading journal.

EXERCISE 10

Reflect upon your reading by writing at least one paragraph (on a separate sheet of paper) about what you gained from the "Group Dynamics and Teamwork" chapter. While reflecting, you might want to consider the following questions: How can you use this information in your career, in your other courses, and/or in your personal life? Did any of the information surprise you? Did the chapter correct any misconceptions you had? Did it reinforce ideas or information you already knew?

EXERCISE 11

On a separate sheet of paper, write your answers to the Internet exercises at the end of the "Group Dynamics and Teamwork" chapter.

In summary, you may want to think about the entire reading process in terms of the **SQ3R System** created in 1941 by Francis P. Robinson. SQ3R stands for:

SURVEY	Preview the chapter's content and organization.
QUESTION	Turn headings into questions.
READ	Find answers to the questions.
RECITE	Say (silently or aloud) the answers to the questions.
REVIEW	Periodically go back over the questions to make sure you can still answer them.

PART 3

"Memory" from *Psychology*

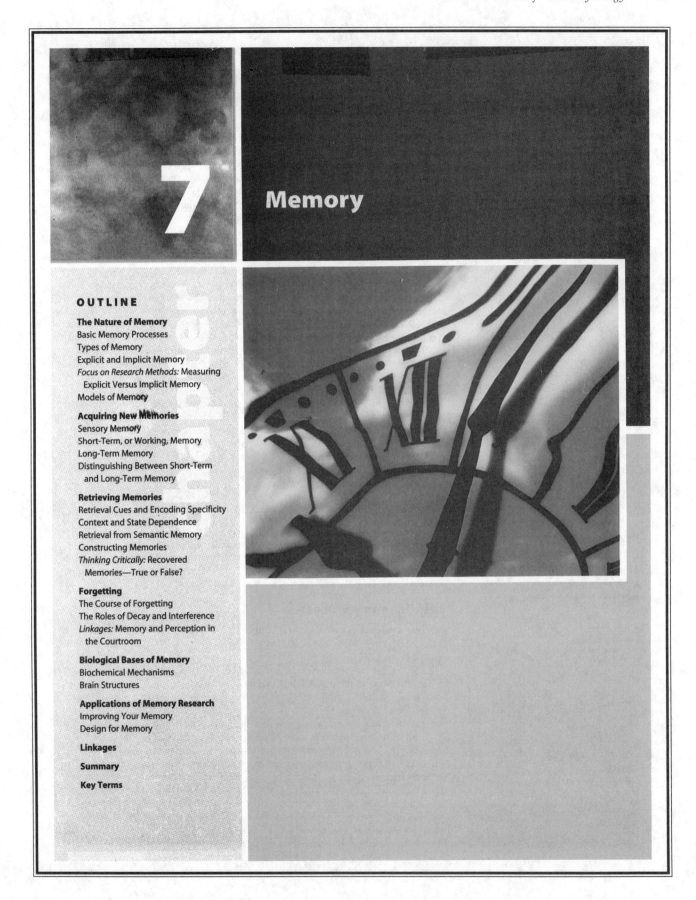

7

Memory

Several years ago an air-traffic controller at Los Angeles International Airport cleared a US Airways flight to land on runway 24L. A couple of minutes later, the US Airways pilot radioed the control tower that he was on approach for runway 24L, but the controller did not reply because she was preoccupied by a confusing exchange with another pilot. After finishing that conversation, the controller told a Sky West commuter pilot to taxi onto runway 24L for takeoff, completely forgetting about the US Airways flight that was about to land on the same runway. The US Airways jet hit the commuter plane, killing thirty-four people. The controller's forgetting was so complete that she assumed the fireball from the crash was an exploding bomb. How could the controller's memory have failed her at such a crucial time?

Memory is full of paradoxes. It is common, for example, for people to remember the name of their first-grade teacher but not the name of someone they met just a minute ago. And consider Rajan Mahadevan. He once set a world's record by reciting from memory the first 31,811 places of pi (the ratio of the circumference of a circle to its diameter), but on repeated visits to the psychology building at the University of Minnesota, he had trouble recalling the location of the nearest restroom (Biederman et al., 1992). Like perception, memory is selective. Whereas people retain a great deal of information, they also lose a great deal (Bjork & Vanhuele, 1992).

Memory plays a critical role in your life. Without memory, you would not know how to shut off your alarm clock, take a shower, get dressed, or recognize objects. You would be unable to communicate with other people because you would not remember what words mean, or even what you had just said. You would be unaware of your own likes and dislikes, and you would have no idea of who you are in any meaningful sense (Kihlstrom, 1993). In this chapter we describe what is known about both memory and forgetting. First, we discuss what memory is—the different kinds of memory and the different ways we remember things. Then we examine how new memories are acquired and later recalled, and why they are sometimes forgotten. We continue with a discussion of the biological bases of memory, and we conclude with some practical advice for improving memory and studying skills.

THE NATURE OF MEMORY

Mathematician John Griffith estimated that, in an average lifetime, a person will have stored roughly five hundred times as much information as can be found in all the volumes of the *Encyclopedia Britannica* (Hunt, 1982). The impressive capacity of human memory depends on the operation of a complex mental system (Schacter, 1999).

Basic Memory Processes

We know a psychologist who sometimes drives to work and sometimes walks. On one occasion, he drove, forgot that he had driven, and walked home. When he failed to find his car in its normal spot the next morning, he reported the car stolen. The police soon called to say that "some college kids" had probably stolen the car because it was found on campus (next to the psychology building!). What went wrong? There are several possibilities, because memory depends on three basic processes—encoding, storage, and retrieval (see Figure 7.1).

First, information must be put into memory, a step that requires **encoding**. Just as incoming sensory information must be coded so that it can be communicated to the brain, information to be remembered must be put in a form that the memory system can accept and use. In the memory system, sensory information is put into various *memory codes*, which are mental representations of physical stimuli. Imagine that you see a billboard that reads "Huey's Going Out of Business Sale," and you want to remember it so you can take advantage of the sale later. If you encode the sound of the words as if they had been spoken, you are using **acoustic encoding**, and the information is represented in your memory as a sequence of sounds. If you encode the image of the letters as they were arranged on the sign, you are using **visual encoding**, and the

Drawing on Memories

The human memory system allows people to encode, store, and retrieve a lifetime of experiences. Without it, you would have no sense of who you are.

FIGURE 7.1

Basic Memory Processes

Remembering something requires, first, that the item be encoded—put in a form that can be placed in memory. It must then be stored and, finally, retrieved, or recovered. If any of these processes fails, forgetting will occur.

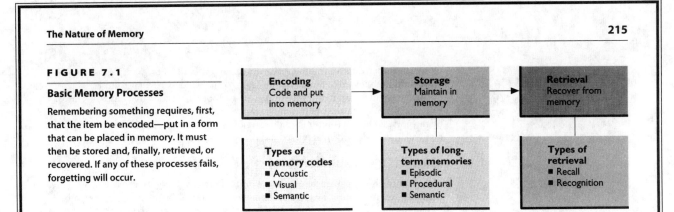

information is represented in your memory as a picture. Finally, if you encode the fact that you saw an ad for Huey's, you are using **semantic encoding**, and the information is represented in your memory by its general meaning. The type of encoding used can influence what is remembered. For example, semantic encoding might allow you to remember that a car was parked in your neighbors' driveway just before their house was robbed. If there was little or no other encoding, however, you might not be able to remember the make, model, or color of the car.

The second basic memory process is **storage**, which refers to the maintenance of information over time, often over a very long time. When you find it possible to use a pogo stick or to recall a vacation from many years ago, you are depending on the storage capacity of your memory.

The third process, **retrieval**, occurs when you locate information stored in memory and bring it into consciousness. Retrieving stored information such as your address or telephone number is usually so fast and effortless that it seems automatic. Only when you try to retrieve other kinds of information—such as the answer to a quiz question that you know but cannot quite recall—do you become aware of the searching process. Retrieval processes include both recall and recognition. To *recall* information, as on an essay test, you have to retrieve it from memory without much help. *Recognition* is retrieval aided by clues, such as the alternatives given in a multiple-choice test item. Accordingly, recognition tends to be easier than recall.

Types of Memory

When was the last time you made a credit card purchase? What part of speech is used to modify a noun? How do you keep your balance when you are skiing? To answer these questions, you must use your memory. However, each may require a different type of memory (Brewer & Pani, 1984). To answer the first question, you must remember a particular event in your life; to answer the second one, you must recall a piece of general knowledge that is unlikely to be tied to a specific event. And the answer to the final question is difficult to put into words but appears in the form of your remembered actions when you get up on skis. How many types of memory are there? No one is sure, but most research suggests that there are at least three basic types. Each is named for the kind of information it handles (Reed, 1992).

Memory of a specific event that happened while you were present—that is, during an "episode" in your life—is called **episodic memory**. Examples are what you had for dinner yesterday, what you did last summer, or where you were last Friday night. Generalized knowledge of the world that does not involve memory of a specific event is called **semantic memory**. For instance, you can answer a question like "Are wrenches pets or tools?" without remembering any specific event in which you learned that wrenches are tools. As a general rule, people convey episodic memories by saying, "I remember when . . . ," whereas they convey semantic memories by saying, "I know that . . ." (Tulving, 1982). Finally, memory of how to do things, such as skiing without falling (and riding a bike, reading a map, tying a shoelace), is called **procedural memory**. Often, procedural memory consists of a complicated sequence of movements that cannot be described adequately in words. For example, a gymnast might find it impossible to describe the exact motions in a particular routine.

Many activities require all three types of memory. Consider the game of tennis. Knowing the official rules or how many sets are needed to win a match involves semantic memory. Remembering which side served last requires episodic memory. Knowing how to lob or volley involves procedural memory.

Explicit and Implicit Memory

Memory can also be categorized in terms of its effects on thoughts and behaviors. For example, you make use of **explicit memory** when you deliberately try to remember something and are consciously aware of doing so (Masson & MacLeod, 1992). Let's say that someone asks you about your last vacation; as you attempt to remember where you went, you would be using explicit memory to recall this episode from your past. Similarly, if you have to answer a question on an examination, you would be using explicit memory to retrieve the information needed to give a correct answer. In contrast, **implicit memory** is the unintentional recollection and influence of prior experiences (Nelson, 1999). For example, while watching a movie about a long car trip, you might begin to feel tense because you subconsciously recall the time you had engine trouble on such a trip. But you are not aware that it is this memory that is making you tense. Implicit memory operates automatically and without conscious effort. As another example, perhaps you've found yourself disliking someone you just met, but didn't know why. One explanation is that implicit memory may have been at work. Specifically, you may have reacted in this way because the person bears a resemblance to someone from your past who treated you badly. In such instances, people are usually unable to recall the person from the past and, indeed, are unaware of any connection between the two individuals (Lewicki, 1985). Episodic, semantic, and procedural memories can be explicit or implicit, but procedural memory usually operates implicitly. This is why, for example, you can skillfully ride a bike even though you cannot explicitly remember all the procedures necessary to do so.

It is not surprising that experience affects how people behave. What is surprising is that they are often unaware that their actions have been influenced by previous events. Because some influential events cannot be recalled even when people try to do so, implicit memory has been said to involve "retention without remembering" (Roediger, 1990).

L I N K A G E S

Learning By Doing

Procedural memories involve skills that can usually be learned only through repetition. This is why parents not only tell children how to tie a shoe but also show them the steps and then let them practice. Factors that enhance skill learning are described in Chapter 6.

FOCUS ON RESEARCH METHODS

Measuring Explicit Versus Implicit Memory

In Canada, Endel Tulving and his colleagues undertook a series of experiments to map the differences between explicit and implicit memory (Tulving, Schacter, & Stark, 1982).

■ What was the researcher's question?

Tulving knew he could measure explicit memory by giving a recognition test in which participants simply said which words on a list they remembered seeing on a previous list. The question was, How would it be possible to measure implicit memory?

■ How did the researcher answer the question?

First, Tulving asked the participants in his experiment to study a long list of words—the "study list." An hour later, they took a recognition test involving explicit memory—saying which words on a new list had been on the original study list. Then, to test their implicit memory, Tulving asked them to perform a "fragment completion" task (Warrington & Weiskrantz, 1970). In this task, participants were shown a "test list" of word fragments, such as *d–l–iu–*, and asked to complete the word (in this case, *delir-*

Making Implicit Memories

By the time they reach adulthood, these boys may have no explicit memories of the interactions they had in early childhood with friends from differing ethnic groups, but research suggests that their implicit memories of such experiences could have an unconscious effect on their attitudes toward and judgments about members of those groups.

FIGURE 7.2

Measures of Explicit and Implicit Memory

This experiment showed that the passage of time greatly affected people's recognition (explicit memory) of a word list but left fragment completion (implicit memory) essentially intact. Results such as these suggest that explicit and implicit memory may be different memory systems.

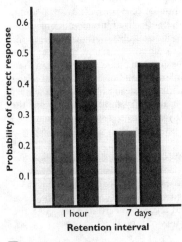

■ Recognition (explicit)

■ Fragment completion (implicit)

Source: Tulving, Schacter, & Stark, 1982.

ium). On the basis of *priming* studies such as those described in Chapter 9, Tulving assumed that memory from a previous exposure to the correct word would improve the participants' ability to complete the fragment, even if they were unable to consciously recall having seen the word before. A week later, all participants took a second test of their explicit memory (recognition) and implicit memory (fragment completion) of the study list. Some of the words on this second test list had been on the original study list, but none had been used in the first set of memory tests. The independent variable in this experiment, then, was the amount of time that elapsed since the participants read the study list (one hour versus one week), and the dependent variable was performance on each of the two types of memory tests, explicit and implicit.

■ **What did the researcher find?**

As shown in Figure 7.2, explicit memory for the study list decreased dramatically over time, but implicit memory was virtually unchanged. Results from several other experiments also show that the passage of time affects one type of memory but not the other (Komatsu & Naito, 1992; Mitchell, 1991). For example, it appears that the aging process has fewer negative effects on implicit memory than on explicit memory (Light, 1991).

■ **What do the results mean?**

The work of Tulving and others supports the idea of a dissociation, or independence, between explicit and implicit memory, suggesting that the two may operate on different principles (Gabrieli et al., 1995). Indeed, some researchers believe that explicit and implicit memory may involve the activity of distinct neural systems in the brain (Squire, 1987; Tulving & Schacter, 1990).

■ **What do we still need to know?**

Psychologists are now studying the role of implicit memory (and dissociations between explicit and implicit memory) in such important psychological phenomena as amnesia (Schacter, Church, & Treadwell, 1994; Tulving, 1993), depression (Elliott & Greene, 1992), problem solving (Jacoby, Marriott, & Collins, 1990), prejudice and stereotyping (Fiske, 1998), the development of self-concept in childhood (Nelson, 1993), and even the power of ads to associate brand names with good feelings (Duke & Carlson, 1993). The results of these studies should shed new light on implicit memory and how it operates in the real world.

While some researchers claim that implicit memory and explicit memory involve different structures in the brain (Schacter, 1992; Squire, 1987; Tulving & Schacter, 1990), others argue that the two types of memory entail different cognitive processes (Nelson, McKinney, & Bennett, in press; Roediger, Guynn, & Jones, 1995). Indeed, some social psychologists are trying to determine whether consciously held attitudes are independent of *implicit social cognitions*—past experiences that unconsciously influence a person's judgments about a group of people (Greenwald & Banaji, 1995). A case in point would be a person whose explicit thoughts about members of some ethnic group are positive but whose implicit thoughts are negative. Early work on implicit memory for stereotypes seemed to indicate that explicit and implicit stereotypes are indeed independent (Devine, 1989), but more recent research suggests that they are to some extent related (Lepore & Brown, 1997). Further research is needed to determine what mechanisms are responsible for implicit versus explicit memory and how they are related to one another (Nelson et al., in press).

Models of Memory

People remember some information far better and longer than other information. For example, suppose your friends throw a surprise party for you. Upon entering the room, you might barely notice, and later fail to recall, the flash from a camera. And you might forget in a few seconds the name of a person you met at the party. But if you live to be a hundred, you will never forget where the party took place or how surprised and pleased you were. Why do some stimuli leave no more than a fleeting impression and others remain in memory forever? In the following sections we examine four theoretical models of memory, each of which provides an explanation for this phenomenon.

Levels of Processing   The **levels-of-processing model** suggests that the most important determinant of memory is how extensively information is encoded or processed when it is first received. Consider situations in which people try to memorize something by mentally rehearsing it. There appear to be two basic types of mental rehearsal: maintenance and elaborative. **Maintenance rehearsal** involves simply repeating an item over and over. This method can be effective for remembering information for a short time. If you need to look up a phone number, walk across the room, and then dial the number, maintenance rehearsal would work just fine. But what if you need to remember something for hours or months or years? Far more effective in these cases is **elaborative rehearsal**, which involves thinking about how new material relates to information already stored in memory. For example, instead of trying to remember a new person's name by simply repeating it to yourself, try thinking about how the name is related to something you already know. If you are introduced to a man named Jim Crews, you might think, "He is as tall as my Uncle Jim, who always wears a crew cut."

Study after study has shown that memory is enhanced when people use elaborative rather than maintenance rehearsal (Anderson, 1990b). According to the levels-of-processing model, this enhancement occurs because of the degree or "depth" to which incoming information is mentally processed during elaborative rehearsal. The more you think about new information, organize it, and relate it to existing knowledge, the "deeper" the processing, and the better your memory of it becomes.

Transfer-Appropriate Processing   Level of processing is not the only factor affecting what we remember (Baddeley, 1992). The **transfer-appropriate processing model** suggests that a critical determinant of memory is how well the encoding process matches up with what is ultimately retrieved. Consider an experiment in which people

FIGURE 7.3

The Match Between Encoding and Retrieval

People who were asked to recognize words seen earlier did better if they had encoded the words on the basis of their meaning (semantic coding) rather than on the basis of what they rhymed with. But if asked to identify words that *rhymed* with those seen before, they did better on those that had been encoded using a rhyming code. These results support the transfer-appropriate processing model of memory.

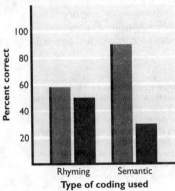

were shown a series of sentences with one word missing and were then asked one of two types of questions about the missing word (Morris, Bransford, & Franks, 1977). Some questions were designed so that participants would use a semantic (meaning) code for the target word. For example, one sentence read "A _____ is a building" and participants were asked whether the target word *house* should go in the blank space. Other questions were designed to elicit a rhyming code, as when participants were shown the sentence "_____ rhymes with *legal*" and asked whether the target word *eagle* rhymed with *legal*.

Later, the participants were given two kinds of memory tasks. On one task, they were asked to select from a list the target words they had been shown earlier. As Figure 7.3 shows, the participants did much better at recognizing the words for which they had used a semantic code rather than a rhyming code. But on the other task, in which they were asked to pick out words that *rhymed* with the ones they had seen (e.g., *grouse*, which rhymes with *house*), they did much better at identifying words that rhymed with those for which they had used a rhyming code rather than a semantic code. Results like these inspired the concept of *transfer-appropriate processing*, which suggests that our memory is better when the encoding process matches up with what we are trying to retrieve.

Parallel Distributed Processing   Still another approach to memory is based on **parallel distributed processing (PDP) models** of memory (Rumelhart & McClelland, 1986). These models suggest that new experiences don't just provide new facts that are

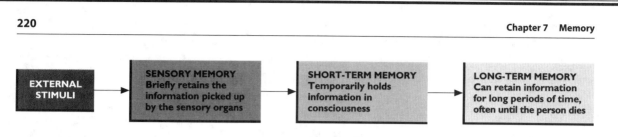

FIGURE 7.4

The Three Stages of Memory

This traditional information-processing model analyzes the memory system into three stages.

later retrieved individually; they also become integrated with people's existing knowledge or memories, changing their overall knowledge base and altering in a more general way their understanding of the world and how it operates. For example, if you compare your knowledge of college life today with what it was when you first arrived, chances are it has changed day by day in a way that is much more general than any single new fact you learned.

PDP memory theorists begin by asking how neural networks might provide a functional memory system (Anderson, 1990b). We describe the essential features of neural networks in Chapters 5 and 6, on perception and learning. In the case of memory, each unit of knowledge is ultimately connected to every other unit, and the connections between units become stronger as they are experienced together more frequently. From this perspective, then, "knowledge" is distributed across a dense network of associations. When this network is activated, *parallel processing* occurs; that is, different portions of the network operate simultaneously, allowing people to quickly and efficiently draw inferences and make generalizations. Just seeing the word *sofa*, for example, allows us immediately to gain access to knowledge about what a sofa looks like, what it is used for, where it tends to be located, who might buy one, and the like.

Information Processing   Historically, the most influential and comprehensive theories of memory have been based on a general **information-processing model** (Roediger, 1990). The information-processing model originally suggested that in order for information to become firmly embedded in memory, it must pass through three stages of mental processing: sensory memory, short-term memory, and long-term memory (Atkinson & Shiffrin, 1968; see Figure 7.4).

In *sensory memory*, information from the senses—sights or sounds, for example—is held in *sensory registers* for a very brief period of time, often less than one second. Information in the sensory registers may be attended to, analyzed, and encoded as a meaningful pattern; this is the process of *perception*. If the information in sensory memory is perceived, it can enter *short-term memory*. If nothing further is done, the information will disappear in about eighteen seconds. But if the information in short-term memory is further processed, it may be encoded into *long-term memory*, where it may remain indefinitely.

Contemporary versions of the information-processing model emphasize the constant interactions among sensory, short-term, and long-term memory (Massaro & Cowan, 1993). For example, sensory memory can be thought of as that part of one's knowledge base (or long-term memory) that is momentarily activated by information

FIGURE 7.5

The Role of Memory in Comprehension

Read the passage shown here, then turn away and try to recall as much of it as possible. Then read the footnote on page 222 and reread the passage. The second reading probably made a lot more sense and was much easier to remember because knowing the title of the passage allowed you to retrieve from long-term memory your knowledge about the topic (Bransford & Johnson, 1972).

The procedure is actually quite simple. First, you arrange items into different groups. Of course, one pile may be sufficient, depending on how much there is to do. If you have to go somewhere else due to lack of facilities that is the next step; otherwise, you are pretty well set. It is important not to overdo things. That is, it is better to do too few things at once than too many. In the short run, this may not seem important, but complications can easily arise. A mistake can be expensive as well. At first, the whole procedure will seem complicated. Soon, however, it will become just another facet of life. It is difficult to foresee any end to the necessity for this task in the immediate future, but then, one never can tell. After the procedure is completed, one arranges the materials into different groups again. Then they can be put into their appropriate places. Eventually they will be used once more, and the whole cycle will then have to be repeated. However, that is part of life.

MODELS OF MEMORY	
Model	**Assumptions**
Levels of processing	The more deeply material is processed, the better the memory of it.
Transfer-appropriate processing	Retrieval is improved when we try to recall material in a way that matches how the material was encoded.
Parallel distributed processing (PDP)	New experiences add to and alter our overall knowledge base; they are not separate, unconnected facts. PDP networks allow us to draw inferences and make generalizations about the world.
Information processing	Information is processed in three stages: sensory, short-term, and long-term memory.

in review

sent to the brain via the sensory nerves. And short-term memory can be thought of as that part of one's knowledge base that is the focus of attention at any given moment. Like perception, memory is an active process, and what is already in long-term memory influences how new information is encoded (Cowan, 1988). To understand this interaction better, try the exercise in Figure 7.5.

For a summary of the four models we have discussed, see "In Review: Models of Memory." Each of these models provides an explanation of why we remember some things and forget others, but which one offers the best explanation? The answer is that more than one model may be required to understand memory. Just as it is helpful for physicists to characterize light in terms of both waves and particles, psychologists find it useful to think of memory as both a serial or sequential process, as suggested by the information-processing model, and a parallel process, as suggested by parallel distributed processing models.

ACQUIRING NEW MEMORIES

The information-processing model suggests that sensory, short-term, and long-term memory each provide a different type of storage system.

Sensory Memory

In order to recognize incoming stimuli, the brain must analyze and compare them to what is already stored in long-term memory. Although this process is very quick, it still takes time. The major function of **sensory memory** is to hold information long enough for it to be processed further. This maintenance is the job of the **sensory registers**, whose storage capability retains an almost complete representation of a sensory stimulus (Best, 1992). There is a separate register for each of the five senses, and every register is capable of storing a relatively large amount of stimulus information.

Memories held in the sensory registers are fleeting, but they last long enough for stimulus identification to begin (Eysenck & Keane, 1995). As you read a sentence, for example, you identify and interpret the first few words. At the same time, subsequent words are being scanned, and these are maintained in your visual sensory register until you can process them as well.

In many ways, sensory memory brings coherence and continuity to the world. To appreciate this fact, turn your head slowly from left to right. Although your eyes may seem to be moving smoothly, like a movie camera scanning a scene, this is not what happens. Your eyes fixate at one point for about one-fourth of a second and then rapidly jump to a new position. The sensation of smoothness occurs because the scene is held in the visual sensory register until your eyes fixate again. Similarly, when you listen to someone speak, the auditory sensory register allows you to experience a smooth flow of information. Information persists for varying amounts of time in the five sensory registers. For example, information in the auditory sensory register lasts longer than information in the visual sensory register. This difference probably reflects humans' adaptation to a world in which visual images can often be looked at again if necessary, whereas sounds tend to be one-time occurrences that may be lost forever if not stored a bit longer.

The fact that sensory memories quickly fade if they are not processed further is another adaptive characteristic of the memory system (Martindale, 1991). One simply cannot deal with all of the sights, sounds, odors, tastes, and tactile sensations that impinge on the sense organs at any given moment. As mentioned in Chapter 5, **selective attention** focuses mental resources on only part of the stimulus field, thus controlling what information is processed further. Indeed, it is through perception that the elusive impressions of sensory memory are captured and transferred to short-term memory.

Short-Term, or Working, Memory

The sensory registers allow your memory system to develop a representation of a stimulus, but they do not allow the more thorough representation and analysis needed if the information is going to be used in some way. These functions are accomplished by **short-term memory (STM)**, the part of our memory system that stores limited amounts of information for up to about eighteen seconds. When you check *TV Guide* for the channel number of a show and then switch to that channel, you are using short-term memory.

Once viewed mainly as a temporary storehouse for information, short-term memory is now recognized as a more complex operation that serves a number of purposes. Accordingly, many researchers refer to STM as **working memory** because it enables people to do much of their mental work, from dialing a phone number to solving a complex math problem (Baddeley, 1992). Suppose, for example, you are buying something for 83 cents. You go through your change and pick out two quarters, two dimes, two nickels, and three pennies. To do this you must remember the price, retrieve the rules of addition from long-term memory, and keep a running count of how much change you have so far. Alternatively, try to recall how many windows there are on the front of the house or apartment where you grew up. In attempting to answer this question, you probably formed a mental image of the building, which required one kind of working-memory process, and then, while maintaining that image in your mind, you "worked" on it by counting the windows.

In other words, more is involved in short-term memory than just storing information. In fact, some researchers view STM as one part of a more elaborate working-memory system whose components function together on a semi-independent basis (Baddeley & Hitch, 1974).

Encoding in Short-Term Memory   The encoding of information in short-term memory is much more elaborative and varied than that in the sensory registers (Brandimonte, Hitch, & Bishop, 1992). Often, *acoustic encoding* seems to dominate. Evidence in support of this assertion comes from an analysis of the mistakes people make when encoding information in short-term memory. These mistakes tend to be acoustically related, which means that they involve the substitution of similar sounds. For example, Robert Conrad (1964) showed people strings of letters and asked them to repeat the letters immediately. Their mistakes tended to involve replacing the correct letter—say, *C*—with another that sounded like it, such as *D*, *P*, or *T*. These mistakes occurred even though the letters were presented visually, without any sound.

Note: The title of the passage on page 220 is "Washing Clothes."

Acquiring New Memories   **223**

FIGURE 7.6

Capacity of Short-Term Memory

Here is a test of your immediate, or short-term, memory span. Ask someone to read to you the numbers in the top row at the rate of about one per second; then try to repeat them back in the same order. Then try the next row, and the one after that, until you make a mistake. Your immediate memory span is the maximum number of items you can repeat back perfectly. Similar tests can be performed using the rows of letters and words.

```
9 2 5                          G M N
8 6 4 2                        S L R R
3 7 6 5 4                      V O E P G
6 2 7 4 1 8                    X W D X Q O
0 4 0 1 4 7 3                  E P H H J A E
1 9 2 2 3 5 3 0                Z D O F W D S V
4 8 6 8 5 4 3 3 2              D T Y N R H E H Q
2 5 3 1 9 7 1 7 6 8            K H W D A G R O F Z
8 5 1 2 9 6 1 9 4 5 0          U D F F W H D Q D G E
9 1 8 5 4 6 9 4 2 9 3 7        Q M R H X Z D P R R E H
```

CAT BOAT RUG
RUN BEACH PLANT LIGHT
SUIT WATCH CUT STAIRS CAR
JUNK LONE GAME CALL WOOD HEART
FRAME PATCH CROSS DRUG DESK HORSE LAW
CLOTHES CHOOSE GIFT DRIVE BOOK TREE HAIR THIS
DRESS CLERK FILM BASE SPEND SERVE BOOK LOW TIME
STONE ALL NAIL DOOR HOPE EARL FEEL BUY COPE GRAPE
AGE SOFT FALL STORE PUT TRUE SMALL FREE CHECK MAIL LEAF
LOG DAY TIME CHESS LAKE CUT BIRD SHEET YOUR SEE STREET WHEEL

Visual as well as acoustic codes are used in short-term memory (Zhang & Simon, 1985). However, information that is coded visually tends to fade much more quickly (Cornoldi, DeBeni, & Baldi, 1989).

Storage Capacity of Short-Term Memory   You can easily determine the capacity of short-term memory by conducting the simple experiment shown in Figure 7.6 (Howard, 1983). The maximum number of items you are able to recall perfectly after one presentation is called your **immediate memory span**. If your memory span is like most people's, you can repeat about six or seven items from the test in this figure. The interesting thing is that you should come up with about the same number whether you estimate your immediate memory span with digits, letters, words, or virtually any type of unit (Pollack, 1953). When George Miller (1956) noticed that studies of a wide variety of tasks showed the same limit on the ability to process information, he pointed out that the limit seems to be a "magic number" of seven plus or minus two. This is the capacity of short-term memory. In addition, the "magic number" refers not to a certain number of discrete elements but to the number of meaningful *groupings* of information, called **chunks**.

To see the difference between discrete elements and chunks, read the following letters to a friend, pausing at each dash: *MT-VVC-RC-IAU-SAB-MW*. The chances are that your friend will not be able to repeat this string of letters perfectly. Why? There are fifteen letters, a total that exceeds most people's immediate memory span. But if you read the letters so that they are grouped as *MTV-VCR-CIA-USA-BMW*, your friend will probably repeat the string easily (Bower, 1975). Although the same fifteen letters are involved, they will be processed as only five meaningful chunks of information.

The Power of Chunking   Chunks of information can become very complex. If someone read to you, "The boy in the red shirt kicked his mother in the shin," you could probably repeat the sentence very easily. Yet it contains twelve words and forty-three letters. How can you repeat the sentence so effortlessly? The answer is that people can build bigger and bigger chunks of information (Ericsson & Staszewski, 1989). In this case, you might represent "the boy in the red shirt" as one chunk of information rather than as six words or nineteen letters. Similarly, "kicked his mother" and "in the shin" represent separate chunks of information.

Chunking in Action

Those who provide instantaneous translation during international negotiations must store long, often complicated segments of speech in short-term memory while searching long-term memory for the equivalent second-language expressions. The task is made easier by chunking the speaker's words into phrases and sentences.

Learning to use bigger and bigger chunks of information can enhance short-term memory. Children's memories improve in part because they gradually become able to hold as many as seven chunks in memory, but also because they become better able to group information into chunks (Servan-Schreiber & Anderson, 1990). Adults, too, can greatly increase the capacity of their short-term memory by more appropriate chunking (Waldrop, 1987); one man increased his immediate memory span to approximately one hundred items (Chase & Ericsson, 1981). In short, although the capacity of short-term memory is more or less constant—five to nine chunks of meaningful information—the size of those chunks can vary tremendously.

Duration of Short-Term Memory   Imagine what life would be like if you kept remembering every phone number you ever dialed or every conversation you ever heard. This does not happen because most people usually forget information in short-term memory quickly unless they continue repeating it to themselves (through maintenance rehearsal). You may have experienced this adaptive, though sometimes inconvenient, phenomenon if you have ever been interrupted while repeating to yourself a new phone number you were about to dial, and then couldn't recall the number.

How long does unrehearsed information remain in short-term memory? To answer this question, John Brown (1958) and Lloyd and Margaret Peterson (1959) devised the **Brown-Peterson procedure**, which is a method for preventing rehearsal. A person is presented with a group of three letters, such as *GRB*, and then counts backward by threes from some number until a signal is given. Counting prevents the person from rehearsing the letters. At the signal, the person stops counting and tries to recall the letters. By varying the number of seconds that the person counts backward, the experimenter can determine how much forgetting takes place over a certain amount of time. As you can see in Figure 7.7, information in short-term memory is forgotten gradually but rapidly: After eighteen seconds, participants can remember almost nothing. Evidence from these and other experiments suggests that *unrehearsed* information can be maintained in short-term memory for no more than about eighteen seconds.

Long-Term Memory

Short-term, or working, memory holds information so briefly that it is not what people usually have in mind when they talk about memory. Usually, they are thinking about **long-term memory (LTM)**, which we now consider.

Encoding in Long-Term Memory   Some information is encoded into long-term memory automatically, without any conscious attempt to memorize it (Ellis, 1991). However, encoding information into long-term memory is often the result of a relatively deep level of conscious processing, which usually involves some degree of *seman-*

FIGURE 7.7

Forgetting in Short-Term Memory

This graph shows the percentage of nonsense syllables recalled after various intervals during which rehearsal was prevented. Notice that virtually complete forgetting occurred after a delay of eighteen seconds.

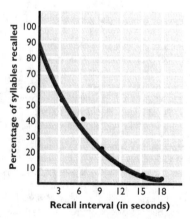

Source: Data from Peterson & Peterson, 1959.

Acquiring New Memories

FIGURE 7.8

Encoding into Long-Term Memory

Which is the correct image of a U.S. penny? (See page 226 for the answer.)

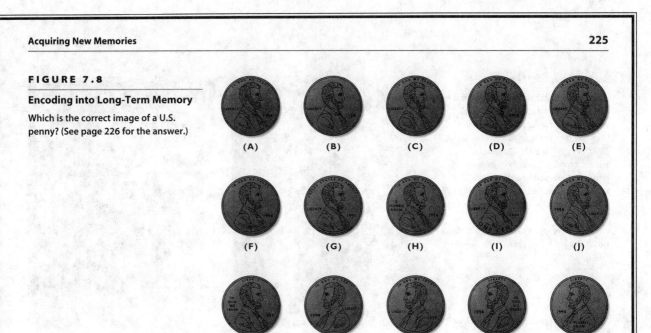

Source: Nickerson & Adams, 1979.

tic encoding. In other words, encoding in long-term memory often ignores details and instead encodes the general, underlying meaning of the information.

The dominance of semantic encoding in long-term memory was demonstrated in a classic study by Jacqueline Sachs (1967). First, people listened to tape-recorded passages. Then Sachs gave them sentences and asked whether each exact sentence had been in the taped passage. People did very well when they were tested immediately (using mainly short-term memory). However, after only twenty-seven seconds, at which point the information had to be retrieved from long-term memory, they could not determine which of two sentences they had heard if both sentences expressed the same meaning. For example, they could not determine whether they had heard "He sent a letter about it to Galileo, the great Italian scientist" or "A letter about it was sent to Galileo, the great Italian scientist." In short, they remembered the general meaning of what they had heard, but not the exact wording.

Counterfeiters depend on the fact that people encode the general meaning of visual stimuli rather than specific details. For example, look at Figure 7.8 and find the correct drawing of the United States penny (Nickerson & Adams, 1979). Most people from the United States are unsuccessful at this task, just as people from Great Britain do poorly at recognizing their country's coins (Jones, 1990). This finding helps explain why the United States Treasury has begun using more distinctive drawings on the paper currencies it distributes.

Long-term memory normally involves semantic encoding, but people can also use visual encoding to process images into long-term memory. In one study, people viewed 2,500 pictures. Although it took sixteen hours just to present the stimuli, the participants later correctly recognized more than 90 percent of the pictures tested (Standing, Conezio, & Haber, 1970). One reason pictures are remembered so well is that these stimuli may be represented in terms of both a visual code and a semantic code. *Dual coding* theory suggests that information is remembered better when it is represented in both codes rather than in only one (Paivio, 1986).

Storage Capacity of Long-Term Memory   Whereas the capacity of short-term memory is limited, the capacity of long-term memory is extremely large; most theorists believe it is literally unlimited (Matlin, 1998). It is impossible to prove this, but

A Photographic Memory

Franco Magnani had been away from his hometown in Italy for more than 30 years, but he could still paint it from memory (see comparison photo; Sacks, 1992). People like Mr. Magnani display *eidetic imagery,* commonly called *photographic memory;* they have automatic, detailed, and vivid images of virtually everything they have ever seen. About 5 percent of all school-age children have eidetic imagery, but almost no adults have it (Haber, 1979; Merritt, 1979).

Drawing (A) shows the correct penny image in Figure 7.8.

there are no cases of people being unable to learn something new because they had too much information stored in long-term memory. We do know for sure that people store vast quantities of information in long-term memory, and that they often remember it remarkably well for long periods of time. For example, people are amazingly accurate at recognizing the faces of their high school classmates after not having seen them for over twenty-five years (Bruck, Cavanagh, & Ceci, 1991), and they do surprisingly well on tests of a foreign language or high school algebra fifty years after having formally studied these subjects (Bahrick & Hall, 1991; Bahrick et al., 1994). However, long-term memories are sometimes subject to distortion. In one study, college students were asked to recall their high-school grades. Even though the students were motivated to be accurate, they correctly remembered 89 percent of their "A" grades but only 29 percent of their "D" grades. And, perhaps not surprisingly, when they made errors, these usually involved recalling grades as being higher than they actually were (Bahrick, Hall, & Berger, 1996).

Distinguishing Between Short-Term and Long-Term Memory

Some psychologists believe that there is no need to distinguish between short-term and long-term memory: What people call short-term, or working, memory is simply that part of memory that they happen to be thinking about at any particular time, whereas long-term memory is the part of memory that they are not thinking about at any given moment. However, other psychologists argue that short-term and long-term memory are qualitatively different, that they obey different laws (Cowan, 1988). Determining whether short-term and long-term memory are functionally separate has become one of the most important topics in memory research. Evidence that information is transferred from short-term memory to a distinct storage system comes from experiments on recall.

Experiments on Recall   To conduct your own recall experiment, look at the following list of words for thirty seconds, then look away and write down as many of the words as you can, in any order: *bed, rest, quilt, dream, sheet, mattress, pillow, night, snore, pajamas.* Which words you recall depends in part on their *serial position*—that is, on where the words are in the list, as Figure 7.9 shows. This figure is a *serial-position curve,* which shows the chances of recalling words appearing in each position in a list. For the first two or three words in a list, recall tends to be very good, a characteristic

FIGURE 7.9

A Serial-Position Curve

The probability of recalling an item is plotted here as a function of its serial position in a list of items. Generally, the first several items and the last several items are most likely to be recalled.

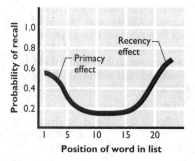

that is called the **primacy effect**. The probability of recall decreases for words in the middle of the list and then rises dramatically for the last few words. The ease of recalling words near the end of a list is called the **recency effect**. It has been suggested that the primacy effect reflects rehearsal that puts early words into *long-term memory*, and that the recency effect occurs because the last few words are still in *short-term memory* when we try to recall the list (Glanzer & Kunitz, 1966; Koppenaal & Glanzer, 1990).

K. Anders Ericsson and Walter Kintsch (1995) have proposed another way of thinking about the relationship between short-term and long-term memory. Studies of people who display unusually good memory abilities—such as waiters or waitresses renowned for their ability to remember dinner orders—suggest the operation of a "long-term working memory." According to these researchers, skilled use of memory appears to be related to an interaction between working memory and long-term memory that enables both the rapid transfer of items into long-term storage and the activation of networks of related information already in long-term storage. The excellent memories exhibited by chess masters, physicians, and, indeed, good restaurant staff, may thus reflect their ability to use chunking and other strategies to manipulate larger amounts of information than is typically associated with working memory by taking advantage of long-term memory stores in a flexible and dynamic way.

RETRIEVING MEMORIES

Have you ever been unable to recall the name of an old television show or movie star, only to think of it the next day? Remembering something requires not only that it be appropriately encoded and stored but also that you have the ability to bring it into consciousness—in other words, to retrieve it.

Retrieval Cues and Encoding Specificity

Stimuli that help people retrieve information from long-term memory are called **retrieval cues**. They allow people to recall things that were once forgotten and help them to recognize information stored in memory. In general, recognition tasks are easier than recall tasks because they contain more retrieval cues. As noted earlier, it is usually easier to recognize the correct alternative on a multiple-choice exam than to recall material for an essay test.

The effectiveness of cues in aiding retrieval depends on the degree to which they tap into information that was encoded at the time of learning (Tulving, 1979; Tulving & Thomson, 1973). This rule, known as the **encoding specificity principle**, is consistent with the transfer-appropriate processing model of memory. Because long-term memories are often encoded semantically, cues that evoke the meaning of the stored information tend to work best. For example, imagine you have learned a long list of sentences, one of which is either (1) "The man lifted the piano" or (2) "The man tuned the piano." Having the cue "something heavy" during a recall test would probably help you remember the first sentence, because you probably encoded something about the weight of a piano, but "something heavy" would probably not help you recall the second sentence. Similarly, the cue "makes nice sounds" would be likely to help you recall the second sentence, but not the first (Barclay et al., 1974).

Context and State Dependence

In general, people remember more when their efforts at recall take place in the same environment in which they learned, because they tend to encode features of the environment where the learning occurred (Richardson-Klavehn & Bjork, 1988). These features may later act as retrieval cues. In one experiment, people studied a series of pictures while in the presence of a particular odor. Later, they reviewed a larger set of photos and tried to identify the ones they had seen earlier. Half of these people were tested in the presence of the original odor and half in the presence of a different odor. Those who smelled the same odor during learning and testing did significantly better

Context-Dependent Memories

Some parents find that being in their child's schoolroom for a teacher conference provides context cues that bring back memories of their own grade school days.

FACTORS AFFECTING RETRIEVAL FROM LONG-TERM MEMORY	
Process	**Effect on Memory**
Encoding specificity	Retrieval cues are effective only to the extent that they tap into information that was originally encoded.
Context dependence	Retrieval is most successful when it occurs in the same environment in which the information was originally learned.
State dependence	Retrieval is most successful when people are in the same psychological state as when they originally learned the information.

on the recognition task than those who were tested in the presence of a different odor. The matching odor served as a powerful retrieval cue (Cann & Ross, 1989).

When memory can be helped or hindered by similarities in environmental context, it is termed **context-dependent**. One study found that students remember better when tested in the classroom in which they learned the material than when tested in a different classroom (Smith, Glenberg, & Bjork, 1978). This context-dependency effect is not always strong (Saufley, Otaka, & Bavaresco, 1985; Smith, Vela, & Williamson, 1988), but some students do find it helpful to study for a test in the classroom where the test will be given.

Like the external environment, the internal psychological environment can be encoded when people learn and thus can act as a retrieval cue. When a person's internal state can aid or impede retrieval, memory is called **state-dependent**. For example, if people learn new material while under the influence of marijuana, they tend to recall it better if they are also tested under the influence of marijuana (Eich et al., 1975). Similar effects have been found with alcohol (Overton, 1984), other drugs (Eich, 1989), and mood states. College students remember more positive incidents from their diaries or from their earlier life when they are in a positive mood at the time of recall (Ehrlichman & Halpern, 1988). More negative events tend to be recalled when people are in a negative mood (Lewinsohn & Rosenbaum, 1987). These *mood congruency effects* are strongest when people try to recall personally meaningful episodes, because such events were most likely to be colored by their mood (Eich & Metcalfe, 1989).

Retrieval from Semantic Memory

All of the retrieval situations we have discussed so far are relevant to episodic memory ("In Review: Factors Affecting Retrieval from Long-Term Memory" summarizes this material). However, *semantic memory*, which stores general knowledge about the world, is also important in everyday functioning. Researchers studying semantic memory typically ask participants general-knowledge questions such as (1) Are fish minerals? (2) Is a beagle a dog? (3) Do birds fly? and (4) Does a car have legs? As you might imagine, most people virtually always respond correctly to such questions. By measuring the amount of time people take to answer the questions, however, psychologists gain important clues about how semantic memory is organized and how information is retrieved.

Semantic Networks   One of the most influential theories of semantic memory suggests that concepts are represented in a dense network of associations (Collins & Loftus, 1975). Figure 7.10 presents a graphic representation of what a fragment of a *semantic memory network* might look like. In general, semantic network theories sug-

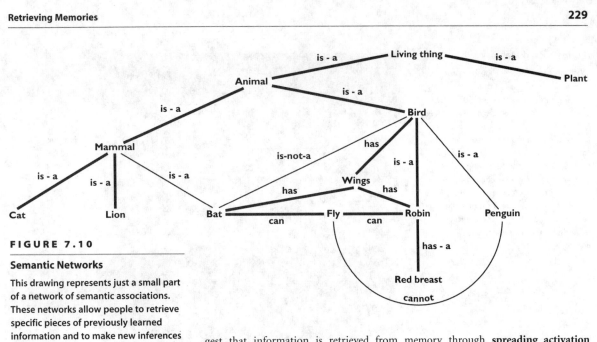

FIGURE 7.10

Semantic Networks

This drawing represents just a small part of a network of semantic associations. These networks allow people to retrieve specific pieces of previously learned information and to make new inferences about concepts.

gest that information is retrieved from memory through **spreading activation** (Eysenck & Keane, 1995). That is, whenever you think about some concept, it is activated in the network, and spreading activation (in the form of neural energy) begins to travel down all the paths related to it. For example, if a person is asked to say whether "A robin is a bird" is true or false, the concepts of both robin and bird will become activated and the spreading activation from each will intersect in the middle of the path between them.

Some associations within the network are stronger than others. Differing strengths are depicted by the varying thicknesses of the lines in Figure 7.10; spreading activation travels more quickly along thick paths than along thin ones. For example, most people probably have a stronger association between "bat" and "can fly" or "has wings" than "bat" and "is a mammal." Accordingly, most people respond more quickly to "Can a bat fly?" than to "Is a bat a mammal?"

Because of the tight organization of semantic networks and the speed at which activation spreads through them, people gain access to an enormous body of knowledge about the world quickly and effortlessly. They retrieve not only facts that they have learned directly but also knowledge that allows them to infer or to compute other facts about the world (Matlin, 1998). For example, imagine answering the following two questions: (1) Is a robin a bird? and (2) Is a robin a living thing? You can probably answer the first question "directly" because you probably learned this fact at some point in your life. However, you may never have consciously thought about the second question, so answering it requires some inference. Figure 7.10 illustrates the path to that inference. Because you know that a robin is a bird, a bird is an animal, and animals are living things, you infer that a robin must be a living thing. As you might expect, however, it takes slightly longer to answer the second question than the first.

Retrieving Incomplete Knowledge   Figure 7.10 also shows that concepts are represented in semantic memory as unique collections of features or attributes. Often, people can retrieve some features but not enough to identify a whole concept. Thus, you might know that there is an animal that has wings, can fly, but is not a bird, and yet be unable to retrieve its name (Connor, Balota, & Neely, 1992). In such cases you are said to be retrieving *incomplete knowledge*.

A common example of incomplete knowledge is the *tip-of-the-tongue phenomenon*. In a typical experiment on this phenomenon, dictionary definitions of words are read to people and they are asked to name each word (Brown & McNeill, 1966). If they cannot recall a defined word, they are asked whether they can recall any feature of it, such

A Constructed Memory

Through constructive memory processes, subjects who waited in this office "remembered" having seen books in it, even though none were present (Brewer & Treyens, 1981). Let a friend examine this photo for a minute or so (cover the caption), then close the book and ask whether each of the following items appeared in the office; chair, wastebasket, bottle, typewriter, coffeepot, and book. If your friend reports having seen a wastebasket or book, you will have demonstrated constructive memory.

PDP Models and Constructive Memory

If you were to hear that "our basketball team won last night," your schema about basketball might prompt you to encode, and later retrieve, the fact that the players were men. Such spontaneous, though often incorrect, generalizations associated with PDP models of memory help account for constructive memory.

as its first letter or how many syllables it has. People are surprisingly good at this task, indicating that they are able to retrieve at least some knowledge of the word (Brennen et al., 1990).

Another example of retrieving incomplete knowledge is the *feeling-of-knowing experience*, which is often studied by asking people trivia questions (Reder & Ritter, 1992). When they cannot answer a question, they are asked to estimate the probability that they could recognize the correct answer if they were given several options. Again, people are remarkably good at this task; even though they cannot recall the answer, they can retrieve enough knowledge to determine whether the answer is actually stored in memory (Costermans, Lories, & Ansay, 1992).

Constructing Memories

The generalized knowledge about the world that each person has stored constantly affects memory (Harris, Sardarpoor-Bascom, & Meyer, 1989). People use their existing knowledge to organize new information as they receive it and to fill in gaps in the information they encode and retrieve. In this way, memories are constructed.

To study this process, which is sometimes called *constructive memory*, William Brewer and James Treyens (1981) asked undergraduates to wait for several minutes in the office of a graduate student. When later asked to recall everything that was in the office, most of the students mistakenly "remembered" that books were present, even though there were none. Apparently, the general knowledge that graduate students read many books influenced the participants' memory of what was in the room.

Relating Semantic and Episodic Memory: PDP Models   Parallel distributed processing models offer one way of explaining how semantic and episodic information become integrated in constructive memories. As noted earlier, PDP models suggest that newly learned facts alter our general knowledge of what the world is like. Figure 7.11 shows a simple PDP network model of just a tiny part of someone's knowledge of the world (Martindale, 1991). At its center lie the intersections of several learned associations between specific facts about five people, each of whom is represented by a circle. Thus, the network "knows" that Joe is a male European-American professor who likes Brie cheese and drives a Subaru. It also "knows" that Claudia is a female African-

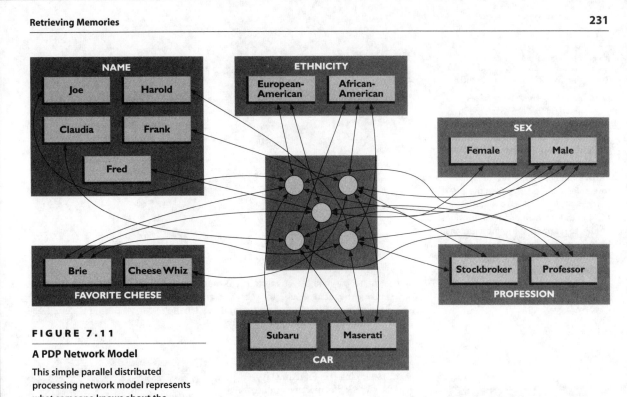

FIGURE 7.11

A PDP Network Model

This simple parallel distributed processing network model represents what someone knows about the characteristics of five people and how they are related to one another. Note that each arrow between a rectangle and a circle connects a characteristic with a person. More complex versions of such network models are capable of accounting not only for what people know but also for the inferences and generalizations they tend to make.

Source: From *Cognitive Psychology*, 1st edition, by C. Martindale, © 1991. Reprinted with permission of Wadsworth Publishing, a division of International Thomson Publishing. Fax 800-730-2215.

American professor who drives a Maserati. Notice that the network has never learned what type of cheese she prefers.

Suppose Figure 7.11 represents your memory and that you now think about Claudia. Because of the connections in the network, the facts that she is a female African-American professor and drives a Maserati would be activated; you would automatically remember these facts about Claudia. However, "likes Brie cheese" would also be activated because it is linked to other professors in the network. If the level of activation for Brie cheese is low, then the proposition that Claudia likes Brie cheese might be considered a hypothesis or an educated guess. But suppose *every other professor* you know likes Brie. In that case, the connection between professors and "likes Brie cheese" would be strong, and the conclusion that Claudia likes Brie cheese would be held so confidently that it would take overwhelming evidence for you to change your mind (Rumelhart & McClelland, 1986).

PDP networks also produce *spontaneous generalizations*. If a friend told you she just bought a new car, you would know without asking that—like all other cars you have experienced—it has four wheels. However, spontaneous generalizations can create significant errors if the network is based on limited or biased experience with a class of objects. For example, if the network in Figure 7.11 were asked what European-American males are like, it would think that all of them drive Japanese cars.

This aspect of PDP networks—generalizing from scanty information—is actually an accurate reflection of human thought and memory. Virtually all people make spontaneous generalizations about males, females, European-Americans, African-Americans, and many other categories (Martindale, 1991).

Schemas   Parallel distributed processing models also help us understand constructive memory by explaining the operation of the schemas that guide it. **Schemas** are mental representations of categories of objects, events, and people. For example, most Americans have a schema for *baseball game*, so that simply hearing these words is likely to activate whole clusters of information in long-term memory, including the rules of the game, images of players, bats, balls, a green field, summer days, and, perhaps, hot dogs and stadiums. The generalized knowledge contained in schemas provides a basis for making inferences about incoming information during the encoding stage. So if

FIGURE 7.12

The Effect of Schemas on Recall

In one early experiment, participants were shown figures like these, along with labels designed to activate certain schemas (Carmichael, Hogan, & Walter, 1932). For example, when showing the top figure, the experimenter said either "This resembles eyeglasses" or "This resembles a dumbbell." When the participants were asked to reproduce the figures from memory, their drawings tended to resemble the items mentioned by the experimenter. In other words, their memory had been altered by the labels.

Figure shown to participants	Group 1		Group 2	
	Label given	Figure drawn by participants	Label given	Figure drawn by participants
◯–◯	Eyeglasses	◯◯	Dumbbell	◯—◯
✕	Hourglass	✕	Table	✕
7	Seven	7	Four	4
🔫	Gun	🔫	Broom	🧹

you hear that a baseball player was injured, your schema about baseball might prompt you to encode the incident as game related, even though the cause was not mentioned. As a result, you are likely to recall the injury as having occurred during a game (see Figure 7.12 for another example).

LINKAGES

Do forgotten memories remain in the subconscious? (a link to Consciousness)

THINKING CRITICALLY

Recovered Memories—
True or False?

In 1989, Eileen Franklin-Lipsker told police in California that, upon looking into her young daughter's eyes one day, she suddenly had a vivid memory of seeing her father kill her childhood friend more than twenty years earlier. Her father, George Franklin, Sr., was sent to prison for murder on the basis of her testimony about that memory (Loftus & Ketcham, 1994). This case sparked a controversy that has continued to grow in intensity, involving not only psychologists but the American legal system as well. The controversy concerns the validity of claims of recovered memory. Some psychologists accept the idea that it is possible for people to repress, or push into unconsciousness, memories of traumatic incidents and then recover these memories many years later. Other psychologists, however, are more skeptical about recovered memory claims.

■ What am I being asked to believe or accept?

The prosecution in the Franklin case successfully argued that Eileen had recovered the memory of a traumatic event. Similar arguments in other cases resulted in the imprisonment of a number of parents whose now-adult children claim to have recovered childhood memories of physical or sexual abuse. The juries in these trials accepted the assertion that people can be unconsciously motivated to forget traumatic events and that, under the right conditions, complete and accurate memories of the events can reappear (Kihlstrom, 1995; Loftus, 1997a). Jurors are not the only believers in this phenomenon. Recently, a news organization in the United States reported that U.S. troops had illegally used nerve gas during the war in Vietnam—a story based, in part, on a Vietnam veteran's recovered memories of a gas attack (*New York Times*, July 3, 1998).

■ What evidence is available to support the assertion?

Proponents of the recovered memory argument point to several lines of evidence to support their claims. First, there is evidence that a substantial amount of mental activity occurs outside conscious awareness (Kihlstrom, 1996; see Chapter 9). Second, research on implicit memory shows that information of which we are unaware can still influence our behavior (Schacter, Chiu, & Ochsner, 1993). Third, research on *motivated*

Exploring Memory Processes

Research by cognitive psychologist Elizabeth Loftus has demonstrated mechanisms through which false memories can be created. Her work has helped to focus scientific scrutiny on reports of recovered memories, especially those arising from contact with therapists who assume that most people have repressed memories of abuse.

forgetting suggests that people may be more likely to forget unpleasant rather than pleasant events (Erdelyi, 1985). In one study, a psychologist kept a detailed record of his daily life over a six-year period. When he later tried to recall these experiences, he remembered more than half of the positive ones, but only one-third of the negative ones. In another study, 38 percent of women who, as children, had been brought to a hospital because of sexual abuse could not recall the incident as adults (Williams, 1994a). Fourth, retrieval cues can help people accurately recall memories that had previously been inaccessible to conscious awareness (Landsdale & Laming, 1995). For example, there are carefully documented cases of soldiers recovering, after many years, vivid and accurate memories of the circumstances in which they were wounded (Karon & Widener, 1997). Finally, there is the confidence with which people report recovered memories; they say they are just too vivid to be anything but real.

■ **Are there alternative ways of interpreting the evidence?**

Those who are skeptical about recovered memories do not deny the operation of subconscious memory and retrieval processes (Greenwald, 1992). They also recognize that, sadly, child abuse and other traumas are all too common. But these facts do not eliminate the possibility that any given "recovered" memory may actually be a distorted, or constructed, memory (Loftus, 1998; Loftus & Pickrell, 1995). As already noted, our recall of past events is affected by what happened at the time, what we knew beforehand, and everything we experience since. The people who "remembered" nonexistent books in a graduate student's office constructed that memory based on what prior knowledge led them to *assume* was there (see photo on page 230).

Research shows that *false memories*—distortions of actual events and the recall of events that didn't actually happen—can be at least as vivid as accurate ones, and people can be just as confident in them (Brainerd & Reyna, 1998; Brainerd, Reyna, & Brandse, 1995; Roediger & McDermott, 1995). In one case study, for example, a teenager named Chris was given descriptions of four incidents from his childhood and asked to write about each of them every day for five days (Loftus, 1997a). One of these incidents—being lost in a shopping mall at age five—never really happened. Yet Chris not only eventually "remembered" this event but added many details about the mall and the stranger whose hand he was supposedly found holding. He also rated this (false) memory as being more vivid than two of the other three (real) incidents. The same pattern of results has appeared in more formal experiments on the planting of emotion-laden false memories (Hyman & Pentland, 1996). For example, researchers have been able to create vivid and striking, but *completely false*, memories of events that people thought they experienced when they were one day old (DuBreuil, Garry, & Loftus, in press). And the "recovered memory" of the Vietnam veteran mentioned earlier appears to have no basis in fact; the news story about the alleged nerve gas attack was later retracted.

Why would anyone "remember" an event that did not actually occur—especially a traumatic one? Elizabeth Loftus (1997b) suggests that, for one thing, popular books such as *The Courage to Heal* (Bass & Davis, 1988) and *Secret Survivors* (Blume, 1990) have planted in many minds the idea that anyone who experiences guilt, depression, low self-esteem, overemotionality, or any of a long list of other problems is harboring repressed memories of abuse. This message, says Loftus, tends to be reinforced and extended by therapists who specialize in using guided imagination, hypnosis, and other methods to "help" clients recover repressed memories (Polusny & Follette, 1996; Poole et al., 1995). In so doing, these therapists may influence people to construct false memories (Olio, 1994). As one client described her therapy, "I was rapidly losing the ability to differentiate between my imagination and my real memory" (Loftus & Ketcham, 1994, p. 25). To such therapists, a client's failure to recover memories of abuse, or refusal to accept their existence, is evidence of "denial" of the truth.

The possibility that recovered memories might actually be false memories has led to dismissed charges or not-guilty verdicts for defendants in some repressed memory cases, and to the release of previously convicted defendants in others (George Franklin's conviction was overturned.) Concern over the potential damage resulting from false memories has led to the establishment of the False Memory Syndrome Foundation, a support group for families affected by abuse accusations stemming from allegedly repressed memories. More than 100 such families have filed lawsuits against therapists and hospitals (False Memory Syndrome Foundation, 1997). In 1994, California winery executive Gary Ramona received $500,000 in damages from two therapists who had "helped" his daughter recall alleged sexual abuse at his hands. A more recent suit led to a $2 million judgment against a Minnesota therapist whose client realized that her "recovered" memories of childhood abuse were false; a similar case in Illinois resulted in a $10.6 million settlement (Loftus, 1998).

■ What additional evidence would help to evaluate the alternatives?

Evaluating reports of recovered memories would be aided by more information about how common it is for people to forget traumatic events. So far, we know that intense emotional experiences usually produce memories that are vivid and long-lasting (Shobe & Kihlstrom, 1997). Some are called *flashbulb memories* because they preserve particular experiences in great detail (Brown & Kulik, 1977). Indeed, many people who live through trauma are *unable* to forget it. In the sexual abuse study mentioned earlier, for example, 62 percent of the abuse victims did recall their trauma. More studies like this one—which track the fate of memories in known abuse cases—would not only help estimate the prevalence of this kind of forgetting but might also offer clues as to the kinds of people and events most likely to be associated with it.

It would also be valuable to know more about what mechanisms might be responsible for recovered memories and how they relate to empirically established theories and models of human memory. Thus far, cognitive psychologists have not found evidence of such mechanisms (Shobe & Kihlstrom, 1997).

■ What conclusions are most reasonable?

An objective reading of the available research evidence supports the view that recovery of memories of trauma is at least possible, but that the implantation of false memories is also possible—and has been demonstrated experimentally.

The intense conflict between the False Memory Syndrome Foundation and those psychologists who accept as genuine most of the memories recovered in therapy reflects a fundamental disagreement about recovered memories: Client reports constitute "proof" for therapists who deal daily with victims of sexual abuse and other traumas, and who rely more on personal experiences than on scientific research findings. Those reports may not be accepted as valid by empirically oriented psychologists.

In short, whether one believes a claim of recovered memory may be determined by the relative weight one assigns to personal experiences and intuition versus empirical evidence. Still, the apparent ease with which false memories can be created should lead judges, juries, and the general public to exercise great caution before accepting as valid unverified memories of traumatic events. At the same time, we should not automatically and uncritically reject the claims of people who appear to have recovered memories. Perhaps the wisest course is to use all the scientific and circumstantial evidence available to carefully and critically examine such claims, while keeping in mind that constructive memory processes *might* have influenced them. This careful, scientific approach is vital if we are to protect the rights and welfare of those who report recovered memories, as well as of those who face accusations arising from them.

FORGETTING

The frustrations of forgetting—where you left your keys, the answer to a test question, an anniversary—are apparent to most people nearly every day. In this section we look more closely at the nature of forgetting, and at some of the mechanisms that are responsible for it.

"As I get older, I find I rely more and more on these sticky notes to remind me."

Durable Memories

This woman has not used a pogo stick since she was ten. Her memory of how to do it is not entirely gone, however, so she will show some "savings": It will take her less time to relearn the skill than it took to learn it initially.

The Course of Forgetting

About a hundred years ago, Hermann Ebbinghaus, a German psychologist, began the systematic study of memory and forgetting, using only himself as the subject of his research. His aim was to study memory in its "pure" form, uncontaminated by emotional reactions and other pre-existing associations between new material and what was already in memory. To eliminate such associations, Ebbinghaus created the *nonsense syllable*, a meaningless set of two consonants and a vowel, such as *POF*, *XEM*, and *QAL*. He read a list of nonsense syllables aloud, to the beat of a metronome—a mechanical device that emits a sound at constant intervals. Then he tried to recall the syllables.

To measure forgetting, Ebbinghaus devised the **method of savings**, which involves computing the difference between the number of repetitions needed to learn a list of items and the number of repetitions needed to relearn it after some time has elapsed. This difference is called the *savings*. If it took Ebbinghaus ten trials to learn a list and ten more trials to relearn it, there would be no savings, and forgetting would have been complete. If it took him ten trials to learn the list and only five trials to relearn it, there would be a savings of 50 percent.

As you can see in Figure 7.13 (on page 236), Ebbinghaus found that savings decline (and forgetting increases) as time passes. However, the most dramatic drop in what people retain in long-term memory occurs during the first nine hours, especially in the first hour. After this initial decline, the rate of forgetting slows down considerably. In Ebbinghaus's study, some savings existed even thirty-one days after the original learning.

Ebbinghaus's research had some important limitations, but it produced two lasting discoveries. One is the shape of the forgetting curve depicted in Figure 7.13. Psychologists have subsequently substituted words, sentences, and even stories for nonsense syllables. In virtually all cases the forgetting curve shows the same strong initial drop in memory, followed by a much more moderate decrease over time (Slamecka & McElree, 1983). Of course, people remember sensible stories better than nonsense syllables, but the shape of the curve is the same no matter what type of material is involved (Davis & Moore, 1935). Even the forgetting of daily events from one's life tends to follow Ebbinghaus's forgetting function (Thomson, 1982).

The second of Ebbinghaus's important discoveries is just how long-lasting "savings" in long-term memory can be. Psychologists now know from the method of savings

FIGURE 7.13

Ebbinghaus's Curve of Forgetting

Ebbinghaus found that most forgetting takes place during the first nine hours after learning, especially in the first hour

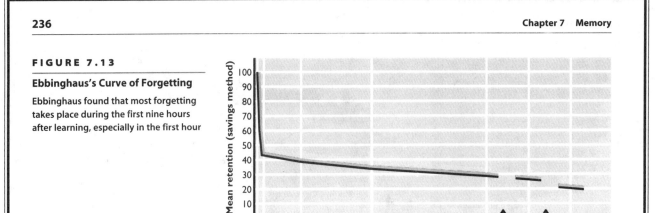

FIGURE 7.14

Procedures for Studying Interference

To recall the two types of interference, remember that the prefixes—*pro* and *retro*—indicate directions in time. In *pro*active interference, previously learned material interferes with *future* learning; *retro*active interference occurs when new information interferes with the recall of *past* learning.

that information about everything from algebra to bike-riding is often retained for decades (Matlin, 1998). Thus, you may forget something you have learned if you do not use the information, but it is easy to relearn the material if the need arises, indicating that the forgetting was not complete (MacLeod, 1988).

The Roles of Decay and Interference

Nothing we have said so far explains why forgetting occurs. In principle, either of two processes can be responsible (Reed, 1992). One process is **decay**, the gradual disappearance of the mental representation of a stimulus, much as letters engraved on a piece of steel are eaten away by rust and become less distinct over time. Forgetting might also occur because of **interference**, a process through which either the storage or retrieval of information is impaired by the presence of other information. Interference might occur either because one piece of information actually *displaces* other information, pushing it out of memory, or because one piece of information makes storing or recalling other information more difficult.

In the case of short-term memory, we noted that if an item is not rehearsed or thought about, memory of it decreases consistently over the course of eighteen seconds or so. Thus decay appears to play a prominent role in forgetting information in short-term memory. But interference through displacement also produces forgetting from short-term memory (Klatzky, 1980). Displacement is one reason why the phone number you just looked up is likely to drop out of short-term memory if you read another

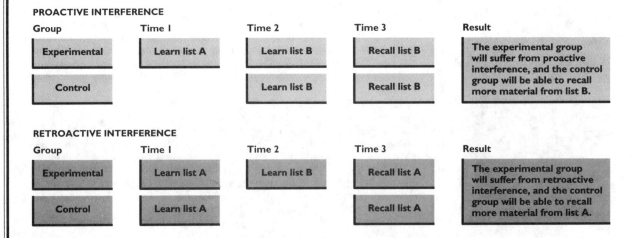

Forgetting **237**

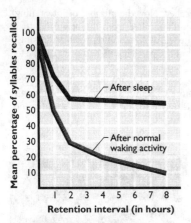

Source: Minimi & Dallenbach, 1946.

FIGURE 7.15

Interference and Forgetting

Forgetting is more rapid if college students engage in normal activity after learning than if they spend the time asleep. These results suggest that interference is more important than decay in forgetting information in long-term memory.

number before dialing. Rehearsal prevents displacement by continually re-entering the same information into short-term memory.

Analyzing the cause of forgetting from long-term memory is more complicated. In long-term memory there can be **retroactive interference**, in which learning of new information interferes with recall of older information, or **proactive interference**, in which old information interferes with learning or remembering new information. For example, retroactive interference would help explain why studying French vocabulary this term might make it more difficult to remember the Spanish words you learned last term. And because of proactive interference, the French words you are learning now might make it harder to learn German next term. Figure 7.14 outlines the types of experiments used to study the influence of each form of interference in long-term memory.

Suppose a person learns something and then, when tested on it after various intervals, remembers less and less as the delay becomes longer. Is this forgetting due to decay or to interference? It is not easy to tell, because longer delays produce both more decay and more retroactive interference as the person is exposed to further information while waiting. To separate the effects of decay from those of interference, Karl Dallenbach sought to create situations in which time passed but there was no accompanying interference. Evidence of forgetting in such a situation would suggest that decay, not interference, was operating.

In one of Dallenbach's studies, college students learned a list of nonsense syllables and then either continued with their waking routine or were sheltered from interference by going to sleep (Jenkins & Dallenbach, 1924). Although the delay (and thus the potential for decay) was held constant for both groups, the greater interference associated with being awake produced much more forgetting, as Figure 7.15 shows.

Results like these suggest that although it is possible that decay sometimes occurs, interference is the major cause of forgetting from long-term memory. But does interference push the forgotten information out of memory, or does it merely hinder the ability to retrieve it? To find out, Endel Tulving and Joseph Psotka (1971) presented people with different numbers of word lists. Each list contained words from one of six semantic categories, such as types of buildings (*hut, cottage, tent, hotel*) or earth formations (*cliff, river, hill, volcano*). Some people learned a list and then recalled as many of the words as possible. Other groups learned the first list and then learned different numbers of other lists before trying to recall the first one.

The results were dramatic. As the number of intervening lists increased, the number of words that people could recall from the original list declined consistently. This finding reflected strong retroactive interference. Then the researchers gave a second test, in which they provided people with a retrieval cue by telling them the category of

FIGURE 7.16

Retrieval Failures and Forgetting

On the initial test in Tulving and Psotka's experiment, people's ability to recall a list of items was strongly affected by the number of other lists they learned before being tested on the first one. When item-category (retrieval) cues were provided on a second test, however, retroactive interference from the intervening lists almost disappeared.

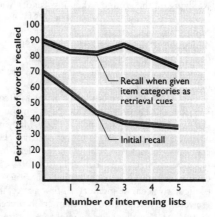

Source: Tulving & Psotka, 1971.

the words (such as types of buildings) to be recalled. Now the number of intervening lists had almost no effect on the number of words recalled from the original list, as Figure 7.16 shows. These results indicate that the words were still represented in long-term memory; they had not been pushed out, but the participants had been unable to recall them without appropriate retrieval cues. In other words, the original forgetting was due to a failure in retrieval. Thus, putting more and more information in long-term memory may be like placing more and more CDs into a storage case. Although none of the CDs disappears, it becomes increasingly difficult to find the specific one you are looking for.

LINKAGES

Memory and Perception in the Courtroom

As described in Chapter 5, in order for incoming information to be encoded into memory, it must first be perceived. Perception, in turn, is influenced by a combination of the stimulus features we find "out there" in the world and what we already know, expect, or want—that is, by both bottom-up and top-down processing. The relationship between memory and perception, especially the impact of top-down processing on memory, is made dramatically evident in the courtroom.

LINKAGES

How accurate is eyewitness testimony? (a link to Perception)

Consider, for example, the accuracy of eyewitness memory and how it can be affected by extraneous information (Loftus, 1993). The most compelling evidence a lawyer can provide is that of an eyewitness, but eyewitnesses make many mistakes (Loftus & Ketcham, 1991). During a federal arson trial in Chicago, for example, a witness was asked if she could identify the man she saw running from a burning building. "That's the guy," she said, looking toward a corner of the courtroom. The judge asked her to single out the man—whereupon she walked over and pointed at an assistant defense attorney (Gottesman, 1992).

Eyewitnesses can remember only what they perceived, and they can have perceived only what they attended to (Backman & Nilsson, 1991). The witnesses' task is to report as accurately as possible what they saw or heard; but no matter how hard they try to be accurate, there are limits to how faithful their reports can be (Kassin, Rigby, & Castillo, 1991). Further, new information, including the form of a lawyer's question, can alter a witness's memory (Loftus, 1979). Experiments show that when witnesses are asked, "How fast was the blue car going when it slammed into the truck?" they are likely to recall a higher speed than when asked, "How fast was the blue car going when it hit the truck?" (Loftus & Palmer, 1974; see Figure 7.17). There is also evidence that an object mentioned after the fact is often mistakenly remembered as having been there in the first place (Dodson & Reisberg, 1991). For example, if a lawyer says that a screwdriver was lying on the ground (when it was not), witnesses often recall with great certainty having seen it (Ryan & Geiselman, 1991). Some theorists have speculated that mentioning an object creates retroactive interference, making the original memory more difficult to retrieve (Tversky & Tuchin, 1989). However, there is now considerable evidence that, when objects are subsequently mentioned, they are integrated into the old memory representation and subsequently are not distinguished from what was originally seen (Loftus, 1992).

For jurors, the credibility of a witness often depends as much (or even more) on *how* the witness presents evidence as on the content or relevance of that evidence (Leippe, Manion, & Romanczyk, 1992). Many jurors are impressed, for example, when a witness can recall a large number of details. Extremely detailed testimony from prosecution witnesses is especially likely to lead to guilty verdicts, even when the details reported are irrelevant (Bell & Loftus, 1989). Apparently, when a witness gives very detailed testimony, jurors infer that the witness paid especially close attention or has a particularly accurate memory. At first glance, these inferences might seem reasonable. However, as discussed in the chapter on perception, the ability to divide attention is limited. As a result, a witness might focus attention on the crime and the criminal or

FIGURE 7.17

The Impact of Leading Questions on Eyewitness Memory

After seeing a filmed traffic accident, people were asked, "About how fast were the cars going when they (smashed, hit, or contacted) each other?" As shown here, the witnesses' responses were influenced by the verb used in the question; "smashed" was associated with the highest average speed estimates. A week later, people who heard the "smashed" question remembered the accident as being more violent than did people in the other two groups (Loftus & Palmer, 1974).

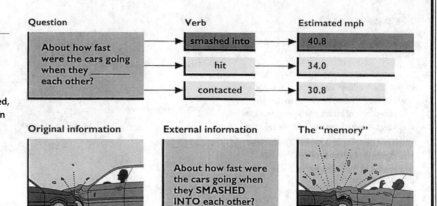

on the surrounding details, but probably not on both. Hence, witnesses who accurately remember unimportant details of a crime scene may not accurately recall the criminal's facial features or other identifying characteristics (Backman & Nilsson, 1991).

Juries also tend to believe a confident witness (Leippe, Manion, & Romanczyk, 1992), but witnesses' confidence about their testimony is frequently much higher than its accuracy (Shaw, 1996). In fact, repeated exposure to misinformation and the repeated recall of misinformation can increase a witness's confidence in objectively incorrect testimony (Lamb, 1998; Mitchell & Zaragoza, 1996; Roediger, Jacoby, & McDermott, 1996).

BIOLOGICAL BASES OF MEMORY

LINKAGES

Where are memories stored? (a link to Biological Aspects of Psychology)

While most psychologists study memory by focusing on conscious and subconscious mental processes, some also consider the physical, electrical, and chemical changes that take place in the brain when people encode, store, and retrieve information. The story of the scientific search for the biological bases of memory begins with the work of Karl Lashley and Donald Hebb, who spent many years studying how memory is related to brain structures and processes. Lashley (1950) taught rats new behaviors and then observed how damage to various parts of the rats' brains changed their ability to perform the tasks they had learned. Lashley hoped that his work would identify the brain area which contained the "engram"—the physical manifestation of memory in the brain. However, after many experiments, he concluded that memories are not localized in one specific region, but, instead, are distributed throughout large areas of brain tissue (Lashley, 1950).

At around the same time, Hebb, who was a student of Lashley's, proposed another biological theory of memory. Hebb believed that a given memory is represented by a group of interconnected neurons in the brain. This set of neurons, which he called a *cell assembly*, formed a network in the cortex. The connections among these neurons were strengthened, he said, when the neurons were simultaneously stimulated through sensory experiences (Hebb, 1949). Though not correct in all its details, Hebb's theory stimulated much research and contributed to an understanding of the physical basis of memory. It is also consistent, in many respects, with contemporary parallel distributed processing models of memory (Hergenhahn & Olson, 1997).

Let's now consider more recent research on the biochemical mechanisms and brain structures that are most directly involved in memory processes.

FIGURE 7.18

Some Brain Structures Involved in Memory

Combined neural activity in many parts of the brain allows us to encode, store, and retrieve memories. The complexity of the biological bases of these processes is underscored by research showing that different aspects of a memory—such as the sights and sounds of some event—are stored in different parts of the cerebral cortex.

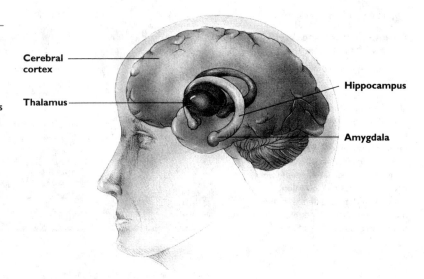

Cerebral cortex

Thalamus

Hippocampus

Amygdala

Biochemical Mechanisms

As described in Chapter 3, communication among brain cells takes place at the synapses between axons and dendrites, and it depends on chemicals, called *neurotransmitters*, released at the synapses. There is evidence that new memories are associated with at least two kinds of changes in synapses.

First, environmental stimulation can promote the formation of new synapses, which increases the complexity of the communication networks through which neurons receive information (Black & Greenough, 1991; Rosenzweig & Bennett, 1996). It is likely that these new synapses are involved in the storage of new memories.

Second, functional changes can occur at existing synapses. The enhancement of existing synapses has been most clearly demonstrated in brain tissue studied in a laboratory dish or in living marine snails. By studying individual synapses as a new memory is formed, researchers have discovered that simultaneous activation of two inputs to a synapse later makes it easier for a signal from a single input to cross the synapse (Sejnowski, Chattarji, & Stanton, 1990). Changing the pattern of electrical stimulation can also weaken synaptic connections (Malenka, 1995).

In the hippocampus (see Figure 7.18), these changes appear to occur at synapses that use glutamate as a neurotransmitter. One type of glutamate receptor is initially activated only if the postsynaptic neuron is being stimulated by input from more than one neuron (Cotman, Monaghan, & Ganong, 1988). After these multiple stimulations are repeated a number of times, this type of glutamate receptor appears to become sensitized so that input from just one neuron is sufficient to produce a response. Such a change in sensitivity could account for the development of conditioned responses, for example.

Acetylcholine also plays a prominent role in memory. The memory problems of Alzheimer's patients appear to be related to a deficiency in neurons that use acetylcholine and send fibers to the hippocampus and the cortex (Muir, 1997). Drugs that interfere with acetylcholine neurotransmission impair memory, and drugs or dietary supplements that increase the amount of acetylcholine in the brain sometimes improve memory in aging experimental animals and humans (Parnetti, Senin, & Mecocci, 1997). However, increasing general acetylcholine levels probably won't improve memory. A more appropriate goal might be to selectively enhance acetylcholine activity at the synapses used in memory. One way of doing so in the future might be to implant in the brain some cells that have been genetically modified to produce acetylcholine. When this procedure was performed on brain-damaged animals, it improved their memory (Li & Low, 1997; Winkler et al., 1995).

In short, research has shown that changes in individual synapses help to strengthen networks that are activated repetitively—specifically, by improving transmission through the networks. This finding provides some support for the ideas formulated by Hebb many years ago.

Brain Structures

Where in the brain do memory-related mechanisms occur? Researchers have concluded that memory involves both specialized regions for memory formation and widespread areas for storage (McCarthy, 1995; Zola-Morgan & Squire, 1990). In the formation of new memories, several brain regions are vital (see Figure 7.18), including the hippocampus and nearby parts of the cortex and the thalamus (Brewer et al., 1998; Squire & Zola, 1996).

The Impact of Brain Damage   Studies of how brain injuries affect memory provide evidence about the brain regions involved in various kinds of memory (Martinez, Scalds, & Weinberger, 1991). For example, damage to the hippocampus, which is part of the limbic system, often results in **anterograde amnesia**, a loss of memory for any event occurring after the injury.

A striking example is seen in the case of H.M. (Milner, 1966). Part of H.M.'s hippocampus had been removed in order to end severe epileptic seizures. Afterward, both his long-term and short-term memory appeared normal, but he had a severe problem. The operation had been performed when he was twenty-seven years old. Two years later, he still believed that he was twenty-seven. When his family moved into a new house, H.M. could not remember the new address or even how to get there. When told that his uncle had died, he grieved in a normal way. But soon thereafter, he began to ask why his uncle had not visited him. Each time he was told of his uncle's death, H.M. became just as upset as when he was first told. In short, the surgery had apparently destroyed the mechanism that transfers information from short-term to long-term memory.

Interestingly, although such patients cannot form new episodic memories following hippocampal damage, they can use their *procedural memory*. For example, H.M. was presented with a complicated puzzle on which mistakes are common and performance gradually improves with practice. Over several days his performance steadily improved, just as it does with normal people, and eventually became virtually perfect. But each time he tried the puzzle, he insisted that he had never seen it before (Cohen & Corkin, 1981; see Figure 9.3 on page 296).

Other researchers, too, have found intact procedural memories in patients who have anterograde amnesia for any new episodic material (Squire & McKee, 1992; Tulving, Hayman, & Macdonald, 1991). These patients are also able to keep information temporarily in working memory, which depends on the activity of dopamine neurons in the prefrontal cortex (Williams & Goldman-Rakic, 1995). Thus, while the hippocampus is crucial in the formation of new episodic memories, procedural memory and working memory appear to be governed by other regions of the brain (Squire, 1992).

Retrograde amnesia, which involves a loss of memory for events *prior* to a brain injury, is also consistent with the idea that memory processes are widely distributed. Often, a person with this condition is unable to remember anything that took place in the months, or even years, before the injury. In most cases, the memories return gradually. The most distant events are recalled first, and the person gradually regains memory for events leading up to the injury. Recovery is seldom complete, however, and the person may never remember the last few seconds before the injury. For example, one man received a severe blow to the head after being thrown from his motorcycle. After regaining consciousness, he claimed that he was eleven years old. Over the next three months, he gradually recovered his memory right up until the time he was riding his motorcycle the day of the accident. But he was never able to remember what happened just before

and rereading (Glover et al., 1990). Repetition may seem effective, because it keeps material in short-term memory; but for retaining information over long periods, repetition alone tends to be ineffective, no matter how much time you spend on it (Bjorklund & Green, 1992). In short, "work smarter, not harder."

In addition, spend your time wisely. *Distributed practice* is much more effective than *massed practice* for learning new information. If you are going to spend ten hours studying for a test, you will be much better off studying for ten one-hour blocks (separated by periods of sleep and other activity) than "cramming" for one ten-hour block. By scheduling more study sessions, you will stay fresh and tend to think about the material from a new perspective each session. This method will help you elaborate the material and remember it.

Reading a Textbook   More specific advice for remembering textbook material comes from a study that examined how successful and unsuccessful college students approach their reading (Whimbey, 1976). Unsuccessful students tend to read the material straight through; they do not slow down when they reach a difficult section; and they keep going even when they do not understand what they are reading. In contrast, successful college students monitor their understanding, reread difficult sections, and periodically stop to review what they have learned. In short, effective learners engage in a deep level of processing. They are active learners, thinking of each new fact in relation to other material, and they develop a context in which many new facts can be organized effectively.

Research on memory suggests two specific guidelines for reading a textbook. First, make sure that you understand what you are reading before moving on (Herrmann & Searleman, 1992). Second, use the SQ3R method (Thomas & Robinson, 1972), which is one of the most successful strategies for remembering textbook material (Anderson, 1990b). SQ3R stands for five activities to engage in when you read a chapter: survey, question, read, recite, review. These activities are designed to increase the depth to which you process the information you read.

1. *Survey*   Take a few minutes to skim the chapter. Look at the section headings and any boldfaced or italicized terms. Obtain a general idea of what material will be discussed, the way it is organized, and how its topics relate to one another and to what you already know. Some people find it useful to survey the entire chapter once and then survey each major section in a little more detail before reading it.

2. *Question*   Before reading each section, ask yourself what content will be covered and what information should be extracted from it.

3. *Read*   Read the text, but think about the material as you read. Are the questions you raised earlier being answered? Do you see the connections between the topics?

4. *Recite*   At the end of each section, recite the major points. Resist the temptation to be passive and say, "Oh, I remember that." Be active. Put the ideas into your own words by reciting them aloud.

5. *Review*   Finally, at the end of the chapter, review all the material. You should see connections not only within a section but also among the sections. The objective is to see how the material is organized. Once you grasp the organization, the individual facts will be far easier to remember. This is because you will be using top-down processing to help you remember.

By following these procedures you will learn and remember the material better and you will also save yourself considerable time.

Lecture Notes   Effective note-taking is an acquired skill. Research on memory suggests some simple strategies for taking and using notes effectively.

Realize first that, in note-taking, more is not necessarily better. Taking detailed notes of everything requires that you pay close attention to unimportant as well as important content, leaving little time for thinking about the material. Note-takers who concentrate on expressing the major ideas in relatively few words remember more than

Understand and Remember

Research on memory suggests that students who simply read their textbooks will not remember as much as those who, like this woman, read for understanding using the SQ3R method. Further, memory for the material is likely to be better if you read and study it over a number of weeks rather than in one marathon session on the night before a test.

IMPROVING YOUR MEMORY	
Domain	**Helpful Techniques**
Lists of items	Use mnemonics. Look for meaningful acronyms. Try the method of loci.
Textbook material	Follow the SQ3R system. Allocate your time to allow for distributed practice. Read actively, not passively.
Lectures	Take notes, but record only the main points. Think about the overall organization of the material. Review your notes as soon after the lecture as possible in order to fill in missing points.
Studying for exams	Write a detailed outline of your lecture notes rather than passively reading them.

in review

those who try to catch every detail (Howe, 1970). In short, the best way to take notes is to think about what is being said, draw connections with other material in the lecture, and then summarize the major points clearly and concisely (Kiewra, 1989).

Once you have a set of lecture notes, review them as soon as possible after the lecture so that you can fill in missing details. (As noted earlier, most forgetting from long-term memory occurs within the first few hours after learning.) When the time comes for serious study, use your notes as if they were a chapter in a textbook. Write a detailed outline. Think about how various points are related. Once you have organized the material, the details will make more sense and will be much easier to remember. ("In Review: Improving Your Memory" summarizes tips for studying.)

Design for Memory

The scientific study of memory has influenced the design of the electronic and mechanical devices that play an increasingly important role in our lives. Designers of computers, VCRs, cameras, and even stoves are faced with a choice: Either place the operating instructions on the devices themselves, or assume that the user remembers how to operate them. Understanding the limits of both working memory and long-term memory has helped designers distinguish between information that is likely to be stored in (and easily retrieved from) the user's memory, and information that should be presented in the form of labels, instructions, or other cues that reduce memory demands (Norman, 1988). Placing unfamiliar or hard-to-recall information in plain view makes it easier to use the device as intended, and with less chance of errors (Segal & Suri, 1999).

Psychologists have influenced advertisers and designers to create many other "user-friendly" systems (Wickens, Gordon, & Liu, 1998). For example, in creating toll-free numbers, they take advantage of chunking, which, as we have seen, provides an efficient way to maintain information in working memory. Which do you think would be easier to remember: "1-800-447-4357" or "1-800-GET-HELP"? Similarly, automobile designers ensure that the turn signals on your car emit an audible cue when turned on, a feature that reduces your memory load while driving, thus leaving you with enough working memory capacity to keep in mind that there is a car in your "blind spot."

As more and more complex devices come into the marketplace, it will be increasingly important that instructions about their operation are presented clearly and memorably. With guidance from research on memory it should be possible for almost anyone to operate such devices efficiently. Yes, even the programming of a VCR will no longer be a mystery!

LINKAGES

As noted in Chapter 1, all of psychology's many subfields are related to one another. Our discussion of the accuracy of eyewitnesses' memories illustrates just one way in which the topic of this chapter, memory, is linked to the subfield of perception (Chapter 5). The Linkages diagram shows ties to two other subfields as well, and there are many more ties throughout the book. Looking for linkages among subfields will help you see how they all fit together and better appreciate the big picture that is psychology.

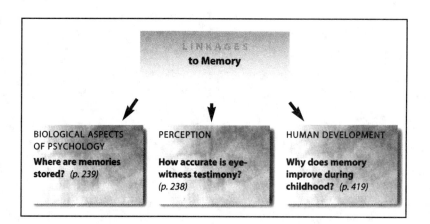

SUMMARY

THE NATURE OF MEMORY

Human memory depends on a complex mental system.

Basic Memory Processes

There are three basic memory processes. *Encoding* transforms stimulus information into some type of mental representation. Encoding can be *acoustic* (by sound), *visual* (by appearance), or *semantic* (by meaning). *Storage* maintains information in the memory system over time. *Retrieval* is the process of gaining access to previously stored information.

Types of Memory

Most psychologists agree that there are at least three types of memory. *Episodic memory* contains information about specific events in a person's life. *Semantic memory* contains generalized knowledge about the world. *Procedural memory* contains information about how to do various things.

Explicit and Implicit Memory

Most research on memory has concerned *explicit memory*, the processes through which people deliberately try to remember

something. Recently, psychologists have also begun to examine *implicit memory*, which refers to the unintentional recollection and influence of prior experiences.

Models of Memory

Four theoretical models of memory have guided most research. According to the *levels-of-processing model*, the most important determinant of memory is how extensively information is encoded or processed when it is first received. In general, *elaborative rehearsal* is more effective than *maintenance rehearsal* in learning new information because it represents a deeper level of processing. According to the *transfer-appropriate processing model*, the critical determinant of memory is not how deeply information is encoded but whether the encoding process produces memory codes that are later accessed at the time of retrieval. *Parallel distributed processing (PDP) models* of memory suggest that new experiences not only provide specific information but also become part of, and alter, a whole network of associations. And the *information-processing model* suggests that in order for information to become firmly embedded in memory, it must pass through three stages of processing: sensory memory, short-term memory, and long-term memory.

Summary **247**

ACQUIRING NEW MEMORIES

Sensory Memory

Sensory memory maintains incoming stimulus information in the *sensory registers* for a very brief time. *Selective attention*, which focuses mental resources on only part of the stimulus field, controls what information in the sensory registers is actually perceived and transferred to short-term memory.

Short-Term, or Working, Memory

Short-term memory (STM), which is also known as *working memory*, has two major functions: It constructs and updates an internal model of the environment, and it provides a system in which people can store, organize, and integrate facts and thereby solve problems and make decisions. Various memory codes can be used in short-term memory, but acoustic codes seem to be preferred in most verbal tasks. Studies of the *immediate memory span* indicate that the capacity of short-term memory is approximately seven *chunks*, or meaningful groupings of information. Studies using the *Brown-Peterson procedure* show that information in short-term memory is usually forgotten within about eighteen seconds if it is not rehearsed.

Long-Term Memory

Long-term memory (LTM) normally involves semantic encoding, which means that people tend to encode the general meaning of information, not specific details, in long-term memory. The capacity of long-term memory to store new information is extremely large, perhaps unlimited.

Distinguishing Between Short-Term and Long-Term Memory

According to some psychologists, there is no need to distinguish between short-term and long-term memory. Still, some evidence suggests that these systems are distinct. For example, the *primacy* and *recency effects* that occur when people try to recall a list of words may indicate the presence of two different systems.

RETRIEVING MEMORIES

Retrieval Cues and Encoding Specificity

Retrieval cues help people remember things that they would otherwise not be able to recall. The effectiveness of retrieval cues follows the *encoding specificity principle:* Cues help retrieval only if they match some feature of the information that was originally encoded.

Context and State Dependence

All else being equal, memory may be better when one attempts to retrieve information in the same environment in which it was learned; this is called *context-dependent* memory. When a person's internal state can aid or impede retrieval, memory is said to be *state-dependent*.

Retrieval from Semantic Memory

Researchers usually study retrieval from semantic memory by examining how long it takes people to answer world knowledge questions. It appears that ideas are represented as associations in a dense semantic memory network, and that the retrieval of information occurs by a process of *spreading activation*. Each concept in the network is represented as a unique collection of features or attributes. The tip-of-the-tongue phenomenon and the feeling-of-knowing experience represent the retrieval of incomplete knowledge.

Constructing Memories

In the process of constructive memory, people use their existing knowledge to fill in gaps in the information they encode and retrieve. Parallel distributed processing models provide one explanation of how people make spontaneous generalizations about the world. They also explain the *schemas* that shape the memories people construct.

FORGETTING

The Course of Forgetting

In his research on long-term memory and forgetting, Hermann Ebbinghaus introduced the *method of savings*. He found that most forgetting from long-term memory occurs during the first several hours after learning and that savings can be extremely long lasting.

The Roles of Decay and Interference

Decay and *interference* are two mechanisms of forgetting. Although there is evidence of both decay and interference in short-term memory, it appears that most forgetting from long-term memory is due to either *retroactive interference* or *proactive interference*.

BIOLOGICAL BASES OF MEMORY

Biochemical Mechanisms

Research has shown that memory can result as new synapses are formed in the brain, and as communication at existing synapses is improved. Several neurotransmitters appear to be involved in the strengthening that occurs at synapses.

Brain Structures

Studies of *anterograde amnesia*, *retrograde amnesia*, Korsakoff's syndrome, and other kinds of brain damage provide information about the brain structures involved in memory. For example, the hippocampus and thalamus are known to play a role in the formation of memories. These structures send nerve fibers to the cerebral cortex, and it is there that memories are probably stored. Memories appear to be both localized and distributed throughout the brain.

APPLICATIONS OF MEMORY RESEARCH

Improving Your Memory

Among the many applications of memory research are *mnemonics*, devices that are used to remember things better. One of the simplest but most powerful mnemonics is the method of loci. It is useful because it provides a context for organizing material more effectively. Guidelines for effective studying have also been derived from memory research. For example, the key to remembering textbook material is to read actively rather than passively. One of the most effective ways to do this is to follow the SQ3R method: survey, question, read, recite, and review. Similarly, to take lecture notes or to study them effectively, organize the points into a meaningful framework and think about how each main point relates to the others.

Design for Memory

Research on the limits of memory has helped product designers to create electronic and mechanical systems and devices that are "user-friendly."

KEY TERMS

acoustic encoding (214)
anterograde amnesia (241)
Brown-Peterson procedure (224)
chunks (223)
context-dependent (228)
decay (236)
elaborative rehearsal (218)
encoding (214)
encoding specificity principle (227)
episodic memory (215)
explicit memory (216)
immediate memory span (223)
implicit memory (216)

information-processing model (220)
interference (236)
levels-of-processing model (218)
long-term memory (LTM) (224)
maintenance rehearsal (218)
method of savings (235)
mnemonics (243)
parallel distributed processing (PDP) models (219)
primacy effect (227)

proactive interference (237)
procedural memory (215)
recency effect (227)
retrieval (215)
retrieval cues (227)
retroactive interference (237)
retrograde amnesia (241)
schemas (231)
selective attention (222)
semantic encoding (215)
semantic memory (215)
sensory memory (221)
sensory registers (221)

short-term memory (STM) (222)
spreading activation (229)
state-dependent (228)
storage (215)
transfer-appropriate processing model (218)
visual encoding (214)
working memory (222)

Textbook Features

Chapter Outline

Some textbooks will provide you with **outlines** of each chapter's content. At the very least, study a chapter outline during your preview step of the reading process to familiarize yourself with the chapter's main ideas and organization. You might also photocopy the outline and keep it beside you for reference as you read. Refer to it often to understand how the specific sections and details fit into the larger framework of ideas.

You can also use a chapter outline as a study tool. It will probably contain only the skeleton of main ideas in the chapter. As you read, you can flesh it out by adding key words or other information to help you remember the contents of each section. For example, you could create a more detailed outline for the first few sections of the "Memory" chapter as follows (the original outline is in bold print):

The Nature of Memory—complex mental system

    Basic Memory Processes (3 steps)
        1. encoding—code sensory info for mental storage
        2. storage—maintain info over time
        3. retrieval—locate info and bring it into consciousness

    Types of Memory (3 types)
        1. episodic—specific event
        2. semantic—general knowledge of world
        3. procedural—how to do things

EXERCISE 1

On a separate sheet of paper, continue adding to the outline begun above for the remainder of "The Nature of Memory" section of the chapter.

Graphics

Graphics—which are also known as visual aids—are visual representations of information. Graphics include photographs, tables, charts, graphs, drawings, diagrams, cartoons, and maps. It's important to note that graphics do not *substitute* for text; instead, they reinforce, emphasize, and summarize information presented in text form, and they also effectively illustrate relationships in that information. Therefore, when a textbook includes graphics, don't ignore them; instead, use them as another tool for helping you understand the content.

To get the most out of the graphics in a textbook, read them in conjunction with the textual explanation. If the author refers you to a graphic, first read the text information, and then locate the graphic to see how that information is presented in visual form. Read the graphic's title and caption, which will indicate the focus and/or conclusion you should understand.

In the "Memory" chapter, a caption explains the main point or conclusion of each graphic. In other words, the authors have done much of the work for you. However, you should still study each graphic until you understand how it conveys that point. Even if a caption or explanation accompanies a visual, try to say in your own words the idea the visual illustrates.

EXERCISE 2

In the space below, list the kinds of graphics included in the "Memory" chapter.

EXERCISE 3

Study Figure 7.11 and its textual explanation in the "Memory" chapter. Then, write a sentence or two to explain, in your own words, the idea illustrated in that figure.

Chapter Summary

A textbook chapter will often include a brief **summary.** As part of your preview process, you should read this summary to get a concise overview of the chapter's main ideas. However, you can also use the summary as a study tool during your review process. Remove most of the key terms from a summary, substituting blanks for those terms. When you feel confident about your understanding of the information, try to fill in the blanks with the correct words. For example, you might remove words from a section of the "Memory" chapter summary as follows:

Short-term memory (STM), which is also known as _____ , has two major functions: It constructs and updates an _____ of the environment, and it provides a system in which people can store, organize, and integrate _____ and thereby solve _____ and make _____ . Various memory codes can be used in short-term memory, but _____ codes seem to be preferred in most verbal tasks. Studies of the _____ indicate that the capacity of short-term memory is approximately seven _____ , or meaning groupings of information. Studies using the _____ procedure show that information in short-term memory is usually forgotten within about _____ seconds if it is not rehearsed.

EXERCISE 4

Write the missing words in the "Memory" chapter summary above.

Tips and Techniques

Active Reading

Part 2 of this book described the basics of **active reading:** turning headings into questions, highlighting the answers, and looking up definitions of unfamiliar words. Using a few additional techniques will increase your comprehension and retention even further.

Writing **notes in the margins** is another effective active reading technique. As you read each paragraph, write in the margin the main idea, a brief summary, or key phrases. For example, in the section of the "Memory" chapter called "Context and State Dependence," you might write:

Context and State Dependence

Environment affects coding and recall

In general, people remember more when their efforts at recall take place in the same environment in which they learned, because they tend to encode features of the environment where the learning occurred (Richardson-Klavehn & Bjork, 1988). These features may later act as retrieval cues. In one experiment, people studied a series of pictures while in the presence of a particular odor. Later, they reviewed a larger set of photos and tried to identify the ones they had seen earlier. Half of these people were tested in the presence of the original odor and half in the presence of a different odor. Those who smelled the same odor during learning and testing did significantly better on the recognition task than those who were tested in the presence of a different odor. The matching odor served as a powerful retrieval cue (Cann & Ross, 1989).

Learning/testing in same classroom

When memory can be helped or hindered by similarities in environmental context, it is termed **context-dependent.** One study found that students remember better when tested in the classroom in which they learned the material than when tested in a different classroom (Smith, Glenberg, & Bjork, 1978). This context-dependency effect is not always strong (Saufley, Otaka, & Bavaresco, 1985; Smith, Vels, & Williamson, 1988), but some students do find it helpful to study for a test in the classroom where the text will be given.

Influence of drugs and moods on recall

Like the external environment, the internal psychological environment can be encoded when people learn and thus can act as a retrieval cue. When a person's internal state can aid or impede retrieval, memory is called **state-dependent.** For example, if people learn new material while under the influence of marijuana, they tend to recall it better if they are also tested under the influence of marijuana (Eich et al., 1975). Similar effects have been found with alcohol (Overton, 1984), other drugs (Eich, 1989), and mood states. College students remember more positive incidents from their diaries or from their earlier life when they are in a positive mood at the time of recall (Ehrlichman & Halpern, 1998). More negative events tend to be recalled when people are in a negative mood (Lewinsohn & Rosenbaum, 1987). These mood *congruency effects* are strongest when people try to recall personally meaningful episodes, because such events were most likely to be colored by their mood (Eich & Metcalfe, 1989).

Completing the extra step of writing down this information may help you remember it better. Marginal notes will also allow you to quickly see important ideas when you review later.

EXERCISE 5

Jot down notes in the margins of the section called "The Course of Forgetting" from the "Memory" chapter.

Another good active reading technique is **outlining** or **diagramming** the information as you read. An outline is a linear representation of the relationships between topics and ideas, You can use either a formal, Roman numeral outline or an informal pattern you create yourself. For example, a formal outline of the section of the "Memory" chapter called "Biological Bases of Memory" might look like this:

I.   Biological Bases of Memory
    A.   Biochemical Mechanisms that Produce New Memories
        1.   Environmental Stimulation Causes New Synapses to Form
        2.   Functional Changes Occur in Existing Synapses
            a.   Glutamate in Hippocampus
            b.   Acelylcholine
    B.   Brain Structure

An informal outline of the same section might look like this:

Biological Bases of Memory
    Biochemical mechanisms
        — Environmental stim → new synapses
        — Existing synapses change functions (glutamate & acelylcholine)

EXERCISE 6

In the space below (or on a separate sheet of paper), create an informal or formal outline for the "Brain Structures" section of the "Memory" chapter.

Rather than outlining a chapter, you may find diagramming to be a more effective study aid. Like an outline, a diagram illustrates relationships; however, it uses more of a visual than a linear structure. For example, you could diagram the "Biological Bases of Memory" section as follows:

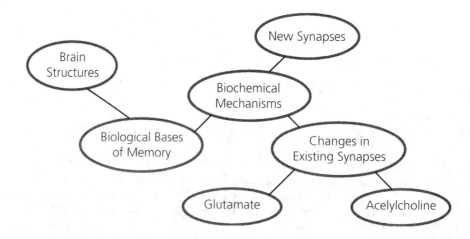

EXERCISE 7

Add to the diagram above by completing the "Brain Structures" section.

One final active reading technique you might consider using is **tape-recording** your notes or outlining and then listening to that recording as part of your review process. Many people find it beneficial to listen to this information as they drive or complete household tasks such as washing dishes. If you try this technique, though, remember that it's not enough to just *hear* the tape; you'll have to *listen* and pay attention to increase your retention.

"Speed" Reading and Efficient Reading

How fast should you be reading? There is no right answer to that question because your reading speed will vary depending on *what* you are reading. Factors such as the complexity of the information, the style of the writing, your prior knowledge of the subject, and your understanding of the vocabulary will all affect how fast you can read. Because of these factors, textbook reading tends to be slower than other types of reading.

Some people who dislike reading textbooks believe they can get the task over with faster by learning to "speed read." It's true that speed and comprehension are related, to some extent. Unusually slow readers may experience more difficulty in forming an understanding of complex ideas. Also, because it's so tedious, slow reading can inhibit the reader's concentration on the material.

However, if your textbook reading skills need improvement, increasing your speed may or may not be the answer. Reading faster is meaningless if you can't remember the information when you're finished, so it's usually much more productive to focus your efforts on improving your concentration and active reading skills. Practice will also improve your reading efficiency.

If you still believe, though, that reading seems to be an unusually slow process for you, many reading experts have produced books and courses that may help you increase your speed. In general, the experts advise you to:

- **Read groups of words instead of each individual word.** If your eyes pause on each word, your reading will be much slower. Practice taking in phrases of two or three words at a time to increase your speed.

- **Stop vocalizing (moving your lips) as you read.** This habit slows down reading.

- **Avoid regression (rereading).** Though you should always reread material that you don't understand, you want to avoid having to reread because your attention wandered. Work on developing your concentration skills to avoid having to regress.

If you are successfully practicing active reading techniques, speed may be important only as a consideration for scheduling your time. You may want to determine your page-per-hour rate to make sure you set aside adequate time to complete your reading assignments. To determine your pages-per-hour rate, simply count the number of pages you were able to read in 1 hour. Divide the number of pages in a reading assignment by that rate to know how much time to schedule. Remember, though, that your rate will likely change for each different textbook, so you'll want to calculate a specific rate for each book.

EXERCISE 8

Do you think unusually slow reading may be inhibiting your concentration? Based on the advice in this section, what could you do to increase your reading speed?

PART 4

"The Enlightenment in the United States" from *The Humanities*

26

*T*he Enlightenment in the United States

*P*olitical events in North America in the last four decades of the eighteenth century fascinated European observers. While the French philosophes were forced to adapt their goals for improving the human condition to the circumstances of a very traditional social and political structure, English-speaking North America presented the situation of a new people in an underdeveloped land largely untrammeled by the weight of past institutions. Once the colonists had thrown off the control imposed on their society by

261

the imperial system of the mother country, the possibilities for political creativity and experimentation seemed limitless. As the new nation emerged from the endless deliberations of the political leadership, European intellectuals watched intently for signs to determine whether the American republic, the most populous and geographically extensive republican government in the history of the world, would succeed or fail.

The history of the creation of the United States, following more than a century of colonial development, can be divided into three basic phases. The first phase began with the defeat of French armies in the New World by combined British and colonial forces, part of a worldwide struggle between rival European powers. When British officials then tried to impose increased taxes on the growing colonies to help cover the rising military and administrative costs of the empire, the colonists resisted in increasing numbers and finally declared themselves politically independent in 1776. The second phase comprises the period from the first years of the war until the creation of the Constitution in 1787, when the dominant minds in America attempted to devise some sort of lasting union among the thirteen loosely confederated states. The final period is that of the first decades after ratification of the Constitution (which went into effect in 1789) as Americans endeavored to make the new government work in the face of forces for decentralization that threatened at times to pull the new federal structure apart.

American Religion

Christianity in prerevolutionary America was the most important cultural and intellectual force in colonial life. Among whites, the predominant allegiance of the colonists was to some form of Protestantism. Even in Maryland, originally founded as a Catholic refuge, Protestants were in the vast majority. The few Jews in the colonies resided largely in the coastal towns. Missionary associations of various churches had achieved little success with the rapidly dwindling Native American population, but from the 1730s on African Americans converted in large numbers. By the revolution, conversion among the enslaved population, now principally being carried out by blacks themselves, created a significant mass of black Christians in the colonies. The African American churches, however, retained many elements of religious practices from the African religious heritage.

The beginning of the conversion of blacks on a large scale in the 1730s was only one aspect of a great religious revival that swept the English colonies in that and the succeeding decade. Known as the Great Awakening, the movement started in New Jersey, was taken up by Jonathan Edwards (1703–1758), a Congregational minister in Northampton, Massachusetts, and within the next few years was spread by a series of fiery preachers the entire length of the Atlantic coast.

Americans in these years were responding to a deeply felt sense that their churches were becoming too institutionalized and too committed to doctrine while the passion of belief that nourished the emotional life of the believer was draining away. By arousing religious feelings at the expense of catechisms and using emotion rather than reasoned argument, the preachers of the Great Awakening, a movement that cut across all doctrinal lines, appealed enormously to those with little education. The spiritual malaise was so general, however, that large numbers from all classes were attracted to the revival movement.

Effect of the Great Awakening

The Great Awakening had a tremendously disruptive effect on established religion in the colonies, dividing congregations into Old Light and New Light groups. The activity of itinerant preachers tended to destroy the identification of churches with particular territories, and because the preachers of the Awakening were marked more by charismatic gifts than by education or status, it undermined the authority of the traditional clergy. The intensity of the Great Awakening abated after 1750, but its effects on American religion were long lasting.

This revival movement contributed to bringing into question two fundamental beliefs of traditional Christianity: that religious conformity was necessary and that the state should lend financial and other support to a particular church. Although some states continued to use tax money to support a designated church or churches, the competition for membership in the spiritual market in the second half of the eighteenth century could not be prevented, and in practice freedom of conscience for all religions became the rule. Unlike in European countries, in which the established church had a guaranteed membership and religion tended to be taken for granted, in the British colonies the competition for souls fostered an almost continual spirit of revival and a rich variety of choices. Consequently, by the time of the revolution the Christian churches were highly decentralized and largely voluntary in membership, and reflected the evolution of republican feeling in a broad sector of the population.

European Influences

From the early eighteen century the dominant stream of ideas shaping politics in America was English. The *empiricism* of English thinkers like Bacon and Newton made a strong impact on Americans, and theory was reinforced by a pioneer culture that respected labor and practical know-how. Products of a highly mobile society with a flexible social structure, the colonists worked well together at the local level in meeting their common needs. The validity of Locke's doctrine of natural rights of humankind seemed borne out by their experience. Beginning as they did in a new environment, the colonists tended to view critically any limitation on their freedom of action unless it could be justified in terms of personal advantage. With the executive power firmly in the hands of British governors, they also found Locke's emphasis on the duty of legislative assemblies to supervise the executive authority to their liking. Characteristically, the Declaration of Independence, which claimed rights to life, liberty, and the pursuit of happiness to be self-evident, justified severance with England on the grounds of George III's tyranny, not because of oppression by Parliament. Furthermore, the Declaration of Independence and the Constitution echo Locke in their statements that governments derive their just powers from the consent of the governed and that when governments exceed their power, the people have the right to institute new governments.

French philosophes were, on the whole, ardent supporters of the American Revolution. They admired versatile diplomats like Benjamin Franklin and Thomas Jefferson, both of whom lived for long periods in France, as the kind of "enlightened" individuals that the New World could produce. People like Turgot, a philosophe minister of Louis XV, used their influence at court to bring the French government into the war on the rebels' side in 1778, and the French intervention was decisive. On the intellectual level, Montesquieu doubtless had the most significant influence on American political thought in the revolutionary period. His conception of a balance of power among the legislative, executive, and judicial branches of government suited the American distrust of the executive and made the Constitution more attractive to many who looked on a strong executive as a potential threat to individual freedom. In the 1780s and 1790s, however, Rousseau's democratic theories provided ammunition against elitist conceptions of political authority held by most American thinkers. For example, property qualifications for voting rights were reduced at this time.

To an extent, the ease with which Americans accepted the ideas of the philosophes stemmed from the fact that much of the philosophy of the French thinkers had been inspired by the English political experience, which Americans had inherited. But more than this, the increasingly voluntaristic character of American religion made Christianity in the colonies compatible with most of their ideas. In France, as we have seen, intellectuals attacked the privileged Church as obscurantist and as the champion of political oppression. Religion itself became tainted by association. On the other hand, in religiously pluralistic America, the Enlightenment lost its antireligious bias. Whereas in France the Enlightenment doctrine of religious toleration aimed at subverting the hold of the Catholic Church on French culture, in America this doctrine was introduced to justify a practical situation created by the existence of conflicting religious groups.

American Federalism

Federalism, perhaps the United States' most original contribution to the theory and practice of republican government, owed little to either the French or the English; it was born of necessity. Under no circumstances able to induce strong, independent state governments to become mere agencies of the central government, the writers of the Constitution established a principle of separation of powers between the central government and the states. Such a system of power division was to have a great future because it permitted unification of large areas of land and supported regional diversity while still limiting the power of local opposition.

The Heritage of Ancient Rome

No account of the ideology of the American revolutionary epoch would be complete without acknowledging the extent to which these patriots thought of themselves and were considered by their European sympathizers as the heirs to the republican tradition of ancient Rome. Since the Renaissance the educated class of the Western world had been deeply imbued with classical culture; one aspect of that culture, clearly defined since the early fifteenth century, was its *republican* tradition. The leaders of the revolution appeared to contemporaries as the simple, honest descendants of Roman leaders like Cato, or the general Cincinnatus, who left his own plow to lead an army against the enemies of the Roman Republic. Americans often signed their letters of protest against English tyranny with Roman names, and Wash-

26-1   *Great Seal of the United States. (Bureau of Engraving and Printing, U.S. Department of the Treasury)*

26-2   *Jean Antoine Houdon,* George Washington, *1788–92. Marble, height 74″, State Capitol, Richmond. (Virginia State Library and Archives)*

ington and other officers of the revolutionary army took part in a controversial Society of Cincinnatus. In their struggle for liberty, the patriots (from Latin *patria*—homeland) seemed to be the modern counterparts of Roman heroes like Horatio and Brutus. The architects of the Constitution drew on words of Latin derivation like *president* and *senate*, and the Great Seal of the new nation and its coinage were marked with Latin phrases and classical emblems (Fig. 26-1). Houdon's statue of Washington in the capitol at Richmond dramatically illustrates these associations of the new republic with the old. In 1786 the French sculptor represented the future president of the United States in modern dress; but he stands beside the Roman *fasces*, a bundle of rods symbolic of power and union, in a pose based on that of a classical statue (Fig. 26-2).

Thomas Jefferson (1743–1826)

The figure who best represents the American Enlightenment is Thomas Jefferson. Jefferson combined the Old World's tradition of scholarship and philosophy with the New World's practicality and readiness to experiment. Both philosopher and plantation manager, he was at home in the salons of Paris and the still untamed parts of Virginia. Like the French *philosophes*, he combined wide learning in the classical humanities with a lively interest in recent scientific developments. He regarded the republic of letters and ideas as an international one.

In addition to his career as a politician, Jefferson was an excellent writer, an educator, a farmer, and an architect. One of his masterpieces is his home near Charlottesville, Virginia, which he called Monticello ("little mountain"; see Fig. 26-3). The house itself is symbolic of the nature of the American Enlightenment. Jefferson used the *Palladian* Villa Rotunda as his model (Fig. 24-1), but the plan of the interior exhibits a functional adaptation of the symmetrical plan to his own particular needs. Similarly, the building, originally designed for stone execution, is rendered in red brick with white wooden trim—an elegant, rich contrast to the building's general simplicity of shape. These adaptations to use and surroundings do not, however, detract from the *portico* and *dome*, the two architectural forms that link it with those of democratic Greece and republican Rome. Facing westward, to the wilderness, dominating but sympathetic to the landscape, the house is almost a metaphor for the man—aristocratic, cosmopolitan, inventive, practical—a farmer and a philosopher.

Designing his own tomb for the grounds at Monticello, Jefferson composed the following inscription: "Here was buried Thomas Jefferson, author of the Declaration of American Independence, of the Statute of Virginia for Religious Freedom, and Father of the University of Virginia." He apparently did not consider that

26-3 *Thomas Jefferson, Monticello, west front. (Thomas Jefferson Memorial Foundation Inc.)*

being the third president of the United States was among his most significant accomplishments. Those that he lists are excellent examples of the application of the principles of the Enlightenment to the American experience.

The Declaration of Independence The Declaration, written largely by Jefferson and approved by the Continental Congress on July 4, 1776, is a statement of political philosophy as well as an act of rebellion. It is in fact typical of the American Enlightenment that theory and its practical application are combined in the same document. The Declaration may be divided into two distinct parts: the first sets forth principles of democratic government and proves, in the abstract, philosophical terms of the Enlightenment, the right of the colonies to rebel. The second part is a specific list of grievances against the king of Great Britain, George III.

A close reading of the first two paragraphs of the Declaration reveals the purpose of the document and a theoretical basis for rebellion.

> When, in the course of human events, it becomes necessary for one people to dissolve the political bands which have connected them with another, and to assume, among the powers of the earth, the separate and equal station to which the laws of nature and of nature's God entitle them, a decent respect to the opinions of mankind requires that they should declare the causes which impel them to the separation.
>
> We hold these truths to be self-evident: That all men are created equal; that they are endowed by their Creator with certain unalienable rights; that among these are life, liberty & the pursuit of happiness; that to secure these rights governments are instituted among men, deriving their just powers from the consent of the governed; that whenever any form of government becomes destructive of these ends, it is the right of the people to alter or to abolish it, and to institute new government, laying its foundation on such principles and organizing its powers in such form, as to them shall seem most likely to effect their safety and happiness.

QUESTIONS

1. Is there any religious basis for the rebellion? Does it seem to be Christian?

2. How do the expressions "laws of nature," "nature's God," and "truths" that are "self-evident" reflect values of the Enlightenment?

3. Did the American political system in fact guarantee the "unalienable rights" that Jefferson lists? What

266   ⌐   *Chapter 26   The Enlightenment in the United States*

do you think that he meant by "the pursuit of happiness"? By "all men are created equal"?

4. How do Jefferson's political ideals differ from, or
resemble, those of Thucydides? (See Chapter 4.)

5. Do the principles of the Enlightenment found here
(such as self-evident truths) seem a valid basis from
which to argue legal and moral questions today?

The questions raised here may be applied to the entire Declaration. The second part of the document pur-
ports to show, by the list of grievances, that George III
deliberately and malevolently attempted to establish an
"absolute tyranny" over the colonies. It is consistent
with Jefferson's idea of a government that derives its
powers from the "consent of the governed" that he
blames all sorts of evils on the tyrannical will of the
king. The last of Jefferson's charges, omitted by the
Congress in the final draft of the Declaration, was an
indictment against the enslavement of Africans.

He has waged cruel war against human nature itself,
violating its most sacred rights of life and liberty in
the persons of a distant people who never offended
him, captivating and carrying them into slavery in
another hemisphere, or to incur miserable death in
their transportation thither. This piratical warfare,
the opprobrium of *infidel* powers, is the warfare of
the *Christian* king of Great Britain. Determined to
keep open a market where MEN should be bought
and sold, he has prostituted his negative[1] for suppressing every legislative attempt to prohibit or to
restrain this execrable commerce; and that this assemblage of horrors might want no fact of distinguished die,[2] he is now exciting these very people to
rise in arms among us, and to purchase that liberty
of which *he* deprived them, by murdering the people
upon whom *he* also obtruded them; thus paying off
former crimes committed against the *liberties* of one
people, with crimes which he urges them to commit
against the *lives* of another.

———

[1]That is, he has conceded to other interests by vetoing.
[2]That is, might be made clear.

26-4   *Thomas Jefferson, University of Virginia. 1856 engraving by C. Bohn. (University of Virginia Library)*

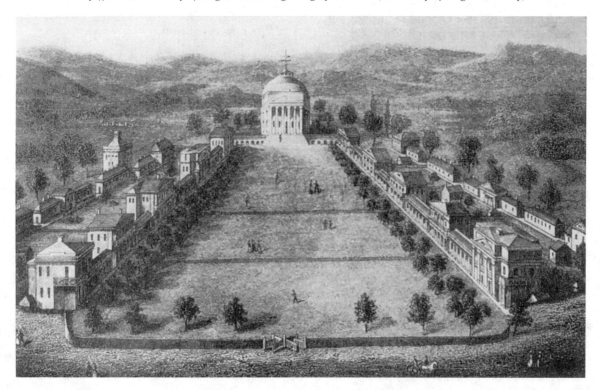

QUESTIONS

1. How does Jefferson's application of the principles of the Enlightenment to the question of slavery differ from and/or resemble that of Montesquieu?

2. Does it make good historical sense to blame the existence of slavery and the slave trade on George III?

3. What important factors does Jefferson omit?

26-5   *Thomas Jefferson, Capitol, Richmond. (Virginia State Library and Archives)*

Jefferson's own position on slavery was fraught with ambiguity. He owned many slaves on his plantation at Monticello. He seems to have been tormented by his contradictory feelings that slavery was a moral wrong and would eventually be abolished, but that the time was not yet ripe for black Americans to be free. Recent biographies of Jefferson wrestle with this and other contradictions in this multifaceted man.

The Virginia Statute and the University of Virginia
The second accomplishment on which Jefferson prided himself, the Virginia Statute of Religious Liberty (October 1785), is in the spirit of Voltaire's *Treatise on Toleration*. The statute was part of the constitution of the state of Virginia, which served as a model for other state constitutions.

Jefferson remained a nominal Anglican until the end of his life but continued to combat what he considered to be superstitions and unnecessary dogmas in Christianity. He respected Jesus as a great moral teacher but did not necessarily believe him to be divine. He made his own edition of the Bible, cutting out references to miracles. Unitarians today consider Jefferson one of their forefathers. In an "unenlightened" age a century or two earlier, he would have been arrested as a heretic.

In keeping with Jefferson's beliefs, his third monumental project, the University of Virginia, was the only early university not to be associated with a church. Jefferson viewed this "academical village" as an opportunity not only to create an ideal educational environment but also to improve the tastes of the Americans who would be educated there (Fig. 26-4).

Jefferson had always scorned the architecture of Williamsburg, where he was educated, and had tried to mold taste with his designs for the capitol of Virginia at Richmond (Fig. 26-5). He used no Renaissance models or sources. Having seen engravings of the Maison Carrée in Nîmes, he adopted the plan of that building for the new capitol.

That the pure temple form was not immediately adopted nationally can be seen by comparing the Virginia State Capitol with the Massachusetts State House in Boston, designed by Charles Bulfinch in 1795 (Fig. 26-6). The sources of the State House are from the English Renaissance as well as from Rome. Both buildings, however, provided strong images of the state.

This belief, that art and architecture reinforce and perpetuate strong, appropriate images for ideals, was much in Jefferson's mind when the university was laid out. The heart of the university is a rectangular quadrangle bounded on each of its long sides by a one-story covered colonnade broken at intervals by the two-story houses of the professors. Students lived in rooms off the colonnades; professors held classes downstairs in their living quarters (Fig. 26-7). The east end of the quadrangle is closed by the library, a domed, porticoed rotunda (Fig. 26-8). Suggested by Benjamin Latrobe, another important architect, the rotunda acted as the focus and capstone, while the west end of the campus was open to the mountains. This very regular pattern for the central campus was relieved by the dining rooms, kitchens, and other service facilities located behind the two parallel rows of colonnades. There were found gardens (which students were expected to help work), pathways, and private walks for the students, who would participate in the educative life in the main quadrangle but still have time for meditation, contemplation, and studies close to nature.

The rotunda and professors' houses were carefully detailed with what Jefferson considered the best forms of the classical *orders*; the Corinthian was reserved for the interior of the rotunda. All are used in correct proportion and with their correct *entablatures* and *moldings*. Jefferson drew on ancient and Renaissance treatises in his planning.

268 ·- *Chapter 26*   *The Enlightenment in the United States*

26-6 *Charles Bulfinch, Massachusetts State House. (Courtesy of the Trustees of the Public Library of the City of Boston)*

26-8 *Thomas Jefferson, University of Virginia, Rotunda. (University of Virginia Library)*

26-7 *Thomas Jefferson, University of Virginia, Pavilion and Colonnade. (University of Virginia Library)*

The architecture of the campus reflects the two areas in which students were supposed to grow to become successful adults—the active and the contemplative life. Conspicuously absent is a chapel or church since religion was to be a personal, private affair. Unlike Harvard, Yale, or Princeton, this early university of the new republic was a monument to free thought.

The ideal behind the University of Virginia was, in typical Enlightenment fashion, universal. "Enlighten the people generally," Jefferson wrote, "and oppressions of body and mind will vanish like evil spirits at the dawn of day." Practically, however, because of the nature of the education planned, it could accommodate only an elite few. Women of all races, blacks, and white males from poor families were excluded. Jefferson, though he educated his daughters, held in fact very conventional ideas regarding women: they should not mix in politics or public meetings or be outspoken in any way; their proper place was in the domestic sphere. The educated elite, who alone were fit to rule the American nation in Jefferson's view, would have been limited to white men of some means if his plan had remained the pattern. Fortunately, as is the case with most important thinkers, Jefferson's ideas outgrew his era's limitations and eventually served the causes of struggles for civil rights in which we are still involved.

The product of Jefferson's old age and retirement years, the University of Virginia opened its doors in 1824, when its founder was eighty-one. It was perhaps natural that the revolutionary, politician, and diplomat should retire into creating an ideal world on a reduced scale. This edifice for the education of the New World elite stands today as a manifestation of the styles and ideals of the Enlightenment, as interpreted by the New World's best example of Enlightenment thinking.

READING SELECTIONS

JONATHAN EDWARDS

FROM *A Faithful Narrative of the Surprising Work of God*

In the following excerpt from *A Faithful Narrative of the Surprising Work of God* (1737), Edwards first describes the effect of his revivalist preaching on his congregation and then the diffusion of its effect to the surrounding countryside in the Connecticut River Valley. Edwards tells us that he had resolved to preach from the pulpit with no ambiguity that humanity is saved by faith alone, and that human beings have absolutely no power to ensure, or even to cooperate in, their own salvation. These sermons had a dazzling and surprising effect.

Although great fault was found with meddling with the controversy in the pulpit, by such a person, at that time, and though it was ridiculed by many elsewhere; yet it proved a word spoken in season here; and was most evidently attended with a very remarkable blessing of heaven to the souls of the people in this town. They received thence a general satisfaction with respect to the main thing in question, which they had in trembling doubts and concern about; and their minds were engaged the more earnestly to seek that they might come to be accepted of God, and saved in the way of the gospel, which had been made evident to them to be the true and only way. And then it was, in the latter part of December [1734], that the Spirit of God began extraordinarily to set in, and wonderfully to work amongst us; and there were, to all appearance, savingly converted, and some of them wrought upon in a very remarkable manner.

Particularly, I was surprised with the relation of a young woman, who had been one of the greatest company keepers in the whole town: when she came to me, I had never heard that she was become in any wise serious, but by the conversation I then had with her, it appeared to me, that what she gave an account of, was a glorious work of God's infinite power and sovereign grace; and that God had given her a new heart, truly broken and sanctified. I could not then doubt of it, and have seen much in my acquaintance with her since to confirm it.

Though the work was glorious, yet I was filled with concern about the effect it might have upon others: I was ready to conclude (though too rashly) that some would be hardened by it, in carelessness and looseness of life; and would take occasion from it to open their mouths, in reproaches of religion.[1] But the event was the reverse, to a wonderful degree; God made it, I suppose, the greatest occasion of awakening to others, of any thing that ever came to pass in the town. I have had abundant opportunity to know the effect it had, by my private conversation with many. The news of it seemed to be almost like a flash of lightning, upon the hearts of young people, all over the town, and upon many others. Those persons amongst us, who used to be farthest from seriousness, and that I most feared would make an ill improvement of it, seemed greatly to be awakened with it; many went to talk with her, concerning what she had met with; and what appeared in her seemed to be to the satisfaction of all that did so.

Presently upon this, a great and earnest concern about the great things of religion, and the eternal world, became universal in all parts of the town, and among persons of all degrees, and all ages; the noise amongst the dry bones waxed louder and louder: all other talk but about spiritual and eternal things was soon thrown by; all the conversation in all companies, and upon all occasions, was upon these things only, unless so much as was necessary for people carrying on their ordinary secular business. Other discourse than of the things of religion, would scarcely be tolerated in any company. The minds of people were wonderfully taken off from the world; it was treated amongst us as a thing

---

[1] Edwards feared that when people were told that they could do nothing to help in their own salvation, they would abandon themselves to pleasure or curse God for his injustice in robbing them of the power of their will.

270

of very little consequence: they seem to follow their worldly business, more as a part of their duty, than from any disposition they had to it; the temptation now seemed to be on that hand, to neglect worldly affairs too much, and to spend too much time in the immediate exercise of religion: which thing was exceedingly misrepresented by reports that were spread in distant parts of the land, as though the people here had wholly thrown by all worldly business, and betook themselves entirely to reading and praying, and such like religious exercises. . . .

This work of God, as it was carried on, and the number of true saints multiplied, soon made a glorious alteration in the town; so that in the spring and summer following, anno 1735, the town seemed to be full of the presence of God: it never was so full of love, nor so full of joy; and yet so full of distress as it was then. There were remarkable tokens of God's presence in almost every house. It was a time of joy in families on the account of salvation's being brought unto them; parents rejoicing over their children as new born, and husbands over their wives, and wives over their husbands. *The goings of God were then seen in his sanctuary, God's day was a delight, and his tabernacles were amiable.* Our public assemblies were then beautiful; the congregation was alive in God's service, every one earnestly intent on the public worship, every hearer eager to drink in the words of the minister as they came from his mouth; the assembly in general were, from time to time, in tears while the word was preached; some weeping with sorrow and distress, others with joy and love, others with pity and concern for the souls of their neighbors. . . .

When this work of God first appeared, and was so extraordinarily carried on amongst us in the winter, others round about us, seemed not to know what to make of it; and there were many that scoffed at, and ridiculed it; and some compared what we called conversion to certain distempers. But it was very observable of many, that occasionally came amongst us from abroad, with disregardful hearts, that what they saw here cured them of such a temper of mind: strangers were generally surprised to find things so much beyond what they had heard, and were wont to tell others that the state of the town could not be conceived of by those that had not seen it. The notice that was taken of it by the people that came to town on occasion of the court, that sat here in the beginning of March, was very observable. And those that came from the neighborhood to our public lectures, were for the most part remarkably affected. Many that came to town, on one occasion or other, had their consciences smitten, and awakened, and went home with wounded hearts, and with those impressions that never wore off till they had hopefully

a saving issue; and those that before had serious thoughts, had their awakenings and convictions greatly increased. And there were many instances of persons that came from abroad, on visits, or on business, that had not been long here before, to all appearance, they were savingly wrought upon, and partook of that shower of divine blessing that God rained down here, and went home rejoicing; till at length the same work began evidently to appear and prevail in several other towns in the county.

In the month of March, the people in South Hadley began to be seized with deep concern about the things of religion; which very soon became universal: and the work of God has been very wonderful there; not much, if any thing, short of what it has been here, in proportion to the bigness of the place. About the same time it began to break forth in the west part of Suffield (where it has also been very great), and it soon spread into all parts of the town. It next appeared at Sunderland, and soon overspread the town; and I believe was for a season, not less remarkable than it was here. About the same time it began to appear in a part of Deerfield, called Green River, and afterwards filled the town, and there has been a glorious work there: it began also to be manifest in the south part of Hatfield, in a place called the Hill, and after that the whole town, in the second week in April, seemed to be seized, as it were at once, with concern about the things of religion: and the work of God has been great there. There has been also a very general awakening at West Springfield, and Long Meadow; and in Enfield, there was, for a time, a pretty general concern amongst some that before had been very loose persons. About the same time that this appeared at Enfield, the Rev. Mr. Bull of Westfield informed me, that there had been a great alternation there, and that more had been done in one week there than in seven years before.—Something of this work likewise appeared in the first precinct in Springfield, principally in the north and south extremes of the parish. And in Hadley old town, there gradually appeared so much of a work of God on souls, as at another time would have been thought worthy of much notice. For a short time there was also a very great and general concern, of the like nature, at Northfield. And wherever this concern appeared, it seemed not to be in vain: but in every place God brought saving blessings with them, and his word attended with his Spirit (as we have all reason to think) returned not void. It might well be said at that time in all parts of the country, *Who are these that fly as a cloud, and as doves to their windows?* . . .

This remarkable pouring out of the Spirit of God, which thus extended from one end to the other of this country, was not confined to it, but many places in Connecticut have partook in the same mercy: as for instance, the first parish in Windsor, under the pastoral care of the Reverend Mr. Marsh, was thus blest about the same time, as we in Northampton, while we had no knowledge of each other's circumstances. . . .

But this shower of Divine blessing has been yet more extensive: there was no small degree of it in some parts of the Jerseys; as I was informed when I was at New-York (in a long journey I took at that time of the year for my health), by some people of the Jerseys, whom I saw: especially the Rev. Mr. William Tennent, a minister, who seemed to have such things much at heart, told me of a very great awakening of many in a place called the Mountains, under the ministry of one Mr. Cross; and of a very considerable revival of religion in another place under the ministry of his brother the Rev. Mr. Gilbert Tennent; and also at another place, under the ministry of a very pious young gentleman, a Dutch minister, whose name as I remember, was Freelinghousen.

QUESTIONS

1. What is meant by "saved by faith alone"?

2. How does Edwards explain the spread of the Great Awakening?

THOMAS JEFFERSON

The Virginia Statute of Religious Liberty

An Act for Establishing Religious Freedom

I. Whereas Almighty God hath created the mind free; that all attempts to influence it by temporal punishments or burthens, or by civil incapacitations, tend only to beget habits of hypocrisy and meanness, and are a departure from the plan of the Holy author of our religion, who being Lord both of body and mind, yet chose not to propagate it by coercions on either, as was in his Almighty power to do; that the impious presumption of legislators and rulers, civil as well as ecclesiastical, who being themselves but fallible and uninspired men, have assumed dominion over the faith of others, setting up their own opinions and modes of thinking as the only true and infallible, and as such endeavouring to impose them on others, hath established and maintained false religions over the greatest part of the world, and through all time; that to compel a man to furnish contributions of money for the propagation of opinions which he disbelieves, is sinful and tyrannical; that even the forcing him to support this or that teacher of his own religious persuasion, is depriving him of the comfortable liberty of giving his contributions to the particular pastor whose morals he would make his pattern, and whose powers he feels most persuasive to righteousness, and is withdrawing from the ministry those temporary rewards, which proceeding from an approbation of their personal conduct, are an additional incitement to earnest and unremitting labours for the instruction of mankind; that our civil rights have no dependence on our religious opinions, any more than our opinions in physics or geometry; that therefore the proscribing any citizen as unworthy the public confidence by laying upon him an incapacity of being called to offices of trust and emolument, unless he profess or renounce this or that religious opinion, is depriving him injuriously of those privileges and advantages to which in common with his fellow-citizens he has a natural right; that it tends only to corrupt the principles of that religion it is meant to encourage, by bribing with a monopoly of worldly honours and emoluments, those who will externally profess and conform to it; that though indeed these are criminal who do not withstand such temptation, yet neither are those innocent who lay the bait in their way; that to suffer the civil magistrate to intrude his powers into the field of opinion, and to restrain the profession or propagation of principles on supposition of their ill tendency, is a dangerous fallacy, which at once destroys all religious liberty, because he being of course judge of that tendency will make his opinions the rule of judgment, and approve or condemn the sentiments of others only as they shall square with or differ from his own; that it is time enough for the rightful purposes of civil government, for its officers to interfere when principles break out into overt acts against peace and good order; and finally, that truth is great and will prevail if left to herself, that she is the proper and sufficient antagonist to error, and has nothing to fear from the conflict, unless by human interposition disarmed of her natural weapons, free argument and debate, errors ceasing to be dangerous when it is permitted freely to contradict them.

II. Be it enacted by the General Assembly, that no man shall be compelled to frequent or support any religious worship, place or ministry whatsoever, nor shall be enforced, restrained, molested, or burthened in his body or goods, nor shall otherwise suffer on account of his religious opinions or belief; but that all men shall be free to profess, and by argument to maintain, their opinions in matters of religion, and that the same shall in no wise diminish, enlarge or affect their civil capacities.

III. And though we well know that this Assembly, elected by the people for the ordinary purposes of legislation only, have no power to restrain the acts of succeeding Assemblies, constituted with powers equal to our own, and that therefore to declare this Act to be irrevocable would be of no effect in law; yet as we are free to declare, and do declare, that the rights hereby asserted are of the natural rights of mankind, and that if any Act shall hereafter be passed to repeal the present, or to narrow its operation, such Act will be an infringement of natural right.

QUESTIONS

1. On what basis does Jefferson seek to establish religious tolerance?

2. Is he critical of Christianity? How?

3. What does Jefferson mean by "truth," and what are his criteria for determining what is true?

4. Does his optimistic belief that truth will inevitably triumph over error strike you as typical of the Enlightenment? As typically American?

5. What specific human rights does Jefferson consider "natural"?

NAME _____ SECTION _____ DATE _____

Chapter 26

The Enlightenment in the United States

VOCABULARY

untrammeled (p. 261) Not restricted or limited; unrestrained.

malaise (p. 262) Uneasiness; discomfort.

obscurantist (p. 263) One who believes in the hindering of progress.

federalism (p. 263) A governmental system in which united provinces or states largely reserve their own authority but also assign some powers to the central government.

republican (p. 263) Characterizing a type of government in which voting citizens have a voice through their elected representatives.

malevolent (p. 265) Malicious or mean; evil.

ambiguity (p. 266) Indefiniteness; vagueness; uncertainty; the quality of being capable of being understood in two or more ways.

Anglican (p. 267) A member of the Church of England.

Unitarian (p. 267) In the twentieth century, a member of a religious denomination that professes no specific creed or system of belief and stresses social action in support of liberal causes.

Review Questions

1. True or false: Citizens of the new American republic were overwhelmingly Protestant, including large numbers of African American slaves (p. 262).

                                                                    Ans. _____

2. The Great Awakening was a mid-eighteenth-century religious movement that stressed _____ versus reasoned argument and appealed to

_____

_____ (p. 262).

3. Not among the influences on the thinking of John Locke was
   a. English empiricism.
   b. ideas about natural rights.
   c. the idea that political authority is based on the consent of the governed.
   d. absolutist theory about royal power.

   Ans. _____

4. Describe the development of the federalist system in the United States, including foreign and historical influences, as well as strictly American contributions (p. 263).

5. Classical Greek and Roman influences on Thomas Jefferson's design for his home, Monticello (Fig. 26-3), which was modeled on the sixteenth-century _____, can be seen in two of its architectural features, the _____ and the _____ (p. 265).

6. Reread the first two paragraphs of the Declaration of Independence and identify, first, the democratic principles of government set forth in the document, and second, the grievances the American colonists had against the British king (p. 265).

   The democratic principles are . . .

   American grievances included . . .

7. Jefferson sought to create an "academical village" at the University of Virginia. Explain how the university's architecture and living arrangements as designed by Jefferson fostered such a community of scholars (p. 267).

NAME _____ SECTION _____ DATE _____

8. True or false: The University of Virginia established by Jefferson excluded women, African Americans, and poor whites (p. 269).

Ans. _____

9. Summarize Jonathan Edwards's statements in each of the following themes (pp. 270–272):

The activity of the spirit of God:

Edwards's concern about the effect of evangelistic preaching:

Spiritual awakening:

Spiritual matters versus worldly affairs:

Criticisms of the revival movement:

The validity of these criticisms:

Conversions:

10. The problem Thomas Jefferson had with the "opinions and modes of thinking" of some European and American leaders was that (p. 272):

11. The "comfortable liberty" about which Jefferson wrote involved the citizen's freedom to choose or not to choose to do what (p. 272)?

12. True or false: American civil rights, Jefferson maintained, should be made dependent on religious beliefs because of the danger of anarchy and the schemes of would-be monarchs (p. 272).

    Ans. _____

13. Jefferson thought that religious freedom should be (p. 272)
    a. completely unqualified.
    b. largely unqualified, allowing a few exceptions.
    c. fairly restricted.
    d. completely restricted, with each state allowed to establish the religion to be observed within its borders.

    Ans. _____

NAME _____ SECTION _____ DATE _____

14. Although Jefferson was a nominal member of the Church of England, his doubts about the divine nature of Jesus, the occurrence of miracles, and other traditional Christian beliefs were similar to those of Unitarians.[1] Explain the ways in which Jefferson's beliefs probably affected his actions.

The Big Picture

Were you acquainted before reading this chapter with the influences on the development of U.S. constitutional democracy? What were the ancient Greek and Roman influences? What about those of the English Enlightenment? Consider the indigenous features of American political culture after the revolution. Was there no way to get the various states, each with a history going back many decades, to fall in line as part of a strong central government, or was federalism the only sensible option?

What about the issue of religion? In your opinion, did Jefferson make a good case for the separation of church and state?

What are your reactions? What questions do you have?

_____

[1] Unitarians profess no creed and see "truth" expressed in science, reason, and scholarship. They also emphasize humanistic goals, and find value in the beliefs and traditions of all major faiths.

Textbook Features

Study Guides

Some textbooks will be accompanied by a **study guide**, a separate book that usually contains exercises, discussion questions, and vocabulary lists or activities for each chapter. Study guides are often in the form of workbooks to allow you to record your answers and even remove pages to submit as assignments to your instructor.

A study guide does not replace the textbook; rather, it is a useful tool you can use *in addition* to reading the chapters. The exercises and vocabulary activities in study guides will steer you toward the most important concepts in the chapters. This direction and emphasis will help increase your understanding and retention of information. The discussion questions in study guides will improve your critical-thinking skills by helping you make new connections or understand the relevance of the information to your own life. Thinking about these questions or going over them in class or with a small study group may also assist you in preparing for writing assignments or research papers.

EXERCISE 1

Complete all of the questions and activities in the study guide for "The Enlightenment in the United States" chapter. Compare your answers to those in the Answer Key at the end of this book.

Tips and Techniques

Critical Reading

Throughout college, you will need to develop and practice **critical-reading** skills. Reading *critically* does not mean finding fault with a text; it means evaluating the text and judging its validity and value. Critical readers are open-minded, yet they do not passively accept everything they see in print. Instead, they maintain a healthy skepticism, expecting the author to convince them to believe or accept his or her ideas. In other words, critical readers think for themselves as they read.

Critical reading offers several benefits. Because it requires analysis, synthesis, and evaluation of ideas and information, it improves your thinking skills. It will also help expand your knowledge and help you decide how to apply that knowledge to your own life. Finally, it will help you prepare for class assignments such as essays and research papers.

Reading critically requires the highest level of concentration. It also requires all three steps—preview, read (actively), and review—of the reading process. While you are reading and reviewing a textbook chapter, practice all of the techniques for increasing comprehension and retention. At the same time, think about the following:

- **Evaluate the information and its sources.**   Authors and publishers take great care to verify the accuracy of the information they include in textbooks, so you don"t necessarily need to question the facts or their sources as you would when you read other types of publications, such as editorials. However, you should evaluate the author's conclusions that are based on this evidence. Ask yourself these questions:

  Is each conclusion supported by enough evidence?
  Does the evidence lead logically to the stated conclusion?
  Could other conclusions arise from the same information?

For example, a critical reading of the following paragraph from "The Enlightenment in the United States" chapter might lead you to write this note beside it:

King

ignores Americans' willing perpetuation of slave trade

(He) has waged cruel war against human nature itself, violating its most sacred rights of life and liberty in the persons of a distant people who never offended him, captivating and carrying them into slavery, in another hemisphere, or to incur miserable death in their transportation thither. This piratical warfare, the opprobrium of *infidel* powers, is the warfare of the *Christian* king of Great Britain. Determined to keep open a market where MEN should be bought and sold, he has prostituted his negative[1] for suppressing every legislative attempt to prohibit or to restrain this execrable commerce; and that this assemblage of horrors might want no fact of distinguished die,[2] he is now exciting these very people to rise in arms among us, and to purchase that liberty of which *he* deprived them, by murdering the people upon whom *he* also obtruded them; thus paying off former crimes committed against the *liberties* of one people, with crimes which he urges them to commit again the *lives* of another.

Try to get in the habit of recording your thoughts in brief marginal notes as you read.

- **Try to make new connections beyond those provided by the author.** When you can connect new information to what you already know, you increase your understanding and your ability to recall new information. As you read about a subject, think of your own related experiences. Do they match the book's ideas and conclusions? Also, try to recall what you've learned about the subject in other courses, in other readings, or from the media. For example, connect what you learn from your humanities textbook to what you studied in your history and government classes, or think of current events in the news that relate to the information you're reading. Strive to create new "webs" of knowledge within your mind.

EXERCISE 2

Preview "The Enlightenment in the United States" chapter. What expectations did you form based on this preview? What do you already know about this topic?

EXERCISE 3

Actively read "The Enlightenment in the United States" chapter by highlighting important information. Also, write marginal notes that either evaluate the information or try to make new connections. For example, look at these sample marginal notes for two different paragraphs from the chapter:

During my visit to Monticello, I learned J. never stopped renovating M.—he never finished—a metaphor for Enlightenment value of continual self-improvement?

Charlottesville, Virginia, which he called Monticello ("little mountain"; see Fig. 26-3). The house itself is symbolic of the nature of the American Enlightenment. Jefferson used the *Palladian* Villa Rotunda as his model (Fig. 24-1), but the plan of the interior exhibits a functional adaptation of the symmetrical plan to his own particular needs. Similarly, the building, originally designed for stone execution, is rendered in red brick with white wooden trim—an elegant, rich contrast to the building's simplicity of shape. These adaptations to use and surroundings do not, however, detract from the *portico and dome*, the two architectural forms that link it with those of democratic Greece and republican Rome. Facing westward, to the wilderness, dominating but sympathetic to the landscape, the house is almost a metaphor for the man—aristocratic, cosmopolitan, inventive, practical—a farmer and a philosopher.

Great Awakening
contributed to
climate of
freedom/choice
that led to
political
revolution

This <u>revival movement</u> contributed to bringing into <u>question two fundamental beliefs</u> of traditional Christianity; that 1) <u>religious conformity</u> was necessary and that the 2) <u>state should lend financial and other support</u> to a particular church. Although some states continued to use tax money to support a designated church or churches, the <u>competition for membership</u> in the spiritual market in the second half of the eighteenth century could not be prevented, and in practice <u>freedom of conscience for all religions</u> became the rule. Unlike in European countries, in which the established church had a guaranteed membership and religion tended to be taken for granted, in the British colonies the competition for souls fostered an almost <u>continual spirit of revival</u> and a <u>rich variety of choices</u>. Consequently, by the time of the revolution the <u>Christian churches were highly decentralized and largely voluntary in membership</u>, and <u>reflected the evolution of republican feeling in a broad sector of the population.</u>

EXERCISE 4

In the space below (or on a separate sheet of paper), write at least one paragraph in response to the chapter on Enlightenment. What did you gain by reading about this topic? How can you use this information in your career, in your other courses, and/or in your personal life? Did any of the information surprise you? Did the chapter correct any misconceptions you had? Did it reinforce ideas or information you already knew?

EXERCISE 5

Many textbooks will include questions that encourage you to read critically. On a separate sheet of paper, write your answers to the two sets of questions within "The Enlightenment in the United States" chapter as well as the two sets of questions following the reading selections at the end of the chapter. Compare your answers to those in the Answer Key at the end of this book.

PART 5

"Transforming Fire: The Civil War, 1861–1865" from *A People and a Nation*

CHAPTER

15

Transforming Fire:
The Civil War
1861–1865

He was a living legend. A frontiersman who fought with Andrew Jackson at the Battle of Horseshoe Bend, he had a distinguished career as lawyer, congressman, and governor of Tennessee. But in 1829 he abruptly resigned his governorship and spent the next three years living among the Cherokees. In 1836 he reemerged as commander-in-chief of the armies winning Texan independence. Then he became president of the new Republic of Texas, holding that office twice. After Texas joined the Union, he served fourteen years as United States senator. In 1859 voters in Texas elected him governor. No one in Texas rivaled the reputation or prestige of Sam Houston, yet in March 1861 he was deposed. Why? Houston opposed secession, warned of defeat, refused to take an oath of allegiance to the Confederacy, and challenged the authority of the secession convention. Its members ended his career by declaring his office vacant.

A similar reversal of fortune befell Nathaniel Banks in Texas. Banks had built a distinguished public career in Massachusetts. Hard-working and self-educated, he had risen from bobbin boy in a cotton mill to lawyer, state legislator, congressman, Speaker of the United States House of Representatives, and governor of Massachusetts. When the Civil War began, Banks promptly volunteered to fight and was commissioned a major general. His troops met defeat in Virginia, however, and his reputation was slipping when he arrived on Texas's coast to try to capture the Rio Grande valley. After some success in 1863, a failed offensive along the Red River in 1864 led to scathing criticism and his departure from the military.

War drastically altered the lives of millions of Americans. Winslow Homer gave the ironic title *Home, Sweet, Home* to this painting of Union soldiers in camp about 1863. *Private Collection, photograph courtesy of Hirschl and Adler Galleries, New York.*

403

404   Chapter 15   Transforming Fire: The Civil War, 1861–1865

The Civil War brought astonishing, unexpected changes not only to Sam Houston and Nathaniel Banks but everywhere in both North and South. For some, wealth changed to poverty and hope to despair; for others, the suffering of war spelled opportunity. Contrasts abounded, between noble and crass motives and between individuals seeking different goals. Even the South's slaves, who hoped that they were witnessing God's "Holy War for liberation," encountered unsympathetic liberators. When a Yankee soldier ransacked a slave woman's cabin, stealing her best quilts, she denounced him as a "nasty, stinkin' rascal" who had betrayed his cause of freedom. Angrily the soldier contradicted her, saying, "I'm fightin' for $14 a month and the Union."

Northern troops were not the only ones to feel anger over their sacrifice. Impoverished by the war, one southern farmer had endured inflation, taxes, and shortages to support the Confederacy. Then an impressment agent arrived to take still more from him—grain and meat, horses and mules, and wagons. In return, the agent offered only a certificate promising repayment sometime in the future. Bitter and disgusted, the farmer declared, "The sooner this damned Government falls to pieces, the better it will be for us."

Many northern businessmen, however, viewed the economic effects of the war with optimism and anticipation. The conflict ensured vast government expenditures, a heavy demand for goods, and lucrative federal contracts. *Harper's Monthly* reported that an eminent financier expected a long war—the kind of war that would mean huge purchases, paper money, active speculation, and rising prices. "The battle of Bull Run," predicted the financier, "makes the fortune of every man in Wall Street who is not a natural idiot."

For these people and millions of others, the Civil War was a life-changing event. It obliterated the normal patterns and circumstances of life. Millions of men were swept away into training camps and battle units. Armies numbering in the hundreds of thousands marched over the South, devastating once-peaceful countrysides. Families struggled to survive without their men; businesses tried to cope with the loss of workers. Women in both North and South took on extra responsibilities in the home and moved into new jobs in the work force. No sphere of life was untouched.

Change was most drastic in the South, where the leaders of the secession movement had launched a revolution for the purpose of keeping things unchanged. Never were men more mistaken: their rev-

olutionary means were fundamentally incompatible with their conservative purpose. Southern whites had feared that a peacetime government of Republicans would interfere with slavery and upset the routine of plantation life. Instead their own actions led to a war that turned southern life upside down and imperiled the very existence of slavery. Jefferson Davis, president of the Confederate States of America, devised policies more objectionable to the elite than any proposed by President-elect Lincoln. Life in the Confederacy proved to be a shockingly unsouthern experience.

War altered the North as well, but less deeply. Because most of the fighting took place on southern soil, northern farms and factories remained virtually unscathed. The drafting of workers and the changing need for products slowed the pace of industrialization somewhat, but factories and businesses remained busy. Workers lost ground to inflation, but the economy hummed. A new probusiness atmosphere dominated Congress, where the seats of southern representatives were empty. To the alarm of many, the powers of the federal government and of the president increased during the war.

The war created social strains in both North and South. Disaffection was strongest in the Confederacy, where poverty and class resentment fed a lower-class antagonism to the war that threatened the Confederacy from within as federal armies assailed it from without. In the North, dissent also flourished, and antiwar sentiment occasionally erupted into violence.

Ultimately, the Civil War forced on the nation new social and racial arrangements. Its greatest effect was to compel leaders and citizens to deal directly with the issue they had debated and argued over but had been unable to resolve: slavery. This issue, in complex and indirect ways, had given rise to the war. Now the scope and demands of the war forced reluctant Americans to confront it.

 ## "Fighting Means Killing": The War in 1861 and 1862

Few Americans understood what they were getting into when the war began. The onset of hostilities sparked patriotic sentiments, optimistic speeches, and joyous ceremonies in both North and South. Northern communities, large and small, raised companies of volunteers eager to save the Union and sent them off with fanfare (a scene captured in the

• *Important Events* •

1861 Battle of Bull Run takes place
General George McClellan organizes Union Army
Union blockade begins
United States Congress passes first confiscation act
Trent affair

1862 Union captures Fort Henry and Fort Donelson
United States Navy captures New Orleans
Battle of Shiloh shows the war's destructiveness
Confederacy enacts conscription
General Robert E. Lee thwarts McClellan's offensive on Richmond
United States Congress passes second confiscation act
Confederacy mounts offensive in Maryland and Kentucky
Battle of Antietam ends Lee's drive into Maryland

1863 Emancipation Proclamation takes effect
United States Congress passes National Banking Act
Union enacts conscription
African-American soldiers join Union Army
Food riots occur in southern cities
Battle of Chancellorsville ends in Confederate victory but General "Stonewall" Jackson's death
Union wins key victories at Gettysburg and Vicksburg
Draft riots take place in New York City
Battle of Chattanooga leaves South vulnerable to General William T. Sherman's march

1864 Battles of the Wilderness and Spotsylvania produce heavy casualties on both sides in the effort to capture and defend Richmond
Battle of Cold Harbor continues carnage in Virginia
Abraham Lincoln requests Republican Party plank abolishing slavery
General Sherman captures Atlanta
Lincoln wins reelection
Jefferson Davis proposes emancipation within the Confederacy
Sherman marches through Georgia

1865 Sherman marches through Carolinas
United States Congress approves Thirteenth Amendment
Hampton Roads Conference
Lee abandons Richmond and Petersburg
Lee surrenders at Appomattox Courthouse
Lincoln assassinated

painting *Departure of the Seventh Regiment*). In the South, confident recruits boasted of whipping the Yankees and returning home in time for dinner, and southern women sewed dashing uniforms for men who soon would be lucky to wear drab gray or butternut homespun.

Through the spring of 1861 both sides scrambled to organize and train their inexperienced, undisciplined armies. On July 21, 1861, the first

Battle of Bull Run

battle took place outside Manassas Junction, Virginia, near a stream called Bull Run. General Irvin McDowell and 30,000 Union troops attacked General

P. G. T. Beauregard's 22,000 southerners (see map, page 407). As raw recruits struggled amid the confusion of their first battle, federal forces began to gain ground. Then they ran into a line of Virginia troops under General Thomas Jackson. "There is Jackson standing like a stone wall," shouted one Confederate. "Stonewall" Jackson's line held, and the arrival of 9,000 Confederate reinforcements won the day for the South. Union troops fled back to Washington and shocked northern congressmen and spectators, who had watched the battle from a point two miles away, suddenly feared their capital would be taken.

The unexpected rout at Bull Run gave northerners their first hint of the nature of the war to come.

In Departure of the Seventh Regiment *(1861), flags and the spectacle of thousands of young men from New York marching off to battle give a deceptively gay appearance to the beginning of the Civil War.*   Museum of Fine Arts, Boston; M. and M. Karolik Collection.

Victory would not be easy, even though the United States enjoyed an enormous advantage in resources. Pro-Union feeling was growing in western Virginia, and loyalties were divided in the four border slave states—Missouri, Kentucky, Maryland, and Delaware. But the rest of the Upper South had joined the Confederacy. Moved by an outpouring of regional loyalty, half a million southerners volunteered to fight; there were so many would-be soldiers that the Confederate government could not arm them all. The United States therefore undertook a massive buildup of troops in northern Virginia.

Lincoln gave command of the army to General George B. McClellan, an officer who proved to be better at organization and training than at fighting. McClellan devoted the fall and winter of 1861 to readying a formidable force of a quarter-million men whose mission would be to destroy southern forces guarding Richmond, the new Confederate capital.

"The vast preparation of the enemy," wrote one southern soldier, produced a "feeling of despondency" in the South for the first time.

While McClellan prepared, the Union began to implement other parts of its overall strategy, which called for a blockade of southern ports and eventual capture of the Mississippi River. Like a constricting snake, this "Anaconda plan" would strangle the Confederacy (see map, page 409). At first the Union Navy had too few ships to patrol 3,550 miles of coastline and block the Confederacy's avenues of commerce and supply. Gradually, however, the navy increased the blockade's effectiveness, though it never bottled up southern commerce completely.

Confederate strategy was essentially defensive. A defensive posture not only was consistent with the South's claim that it merely wanted to be left alone, but also took into account the North's advantage in resources (see figure, page 410). Furthermore, communities all across the South demanded to be defended. Jefferson Davis, however, wisely rejected a static or wholly defensive strategy. The South would pursue an "offensive defensive," taking advantage of opportunities to attack and using its interior lines of transportation to concentrate troops at crucial points.

Strategic thinking on both sides slighted the importance of "the West," that vast expanse of territory between Virginia and the Mississippi River. When the war began, both sides were unprepared for large-scale and sustained operations in the West, but before the end of the war it would prove to be a crucial theater. North and South also shared a fondness for "turning movements," in which an army marched around its opponent to force a withdrawal or unleashed a flank attack in battle. In the Far West, beyond the Mississippi River, the Confederacy hoped to gain an advantage by negotiating treaties with the Creeks, Choctaws, Chickasaws, Cherokees, Seminoles, and smaller tribes of Plains Indians.

The last half of 1861 brought no major land battles, but the North made gains by sea. Late in the summer Union naval forces captured Cape Hatteras and then seized Hilton Head, one of the Sea Islands off Port Royal, South Carolina. A few months later, similar operations secured vital coastal points in North Carolina, as well as Fort Pulaski, which defended Savannah. Federal naval operations were biting into the Confederate coastline (see map, page 409).

Union Naval Campaign

The coastal victories off South Carolina foreshadowed major changes in slave society. At the federal gunboats' approach, frightened planters abandoned their lands and fled. Their slaves greeted what they hoped to be freedom with rejoicing and broke the hated cotton gins. Their jubilation and the constantly growing stream of runaways who poured into the Union lines eliminated any doubt about which side slaves would support, given the opportunity. Unwilling at first to wage a war against slavery, the federal government did not acknowledge the slaves' freedom—though it began to use their labor in the Union cause.

The coastal incursions worried southerners, but the spring of 1862 brought even stronger evidence of the war's seriousness. In March two ironclad ships—the *Monitor* (a Union warship) and the *Merrimack* (a Union ship recycled by the Confederacy)—fought each other for the first time; their battle, though indecisive, ushered in a new era in naval de-

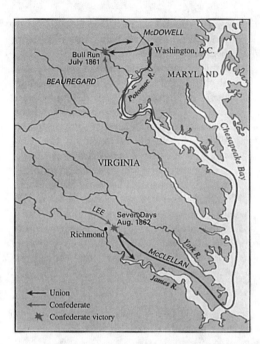

McClellan's Campaign   *The water route chosen by McClellan to threaten Richmond during the peninsular campaign.*

sign. In April Union ships commanded by Admiral David Farragut smashed through log booms blocking the Mississippi River and fought their way upstream to capture New Orleans. Farther west a Union victory at Elkhorn Tavern, Arkansas, shattered Confederate control of Indian Territory. (Thereafter, dissension within Native American groups and a Union victory the following year at Honey Springs, Arkansas, reduced Confederate operations in Indian Territory to guerrilla raids.)

In February 1862 land and river forces in northern Tennessee won significant victories for the Union. A hard-drinking, hitherto unsuccessful general named Ulysses S. Grant saw the strategic importance of Fort Henry and Fort Donelson, the Confederate outposts guarding the Tennessee and Cumberland Rivers. If federal troops could capture these forts, Grant realized, two prime routes into the heartland of the Confederacy would lie open. In just ten days he seized the forts, using his forces so well that he was in a position to demand

Grant's Campaign in Tennessee

408   Chapter 15   Transforming Fire: The Civil War, 1861–1865

unconditional surrender of Fort Donelson's defenders. A path into Tennessee, Alabama, and Mississippi now lay open before the Union Army.

Grant moved on into southern Tennessee and the first of the war's shockingly bloody encounters, the Battle of Shiloh. On April 6, Confederate General Albert Sidney Johnston caught federal troops in an undesirable position on the Tennessee River. With their backs to the water, Grant's men were awaiting reinforcements. The Confederates attacked early in the morning and inflicted heavy damage all day. Close to victory, General Johnston was struck and killed by a ball that severed an artery in his thigh. Southern forces almost achieved a breakthrough, but Union reinforcements arrived that night. The next day the tide of

Battle of Shiloh

battle turned, and after ten hours of heavy combat, Grant's men forced the Confederates to withdraw. Neither side won a victory, yet the losses were staggering. Northern troops lost 13,000 men (killed, wounded, or captured) out of 63,000; southerners sacrificed 11,000 out of 40,000. Total casualties in this single battle exceeded those in all three of America's previous wars combined. Now both sides were beginning to sense the true nature of the war. Shiloh utterly changed Grant's thinking about it. He had hoped that southerners soon would be "heartily tired" of the conflict. After Shiloh, he recalled, "I gave up all idea of saving the Union except by complete conquest."

Meanwhile, on the Virginia front, President Lincoln had a different problem. Conquest was impossible without battles, but General McClellan seemed

Both armies experienced religious revivals during the war. This photograph shows members of a largely Irish regiment from New York celebrating Mass at the beginning of the war. Notice the presence of some female visitors in the left foreground.   Library of Congress.

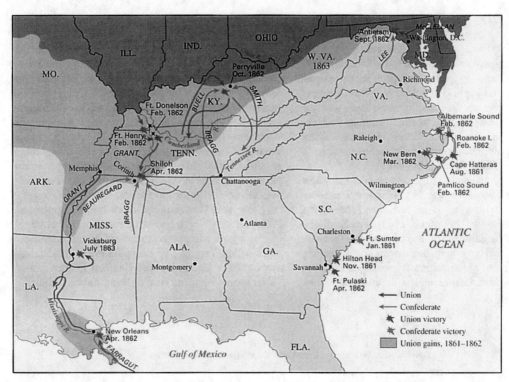

Anaconda Plan   *An overview of the Union's "Anaconda Plan" and key battles on the coast and in the West, 1861–1863.*

unwilling to fight. Only thirty-six, McClellan had already achieved notable success as an army officer and railroad president. Keenly aware of his historic role, he did not want to fail and insisted on having everything in order before he attacked. Habitually overestimating the size of enemy forces, McClellan called repeatedly for reinforcements and ignored Lincoln's directions to advance. Finally McClellan chose to move by a roundabout water route, sailing his troops around the York peninsula and advancing on Richmond from the east (see map, page 407).

By June the sheer size of the federal armies outside the Confederacy's capital was highly threatening. But southern leaders foiled McClellan's legions. First, Stonewall Jackson moved north into the Shenandoah valley behind Union forces and threatened Washington, D.C., drawing some of the federal troops away from Richmond to protect their own capital. Then, in a series of engagements known as the Seven Days Battles, Confederate general Robert E. Lee struck at McClellan's army. Lee never managed to close his pincers around the retreating Union forces, but on August 3 McClellan withdrew to the Potomac. Richmond remained safe for almost two more years.

Buoyed by these results, Jefferson Davis conceived an ambitious plan to turn the tide of the war and gain recognition of the Confederacy by European nations. He ordered a general offensive, sending Lee north into Maryland and Generals Kirby Smith and Braxton Bragg into Kentucky. Calling on residents of Maryland and Kentucky to make a separate peace with his government, Davis also invited northwestern states like Indiana, which sent much of their trade down the Mississippi to New Orleans, to leave the Union.

Confederate Offensive in Maryland and Kentucky

The plan was promising, but every part of the offensive failed. In the bloodiest day of the entire war, September 17, 1862, McClellan turned Lee back

410   Chapter 15   Transforming Fire: The Civil War, 1861–1865

from Sharpsburg, Maryland. In the Battle of Antietam 5,000 men died (3,500 had died at Shiloh), and another 18,000 were wounded. Lee was lucky to escape destruction, for McClellan had obtained a copy of Lee's marching orders. But McClellan moved slowly, failed to use his larger forces in simultaneous attacks all along the line, and allowed Lee's stricken army to retreat to safety across the Potomac. In Kentucky Generals Smith and Bragg had to withdraw just one day after Bragg attended the inauguration of a provisional Confederate governor.

Confederate leaders had marshaled all their strength for a breakthrough but had failed. Outnumbered and disadvantaged in resources, the South could not continue the offensive. Profoundly disappointed, Davis admitted to a committee of Confederate representatives that southerners were entering "the darkest and most dangerous period we have yet had." Tenacious defense and stoic endurance now

seemed the South's only long-range hope. Perceptive southerners shared their president's despair.

But 1862 also brought painful lessons to the North. Confederate General James E. B. (Jeb) Stuart executed a daring cavalry raid into Pennsylvania in October. Then on December 13 Union general Ambrose Burnside unwisely ordered his soldiers to attack Lee's army, which held fortified positions on high ground at Fredericksburg, Virginia. Lee's men performed so coolly and controlled the engagement so thoroughly that Lee, a restrained and humane man, was moved to say, "It is well that war is so terrible. We should grow too fond of it."

The rebellion was far from being suppressed. Although the North had large reserves, it was learning just how high were the costs of the war. Both sides would have to pay a terrible price. As Confederate cavalry leader Nathan Bedford Forrest put it, "War means fighting. And fighting means killing."

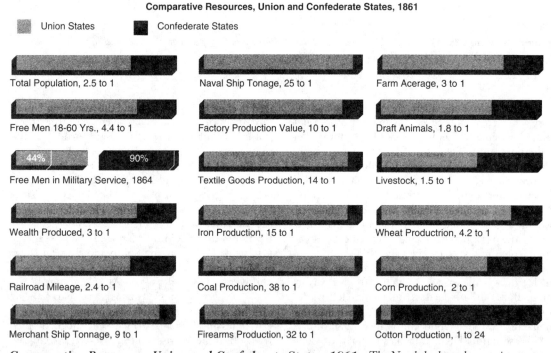

Comparative Resources, Union and Confederate States, 1861

Union States   Confederate States

Total Population, 2.5 to 1

Naval Ship Tonage, 25 to 1

Farm Acerage, 3 to 1

Free Men 18-60 Yrs., 4.4 to 1

Factory Production Value, 10 to 1

Draft Animals, 1.8 to 1

44%   90%

Free Men in Military Service, 1864

Textile Goods Production, 14 to 1

Livestock, 1.5 to 1

Wealth Produced, 3 to 1

Iron Production, 15 to 1

Wheat Productrion, 4.2 to 1

Railroad Mileage, 2.4 to 1

Coal Production, 38 to 1

Corn Production, 2 to 1

Merchant Ship Tonnage, 9 to 1

Firearms Production, 32 to 1

Cotton Production, 1 to 24

Comparative Resources, Union and Confederate States, 1861 *The North had vastly superior resources. Although the North's advantages in manpower and industrial capacity proved very important, the South could not really be conquered until it chose to give up the fight.*   Source: From *The Times Atlas of World History.* Time Books, London, 1978. Used with permission.

In October 1862 in New York City, photographer Matthew Brady opened an exhibition of photographs from the Battle of Antietam. The camera, whose modern form had been invented only in 1826, made war's carnage hideously real. Although few knew it, Brady's vision was very poor, and this photograph of Confederate dead was actually made by his assistants, Alexander Gardner and James F. Gibson. Confederate dead: Library of Congress; camera: George Eastman House Collection.

 ## War Transforms the South

Even more than the fighting itself, disruptions in civilian life robbed southerners of their gaiety and nonchalance. The war altered southern society beyond all expectations and with astonishing speed. One of the first traditions to fall was the southern preference for local government. The South had been characterized by limited government. States' rights had been its motto, but by modern standards even the state governments were weak and sketchy affairs. The average citizen, on whom the hand of government had rested lightly, probably knew county authorities best. To withstand the massive power of the North, however, the South needed to centralize;

like the colonial revolutionaries, southerners faced a choice of join or die. No one saw the necessity of centralization more clearly than Jefferson Davis. If the states of the Confederacy insisted on fighting separately, said Davis, "we had better make terms as soon as we can."

Promptly Davis moved to bring all arms, supplies, and troops under his control. But by early 1862 the scope and duration of the conflict required

Confederacy Resorts to a Draft

something more. Tens of thousands of Confederate soldiers had volunteered for just one year's service, planning to return home in the spring to plant their crops. To keep southern armies in the

412   Chapter 15   Transforming Fire: The Civil War, 1861–1865

field, the War Department encouraged reenlistments and called for new volunteers. However, as one official admitted, "the spirit of volunteering had died out." Three states threatened or instituted a draft. Finally, faced with a critical shortage of troops, in April 1862 the Confederate government enacted the first national conscription (draft) law in American history. Thus the war forced unprecedented change on states that had seceded out of fear of change.

Though Jefferson Davis was careful to observe the Confederate constitution, he was a strong chief executive. He adopted a firm leadership role toward the Confederate Congress, which raised taxes and later passed a tax-in-kind—a tax paid in farm products. Almost three thousand agents dispersed to collect the tax, assisted by almost fifteen hundred appraisers. Where opposition arose, the government suspended the writ of habeas corpus (which prevented individuals from being held without trial) and imposed martial law. In the face of political opposition that cherished states' rights, Davis proved unyielding.

Centralization of Power

To replace the food that men in uniform would have grown, Davis exhorted farmers to switch from cash crops to food crops; he encouraged the states to require them to do so. But the army remained short of food and labor. In emergencies the War Department resorted to impressing slaves to work on fortifications, and after 1861 the government relied heavily on confiscation of food to feed the troops. Officers swooped down on farms in the line of march and carted away grain, meat, wagons, and draft animals.

Soon the Confederate administration in Richmond was exercising virtually complete control over the southern economy. Because it controlled the supply of labor through conscription, the administration could compel industry to work on government contracts and supply the military's needs. The Confederate Congress also gave the central government almost complete control of the railroads; in 1864 shipping, too, came under extensive regulation. New statutes even limited corporate profits and dividends. A large bureaucracy sprang up to administer these operations: over seventy thousand civilians staffed the Confederate administration. By the war's end, the southern bureaucracy was larger in proportion to population than its northern counterpart.

Clerks and subordinate officials crowded the towns and cities where Confederate departments had their offices. The sudden population booms that resulted overwhelmed the housing supply and stimulated new construction. The pressure was especially great in Richmond, whose population increased 250 percent. Before the war's end, Confederate officials were planning the relocation of entire departments to lessen crowding in Richmond. Mobile's population jumped from 29,000 to 41,000; Atlanta began to grow; and 10,000 people poured into war-related industries in little Selma, Alabama.

Effects of War on Southern Cities and Industry

Another prime cause of urban growth in the South was industrialization. The Union blockade disrupted imports of manufactured products and caused the traditionally agricultural South to become interested in industry. Davis exulted that manufacturing was making the South "more and more independent of the rest of the world." Many planters shared his hope that industrialization would bring "deliverance, full and unrestricted, from all commercial dependence" on the North. Indeed, beginning almost from scratch, the Confederacy achieved tremendous feats of industrial development. Chief of Ordnance Josiah Gorgas increased the capacity of Richmond's Tredegar Iron Works and other factories to the point that by 1865 his Ordnance Bureau was supplying all Confederate small arms and ammunition. Meanwhile, the government constructed new railroad lines to improve the efficiency of the South's transportation system.

Southerners adopted new ways in response to these changes. Women, restricted to narrow roles in antebellum society, gained substantial new responsibilities. The wives and mothers of soldiers now headed households and performed men's work, adding to their traditional chores the tasks of raising crops and tending animals. Women in nonslaveowning families cultivated fields themselves, while wealthier women suddenly had to manage field hands unaccustomed to female overseers. Only the very rich had enough servants to allow a woman's routine to continue undisturbed. In the cities, white women—who had been virtually excluded from the labor force—found a limited number of respectable new paying jobs. Clerks had always been males, but the war changed that, too. "Government girls" staffed the Confederate bureaucracy, and female schoolteachers became commonplace in the South for the first time.

Change in the Role of Southern Women

Some women gained confidence from their new responsibilities. Among these was Janie Smith, a young North Carolinian. Raised in a rural area by prosperous parents, she had faced few challenges or grim realities before the war reached her farm and troops turned her home into a hospital. "It makes me shudder when I think of the awful sights I witnessed that morning," she wrote to a friend. "Ambulance after ambulance drove up with our wounded. . . . Under every shed and tree, the tables were carried for amputating the limbs. . . . The blood lay in puddles in the grove; the groans of the dying and complaints of those undergoing amputation were horrible." But Janie Smith learned to cope with crisis. She ended her account with the proud words, "I can dress amputated limbs now and do most anything in the way of nursing wounded soldiers."

Patriotic sacrifice appealed to some women, but others resented their new burdens. Many among the wealthy found their new tasks difficult and their changed situation distasteful. North Carolina diarist Catherine Devereux Edmondston was enthusiastic for the southern cause but wanted her husband to remain at home. A Texas woman who had struggled to discipline slaves pronounced herself "sick of trying to do a man's business." Others grew angry over shortages and resented cooking and unfamiliar contact with lower-class women.

Yet the Confederate experience produced some new values. Legislative bodies yielded power to the executive branch of government, which could act more decisively in time of war. Achievement and bravery under fire began to take precedence over aristocratic lineage. Men such as Josiah Gorgas, Stonewall Jackson, and Nathan Bedford Forrest gained renown by distinguishing themselves in industry and on the battlefield.

For millions of ordinary southerners, however, change brought privation and suffering. Mass poverty descended for the first time on a large minority of the white population. Many

Human Suffering

yeoman families had lost their breadwinners to the army. As a South Carolina newspaper put it, "The duties of war have called away from home the sole supports of many, many families. . . . Help must be given, or the poor will suffer." The poor sought help from relatives, neighbors, friends, anyone. Sometimes they pleaded their cases to the Confederate government. "In the name of humanity," begged one woman, "discharge my husband he is not able to do your government much

This Confederate soldier, like thousands of his comrades, took advantage of an opportunity to pose with his wife and brother. As the death toll mounted and suffering increased, southern women grew less willing to urge their men into battle. Collection of Larry Williford.

good and he might do his children some good . . . my poor children have no home nor no Father."

Other factors aggravated the effect of the labor shortage. The South was in many places so sparsely populated that the conscription of one skilled craftsman could work a hardship on the people of an entire county. Often they begged in unison for the exemption or discharge of the local miller or the neighborhood tanner, wheelwright, or potter. Physicians also were in short supply. Most serious, however, was the loss of a blacksmith. As a petition from Alabama explained, "our Section of County [is] left entirely Destitute of any man that is able to keep in order any kind of Farming Tules."

The blockade of Confederate shipping created shortages of common but important items—salt, sugar, coffee, nails—and speculation and hoarding made the shortages worse. Greedy

Hoarding and Runaway Inflation

businessmen cornered the supply of some commodities; prosperous citizens stocked up on food. The *Richmond Enquirer* criticized one man for hoarding seven hundred barrels of flour; another man, a planter, purchased so many wagonloads of supplies that his "lawn and paths looked like a wharf covered with a ship's loads." "This disposition to speculate upon the yeomanry of the country," lamented the *Richmond Examiner*, "is the most mortifying feature of the war." North Carolina's Governor Zebulon Vance worried about "the cry of distress . . . from the poor wives and children of our soldiers. . . . What will become of them?"

Inflation raged out of control, fueled by the Confederate government's heavy borrowing and inadequate taxes, until prices had increased almost 7,000 percent. Inflation particularly imperiled urban dwellers and the many who could no longer provide for themselves. As early as 1861 and 1862, newspapers reported that "want and starvation are staring thousands in the face," and troubled officials predicted that "women and children are bound to come to suffering if not starvation." Some concerned citizens tried to help. "Free markets," which disbursed goods as charity, sprang up in various cities. Some families came to the aid of their neighbors. But other people would not cooperate: "It is folly for a poor mother to call on the rich people about here," raged one woman. "Their hearts are of steel they would sooner throw what they have to spare to the dogs than give it to a starving child." The need was so vast that it overwhelmed private charity. A rudimentary relief program organized by the Confederacy offered hope but was soon curtailed to supply the armies. Thus southern yeomen sank into poverty and suffering.

As their fortunes declined, people of once-modest means looked around and found abundant evidence that all classes were not sacrificing equally.

Inequities of the Confederate Draft

They saw that the wealthy gave up only their luxuries, while many poor families went without necessities. And they noted that the Confederate government contributed to these inequities through policies that favored the upper class. Until the last year of the war, for example, prosperous southerners could avoid military service by hiring substitutes. Prices for substitutes skyrocketed until it cost a man $5,000 or $6,000 to send someone to the front in his place. Well over 50,000 upper-class southerners purchased such substitutes. South Carolina's Mary Boykin Chesnut knew of one young aristocrat who "spent a fortune in substitutes. Two have been taken from him [when *they* were conscripted], and two he paid to change with him when he was ordered to the front. He is at the end of his row now, for all ablebodied men are ordered to the front. I hear he is going as some general's courier." As Chesnut's last remark indicates, the rich also traded on their social connections to avoid danger. "It is a notorious fact," complained an angry Georgian, that "if a man has influential friends—or a little money to spare he will never be enrolled." A Confederate senator from Mississippi, James Phelan, informed Jefferson Davis that apparently "nine tenths of the youngsters of the land whose relatives are conspicuous in society, wealthy, or influential obtain some safe perch where they can doze with their heads under their wings."

Anger at such discrimination exploded in October 1862 when the Confederate Congress exempted from military duty anyone who was supervising at least twenty slaves. "Never did a law meet with more universal odium," observed one representative. "Its influence upon the poor is most calamitous." Protests poured in from every corner of the Confederacy, and North Carolina's legislators formally condemned the law. Its defenders argued, however, that the exemption preserved order and aided food production, and the statute remained on the books.

Dissension spread as growing numbers of citizens concluded that the struggle was "a rich man's war and a poor man's fight." Alert politicians and newspaper editors warned that class resentment was building to a dangerous level. The bitterness of letters to Confederate officials during this period suggests the depth of the people's anger. "If I and my little children suffer [and] die while there Father is in service," threatened one woman, "I invoke God Almighty that our blood rest upon the South." Another woman swore to the secretary of war that unless help was provided to poverty-stricken wives and mothers "an allwise god . . . will send down his fury and judgment in a very grate manar . . .[on] those that are in power." War was magnifying social tensions in the Confederacy.

 ## The Northern Economy Copes with War

With the onset of war, a tidal wave of change rolled over the North as well. Factories and citizens' associations geared up to support the war, and the federal government and its executive branch gained new powers. The energies of an industrializing, cap-

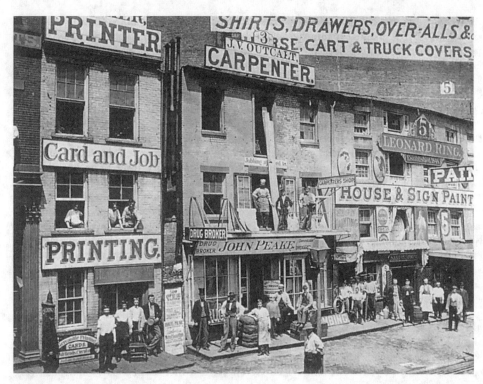

Despite initial problems, the task of supplying a vast war machine kept the northern economy humming. This photograph shows businesses on the west side of Hudson Street in New York City in 1865.   New-York Historical Society.

italist society were harnessed to serve the cause of the Union. Idealism and greed flourished together, and the northern economy proved its awesome productivity. Northern factories ran overtime, and unemployment was low. The war did not destroy the North's prosperity. Northern farms and factories came through the war unharmed, whereas most of the South suffered extensive damage. To Union soldiers on the battlefield, sacrifice was a grim reality, but northern civilians experienced only the bustle and energy of wartime production.

At first the war was a shock to business. Northern firms lost their southern markets, and many companies had to change their products and find new customers in order to remain open. Southern debts became uncollectible, jeopardizing not only northern merchants but also many western banks. In farming regions, families struggled with an aggravated shortage of labor. A few enterprises never pulled out of the tailspin caused by the war.

Initial Slump in Northern Business

Cotton mills lacked cotton; construction declined; shoe manufacturers sold few of the cheap shoes that planters had bought for their slaves.

Overall the war slowed the pace of industrialization in the North, but its economic impact was not all negative. Certain entrepreneurs, such as wool producers, benefited from shortages of competing products, and soaring demand for war-related goods swept some businesses to new heights of production. To feed the hungry war machine, the federal government pumped unprecedented sums into the economy. The Treasury issued $3.2 billion in bonds and paper money called greenbacks, and the War Department spent over $360 million in revenues from new taxes (including a broad excise tax and the nation's first income tax). Government contracts soon totaled more than $1 billion.

Secretary of War Edwin M. Stanton's list of the supplies needed by the Ordnance Department indicates the scope of government demand: "7,892 cannon, 11,787 artillery carriages, 4,022,130 small-arms, . . . 1,022,176,474 cartridges for small-arms,

416   Chapter 15   Transforming Fire: The Civil War, 1861–1865

1,220,555,435 percussion caps, . . . 26,440,054 pounds of gunpowder, 6,395,152 pounds of niter, and 90,416,295 pounds of lead." Stanton's list covered only weapons; the government also purchased huge quantities of uniforms, boots, food, camp equipment, saddles, ships, and other necessities. War-related spending revived business in many northern states. In 1863, a merchants' magazine examined the effects of the war in Massachusetts: "Seldom, if ever, has the business of Massachusetts been more active or profitable than during the past year. . . . In every department of labor the government has been, directly or indirectly, the chief employer and paymaster." Government contracts had a particularly beneficial impact on the state's wool, metal, and shipbuilding industries, and also saved Massachusetts shoe manufacturers from ruin.

Nothing illustrated the wartime partnership between business and government better than the work of Jay Cooke, a wealthy New York financier. Cooke threw himself into the marketing of government bonds to finance the war effort. With great imagination and energy, he convinced both large investors and ordinary citizens to invest enormous sums in the war effort, in the process earning hefty commissions for himself. But the financier's profit served the Union cause, as the interests of capitalism and government, finance and patriotism, merged. The booming economy, the Republican alliance with business, and the frantic wartime activity combined to create a new atmosphere in Washington. The notion spread that government should aid businessmen and not interfere with them. Noting the favorable atmosphere, railroad builders and industrialists—men such as Leland Stanford, Collis P. Huntington, John D. Rockefeller, John M. Forbes, and Jay Gould—took advantage of it. Their enterprises grew with the aid of government loans, grants, and tariffs.

War production aided some heavy industries in the North. Coal output rose substantially. Iron makers improved the quality of their product while boosting the production of pig iron from 920,000 tons in 1860 to 1.1 million tons in 1864. Foundries developed new and less expensive ways to make steel. Although new railroad construction slowed, repairs helped the manufacture of rails to increase. Of considerable significance for the future was the railroad industry's adoption of a standard gauge (width) for

Effects of War on Northern Industry and Agriculture

track, which eliminated the unloading and reloading of boxcars and created a unified transportation system.

Another strength of the northern economy was the complementary relationship between agriculture and industry. Mechanization of agriculture had begun before the war. Wartime recruitment and conscription, however, gave western farmers an added incentive to purchase labor-saving machinery. The shift from human labor to machines created new markets for industry and expanded the food supply for the urban industrial work force. The boom in the sale of agricultural tools was tremendous. Cyrus and William McCormick built an industrial empire in Chicago from the sale of their reapers. Between 1862 and 1864 the manufacture of mowers and reapers doubled to 70,000 yearly; even so, manufacturers could not satisfy the demand. By the end of the war, 375,000 reapers were in use, triple the number in 1861. Large-scale commercial agriculture had become a reality. As a result, northern farm families whose breadwinners went to war did not suffer as their counterparts did in the South. "We have seen," one magazine observed, "a stout matron whose sons are in the army, cutting hay with her team . . . and she cut seven acres with ease in a day, riding leisurely upon her cutter."

Northern industrial and urban workers did not fare as well. After the initial slump, jobs became plentiful, but inflation ate up much of a worker's paycheck. By 1863 9-cent-a-pound beef cost 18 cents. The price of coffee had tripled; rice and sugar had doubled; and clothing, fuel, and rent had all climbed. Between 1860 and 1864 consumer prices rose at least 76 percent, while daily wages rose only 42 percent. Workers' families consequently suffered a substantial decline in their standard of living.

As their real wages shrank, industrial workers lost job security. To increase production, some employers were replacing workers with labor-saving machines. Other employers urged the government to promote immigration so they could import cheap labor. Workers responded by forming unions and sometimes by striking. Skilled craftsmen organized to combat the loss of their jobs and status to machines; women and unskilled workers, excluded by the craftsmen, formed their own unions. In recognition of the increasingly national scope of business activity, thirteen occupational groups—including tailors, coal miners, and

New Militancy Among Northern Workers

Wartime Society in the North **417**

railway engineers—formed national unions during the Civil War. Because of the tight labor market, unions won many of their demands without striking, but the number of strikes also rose steadily.

Employers reacted with hostility to this new spirit among workers—a spirit that William H. Sylvis, leader of the iron molders, called a "feeling of manly independence." Manufacturers viewed labor activism as a threat to their property rights and freedom of action, and accordingly formed statewide or craft-based associations to cooperate and pool information. These employers shared blacklists of union members and required new workers to sign "yellow dog" contracts (promises not to join a union). To put down strikes, they hired strikebreakers from the ranks of the poor and desperate—blacks, immigrants, and women—and sometimes received additional help from federal troops.

Troublesome as unions were, they did not prevent many employers from making a profit. The highest profits were made from profiteering on government contracts. Unscrupulous businessmen took advantage of the suddenly immense demand for army supplies by selling clothing and blankets made of "shoddy"—wool fibers reclaimed from rags or worn cloth. Shoddy goods often came apart in the rain; most of the shoes purchased in the early months of the war were worthless, too. Contractors sold inferior guns for double the usual price and passed off tainted meat as good. Corruption was so widespread that it led to a year-long investigation by the House of Representatives. A group of contractors that had demanded $50 million for their products dropped their claims to $17 million as a result of the findings of the investigation.

Legitimate enterprises also made healthy profits. The output of woolen mills increased so dramatically that dividends in the industry nearly tripled.

Wartime Benefits to Northern Business Some cotton mills made record profits on what they sold, even though they reduced their output. Brokerage houses worked until midnight and earned unheard-of commissions. Railroads carried immense quantities of freight and passengers, increasing their business to the point that railroad stocks doubled or even tripled in value. The price of Erie Railroad stock rose from $17 to $126 a share during the war.

Railroads also were a leading beneficiary of government largesse. Congress had failed in the 1850s to resolve the question of a northern versus a southern route for the first transcontinental railroad. With the South absent from Congress, the northern route quickly prevailed. In 1862 and 1864 Congress chartered two corporations, the Union Pacific Railroad and the Central Pacific Railroad, and assisted them financially in connecting Omaha, Nebraska, with Sacramento, California. For each mile of track laid, the railroads received a loan of from $16,000 to $48,000 in government bonds plus 20 square miles of land along a free 400-foot-wide right of way. Overall, the two corporations gained approximately 20 million acres of land and nearly $60 million in loans.

Morrill Land Grant Act Other businessmen benefited handsomely from the Morrill Land Grant Act (1862). To promote public education in agriculture, engineering, and military science, Congress granted each state 30,000 acres of federal land for each of its congressional districts. The states could sell the land, as long as they used the income for the purposes Congress had intended. The law eventually fostered sixty-nine colleges and universities, but one of its immediate effects was to enrich a few prominent speculators. Hard-pressed to meet wartime expenses, some states sold their land cheaply to wealthy entrepreneurs. For example, Ezra Cornell, a leader in the telegraph industry, invested in 500,000 acres in the Midwest.

Higher tariffs also pleased many businessmen. Northern businesses did not uniformly favor high import duties; some manufacturers desired cheap imported raw materials more than they feared foreign competition. But northeastern congressmen traditionally supported higher tariffs, and after southern lawmakers left Washington, they had their way: the Tariff Act of 1864 raised tariffs generously. According to one scholar, manufacturers had only to mention the rate they considered necessary and that rate was declared. Some healthy industries earned artificially high profits by raising their prices to a level just below that of the foreign competition. By the end of the war, tariff increases averaged 47 percent, and rates were more than double those of 1857.

 ## Wartime Society in the North

The outbreak of war stimulated patriotism in the North just as it initially had done in the South. Northern society, which had suffered the stresses associated with industrialization, immigration, and widespread social change, found a unifying cause in the preservation of the nation and the American form of government. In thousands of self-governing towns and communities, northern citizens felt a personal connection to representative government. Secession threatened to destroy their system, and northerners rallied to its defense. Secular and church leaders supported the cause, and even ministers who preferred to separate politics and pulpit denounced "the iniquity of causeless rebellion."

Such enthusiasm proved useful as northerners encountered a multitude of wartime changes. The powers of the federal government and the president grew steadily during the crisis.

Expanded Powers of the United States President

Abraham Lincoln, like Jefferson Davis, found that war required active presidential leadership. At the beginning of the conflict, Lincoln launched a major shipbuilding program without waiting for Congress to assemble. The lawmakers later approved his decision, and Lincoln continued to act in advance of Congress when he deemed such action necessary. In one striking exercise of executive power, Lincoln suspended the writ of habeas corpus for everyone living between Washington D.C., and Philadelphia. There was scant legal justification for this act, but the president's motive was practical: to ensure the loyalty of Maryland. Later in the war, with congressional approval, Lincoln repeatedly suspended habeas corpus and invoked martial law, mainly in the border states but elsewhere as well. Between fifteen and twenty thousand United States citizens were arrested on suspicion of disloyal acts.

On occasion Lincoln used his wartime authority to bolster his own political fortunes. He and his generals proved adept at furloughing soldiers so they could vote in close elections; those whom Lincoln furloughed, of course, usually voted Republican. He also came to the aid of other officeholders in his party. When the Republican governor of Indiana, who was battling propeace Democrats in his legislature, ran short of funds, Lincoln had the War Department supply $250,000. This procedure lacked constitutional sanction, but it advanced the Union cause.

Among the clearest examples of the wartime expansion of federal authority were the National Banking Acts of 1863, 1864, and 1865. Before the Civil War, the nation lacked a uniform currency, for the federal government had never exercised its authority in this area. Banks operating under state charters issued no fewer than seven thousand different kinds of notes, which were difficult to distinguish from a variety of forgeries. On the recommendation of Secretary of the Treasury Salmon Chase, Congress established a national banking system empowered to issue national bank notes. At the close of the war in 1865, Congress imposed a prohibitive tax on state bank notes and forced most state institutions to join the national system. This process created a sounder currency and a simpler monetary system—but also inflexibility in the money supply and an eastern-oriented financial structure.

Social attitudes on the home front evolved in directions that would have shocked the soldiers in the field. In the excitement of moneymaking, an eagerness to display one's wealth flourished in the largest cities. A visitor to Chicago commented that "so far as lavish display is concerned, the South Side in some portions has no rival in Chicago, and perhaps not outside New York." *Harper's Monthly* reported that "the suddenly enriched contractors, speculators, and stock-jobbers . . . are spending money with a profusion never before witnessed in our country, at no time remarkable for its frugality. . . . The men button their waistcoats with diamonds . . . and the women powder their hair with gold and silver dust." The *New York Herald* summarized that city's atmosphere: "The richest silks, laces and jewelry are the soonest sold. . . . Not to keep a carriage, not to wear diamonds, . . . is now equivalent to being a nobody. This war has entirely changed the American character. . . . The individual who makes the most money— no matter how—and spends the most—no matter for what—is considered the greatest man."

Extravagance Amid War

Yet idealism coexisted with ostentation. Many churches endorsed the Union cause as God's cause. One Methodist newspaper described the war as a contest between "equalizing, humanizing Christianity" and "disunion, war, selfishness, [and] slavery." Abolitionists, after initial uncertainty over whether to let the South go, campaigned to turn the war into a crusade against slavery. Free black communities and churches both black and white responded to the needs of slaves who flocked to the Union lines, sending clothing, ministers, and teachers to aid the runaways.

Northern women, like their southern counterparts, took on new roles. Those who stayed home organized over ten thousand soldiers' aid societies, rolled innumerable bandages, and raised $3 million to aid injured troops. Thousands served as nurses in front-line hospitals, where they pressed for better care of the wounded. Yet women were only a small minority of all nurses, and they had to fight for a chance to serve at all. The professionalization of medicine since the Revolution had created a medical system dominated by men, and many male physicians did not want women's aid. Female nurses proved their worth, but only the wounded welcomed them. Even Clara Barton, the most famous female nurse, was ousted from her post in 1863.

The poet Walt Whitman left a record of his experiences as a volunteer nurse in Washington, D.C. As he dressed wounds and tried to comfort suffering and lonely men, Whitman found

Walt Whitman

"the marrow of the tragedy concentrated in those Army Hospitals." But despite "indescribably horrid wounds," he also found in the hospitals inspiration and a deepening faith in American democracy. Whitman celebrated the "incredible dauntlessness" and sacrifice of the common soldier who fought for the Union. As he had written in the preface to his great work *Leaves of Grass* (1855), "The genius of the United States is not best or most in its executives or legislatures, but always most in the common people." Whitman worked this idealization of the common man into his poetry, which also explored homoerotic themes and rejected the lofty meter and rhyme of European verse to strive for a "genuineness" that would appeal to the masses.

Thus northern society embraced strangely contradictory tendencies. Materialism and greed flourished alongside idealism, religious conviction, and self-sacrifice. While some soldiers risked their lives willingly out of a desire to preserve the Union or extend freedom, many others openly sought to avoid service. Under the law, a draftee could stay at home by providing a substitute or paying a $300 commutation fee. Many wealthy men chose these options, and in response to popular demand, clubs, cities, and states provided the money for others. In all, 118,000 substitutes were provided and 87,000 commutations paid before Congress ended the commutation system in 1864.

The Strange Advent of Emancipation

At the highest levels of government in the United States and in the Confederacy there was a similar lack of clarity about the purpose of the war. Throughout the first several months of the struggle, both Davis and Lincoln studiously avoided references to slavery. Davis realized that emphasis on the issue could increase class conflict in the South. To avoid identifying the Confederacy only with the interests of slaveholders, he articulated a broader, traditional ideology. Davis told southerners that they were fighting for constitutional liberty: northerners had betrayed the founders legacy, and southerners had seceded to preserve it. As long as Lincoln also avoided making slavery an issue, Davis's line seemed to work.

Lincoln had his own reasons for not mentioning slavery. It was crucial at first not to antagonize the Union's border slave states, whose loyalty was tenuous. Also for many months Lincoln hoped that a pro-Union majority would assert itself in the South. It might be possible, he thought, to coax the South back into the Union and stop the fighting. Raising the slavery issue would severely undermine both goals. Powerful political considerations also dictated that Lincoln remain silent. The Republican Party was a young and unwieldy coalition. Some Republicans burned with moral outrage over slavery; others were frankly racist, dedicated to protecting free whites from the Slave Power and the competition of cheap slave labor; still others saw the tariff or immigration or some other issue as paramount. A forthright stand by Lincoln on the subject of slavery could split the party, gratifying some groups and alienating others. Until a consensus developed or Lincoln found a way to appeal to all the elements of the party, silence was the best approach.

The president's hesitancy ran counter to some of his personal feelings. Lincoln was a sensitive and compassionate man whose humility and moral anguish during the war were evident in his speeches and writings. But as a politician, Lincoln distinguished between his own moral convictions and his official acts. His political positions were studied and complex, calculated for maximum advantage. Frederick Douglass, the astute and courageous black protest leader, sensed that Lincoln was without prejudice toward black people. Yet Douglass judged him "pre-eminently the white man's president."

Lincoln first broached the subject of slavery in a substantive way in March 1862, when he proposed that the states consider emancipation on their own. He

Lincoln's Plan for Gradual Emancipation

asked Congress to promise aid to any state that decided to emancipate, and he appealed to border-state representatives to consider this course seriously. What Lincoln proposed was gradual emancipation, with compensation for slaveholders and colonization of the freed slaves outside the United States. To a delegation of free blacks he explained that "it is better for us both . . . to be separated." Until well into 1864 Lincoln steadfastly promoted an unpromising and wholly impractical scheme to colonize blacks in some region like Central America. Despite Secretary of State William H. Seward's care to insert phrases such as "with their consent," the word *deportation* crept into one of Lincoln's speeches in place of *colonization*. Thus his was as conservative a scheme as could be devised. Moreover, since the states would make the decision voluntarily, no responsibility for it would attach to Lincoln.

Others wanted to go much further. A group of Republicans in Congress, known as the Radicals and led by men such as George Julian, Charles Sumner, and Thaddeus Stevens, dedicated themselves to seeing that the war was prosecuted vigorously. They were instrumental in creating a special House-Senate committee on the conduct of the war, which investigated Union reverses, sought to make the war effort more efficient, and prodded the president to take stronger measures. Early in the war these Radicals, with support from other representatives, turned their attention to slavery.

In August 1861, at the Radicals' instigation, Congress passed its first confiscation act. Designed to punish the Confederate rebels, the law confiscated all property used for "insurrectionary purposes." Thus if the

Confiscation Acts

South used slaves in a hostile action, those slaves were declared seized and liberated. A second confiscation act (July 1862) was much more drastic: it confiscated the property of all those who supported the rebellion, even those who merely resided in the South and paid Confederate taxes. Their slaves were declared "forever free of their servitude, and not again [to be] held as slaves." The logic behind these acts was that the insurrection—as Lincoln always termed it—was a serious revolution requiring strong measures. Let the government use its full powers, free the slaves, and crush the revolution, urged the Radicals.

Lincoln refused to adopt that view. He stood by his proposal of voluntary gradual emancipation by the states and made no effort to enforce the second confiscation act. His stance provoked a public protest from Horace Greeley, editor of the powerful *New York Tribune*. In an open letter to the president entitled "The Prayer of Twenty Millions," Greeley pleaded with Lincoln to "execute the laws" and declared, "On the face of this wide earth, Mr. President, there is not one disinterested, determined, intelligent champion of the Union cause who does not feel that all attempts to put down the Rebellion and at the same time uphold its inciting cause are preposterous and futile."

Lincoln's reply was an explicit statement of his complex and calculated approach to the question. He disagreed, he said, with all those who would make the maintenance or destruction of slavery the paramount issue of the war. "I would save the Union," announced Lincoln. "If I could save the Union without freeing *any* slave I would do it, and if I could save it by freeing *all* the slaves I would do it; and if I could save it by freeing some and leaving others alone I would also do that. What I do about slavery, and the colored race, I do because I believe it helps to save the Union." Lincoln closed with a personal disclaimer: "I have here stated my purpose according to my view of *official* duty; and I intend no modification of my oft-expressed *personal* wish that all men everywhere could be free."

When he wrote those words, Lincoln had already decided on a new step: issuance of the Emancipation Proclamation. On the advice of the cabinet, however, he was waiting for a Union victory before announcing the proclamation, so that it would not appear to be an act of desperation. Yet the letter to Greeley was not simply an effort to stall; it was an integral part of Lincoln's approach to the future of slavery, as the text of the Emancipation Proclamation would show.

On September 22, 1862, shortly after the Battle of Antietam, Lincoln issued the first part of his two-part proclamation. Invoking his powers as commander-in-chief of the armed forces, he announced that on January 1, 1863, he would emancipate the slaves in states whose people "shall then be in rebellion against the United States." Lincoln made plain that he would judge a state to be in rebellion in January if it lacked bona fide representatives in the United States Congress. Thus his September proclamation was less a declaration of the right of slaves to be free than a threat to southerners: unless they stopped fighting and returned to Congress, they would lose their slaves. "Knowing the value that was set on the slaves by the rebels," said Garrison Frazier, a black Georgian, "the President thought that his proclamation would stimulate them to lay down their arms . . . and their not

Emancipation Proclamations

doing so has now made the freedom of the slaves a part of the war." Lincoln may not actually have expected southerners to give up their effort, but he was careful to offer them the option, thus putting the onus of emancipation on them.

When Lincoln designated the areas in rebellion on January 1, his proclamation excepted every Confederate county or city that had fallen under Union control. Those areas, he declared, "are, for the present, left precisely as if this proclamation were not issued." Nor did Lincoln liberate slaves in the border slave states that remained in the Union. "The President has purposely made the proclamation inoperative in all places where . . . the slaves [are] accessible," charged the anti-administration *New York World*. "He has proclaimed emancipation only where he has notoriously no power to execute it." Partisanship aside, even Secretary of State Seward, a moderate Republican, said sarcastically, "We show our sympathy with slavery by emancipating slaves where we cannot reach them and holding them in bondage where we can set them free." A British official, Lord Russell, commented on the "very strange nature" of the document, noting that it did not declare "a principle adverse to slavery."

By making the liberation of the slaves "a fit and necessary war measure," furthermore, Lincoln raised a variety of legal questions. How long did a war measure remain in force? Did it expire with the suppression of a rebellion? The proclamation did little to clarify the status or citizenship of the freed slaves. And a reference to garrison duty in one of the closing paragraphs suggested that former slaves would have inferior duties and rank in the army. For many months, in fact, their pay and treatment were inferior.

Thus the Emancipation Proclamation was a puzzling and ambiguous document that said less than it seemed to say. It freed no slaves, and serious limitations were embedded in its language. But if as a moral and legal document it was wanting, as a political document it was nearly flawless. Because the proclamation defined the war as a war against slavery, radicals could applaud it, even if the president had not gone as far as Congress. Yet at the same time it protected Lincoln's position with conservatives, leaving him room to retreat if he chose and forcing no immediate changes on the border slave states.

The need for men soon convinced the administration to recruit northern and southern blacks for the Union Army. By the spring of 1863, African-American troops were proving their value. Lincoln came to see them as "the great *available* and yet *un-*

availed of force for restoring the Union." African-American leaders hoped that military service would secure equal rights for their people. Once the black soldier had fought for the Union, wrote Frederick Douglass, "there is no power on earth which can deny that he has earned the right of citizenship in the United States." If black soldiers turned the tide, asked another man, "would the nation refuse us our rights?"

In June 1864, Lincoln gave his support to a constitutional ban on slavery. Reformers such as Elizabeth Cady Stanton and Susan B. Anthony were pressing for an amendment that would write emancipation into the Constitution. On the eve of the Republican national convention, Lincoln called the party's chairman to the White House and instructed him to have the party "put into the platform as the keystone, the amendment of the Constitution abolishing and prohibiting slavery forever." The party promptly called for a new amendment, the Thirteenth. Republican delegates probably would have adopted such a plank without his urging, but Lincoln demonstrated his commitment by lobbying Congress for quick approval of the measure. The proposed amendment passed in 1865 and was sent to the states for ratification or rejection. Lincoln's strong support for the Thirteenth Amendment—an unequivocal prohibition of slavery—constitutes his best claim to the title "Great Emancipator."

Yet Lincoln soon clouded that clear stand, for in 1865 the newly reelected president considered allowing the defeated southern states to reenter the Union and delay or defeat the amendment. In February he and Secretary of State Seward met with three Confederate commissioners at Hampton Roads, Virginia. The end of the war was clearly in sight, and southern representatives angled vainly for an armistice that would allow the South to remain a separate nation. But Lincoln was doing some political maneuvering of his own, apparently contemplating the creation of a new national party based on a postwar alliance with southern Whigs and moderate and conservative Republicans. The cement for the coalition would be concessions to planter interests.

Hampton Roads Conference

Pointing out that the Emancipation Proclamation was only a war measure, Lincoln predicted that the courts would decide whether it had granted all, some, or none of the slaves their freedom. Seward observed that the Thirteenth Amendment, which would be definitive, was not yet ratified and that reentry

422 Chapter 15 Transforming Fire: The Civil War, 1861–1865

into the Union would allow the southern states to defeat it. Lincoln did not contradict Seward but spoke in favor of "prospective" ratification: approval with the effective date postponed for five years. He also promised to seek $400 million in compensation for slaveholders and to consider their views on related questions such as confiscation. Such financial aid would provide an economic incentive for planters to rejoin the Union and capital to cushion the economic blow of emancipation.

These were startling propositions from a president on the verge of military victory. Most northerners opposed them, and only the opposition of Jefferson Davis, who set himself against anything short of independence, prevented discussion of the proposals in the South. Even at the end of the war, Lincoln was keeping his options open and maintaining the distinction he had drawn between "*official* duty" and "*personal* wish." Lincoln did not attempt to mold public opinion on race, as did advocates of equality in one direction and racist Democrats in the other. Instead, he moved cautiously, constructing complex and ambiguous positions and avoiding the risks inherent in challenging, educating, or inspiring the nation's conscience.

Before the war was over, the Confederacy, too, addressed the issue of emancipation. Jefferson Davis himself offered a strong proposal in favor of liberation.

Davis's Plan for Emancipation

Though emancipation was less popular in the South than in the North, Davis did not flinch or conceal his purpose. He was dedicated to independence, and he was willing to sacrifice slavery to achieve that goal. After considering the alternatives for some time, Davis concluded late in 1864 that the military status of the Confederacy was desperate and that independence with emancipation was preferable to defeat with emancipation. He proposed that the Confederate government purchase forty thousand slaves to work for the army as laborers, with a promise of freedom at the end of their service. Soon Davis upgraded his proposal, calling for the recruitment and arming of slaves as soldiers, who likewise would gain their freedom at the end of the war. The wives and children of these soldiers, he made plain, must also receive freedom from the states. Davis and his advisers did not favor full equality—they envisioned "an intermediate state of serfage or peonage." Thus they shared with Lincoln and their entire generation racial attitudes that blinded them to the massive changes taking place around them.

Still, Davis had proposed a radical change for the slaveholding South. Bitter debate resounded through the Confederacy, but Davis stood his ground. When the Confederate Congress approved slave enlistments without the promise of freedom, Davis insisted on more. He issued an executive order to guarantee that owners would emancipate slave soldiers, and his allies in the states started to work for emancipation of the soldiers' families. Some black troops had started to drill as the end of the war approached.

Confederate emancipation began too late to revive southern armies or win diplomatic advantages with antislavery Europeans. By contrast, Lincoln's Emancipation Proclamation stimulated a vital infusion of forces into the Union armies. Beginning in 1863 slaves from the Confederacy and the border states shouldered arms for the North. Before the war was over, 134,000 slaves (and 52,000 free African-Americans) had fought for freedom and the Union. Their participation aided northern victory while it discouraged recognition of the Confederacy by foreign governments. Lincoln's policy, whatever its limitations and lack of clarity, had profound practical effects.

 The Soldier's War

The intricacies of policymaking were far from the minds of ordinary soldiers. Military service completely altered their lives. Enlistment took young men from their homes and submerged them in large organizations whose military discipline ignored their individuality. Army life meant tedium, physical hardship, and separation from loved ones even in the best of times. Soldiers in battle confronted fear and danger, and the risk of death from wounds or disease was very high. Yet the military experience had powerful attractions as well. It molded men on both sides so thoroughly that they came to resemble each other far more than they resembled civilians back home. Many soldiers forged amid war a bond with their fellows and a connection to a noble purpose that they cherished for years afterward.

Union soldiers may have sensed most clearly the massive scale of modern war. Most were young; eighteen was the most common age, followed by twenty-one. Many went straight from small towns and farms into large armies supplied by extensive bureaucracies. By late 1861 there were 640,000 volunteers in arms, a stupendous increase over the regular

How do historians know what the average soldier thought and felt? A vast number of diaries and letters written by soldiers have been preserved in archives and libraries and reveal a wide range of experiences. Many soldiers acted on noble ideals, but others did not. Papers at the University of Michigan document one Union soldier's worry that "If this experiment in self-government by the people shall fail, where are the oppressed and the downtrodden millions of the earth to look for hope of better days?" They also contain letters from Private Robert Sherry of New York, shown here. *Sherry cared little for the Republican Party. The enlisted men and officers in his regiment rarely got along, and after twenty soldiers were sent to Dry Tortugas, in the Gulf of Mexico, as punishment for a mutiny, Sherry wrote bitterly that he hoped "to see the day when we will get into some battle that will be the means of getting a great portion of our Officers killed or wounded." A rough man in a rough regiment, Sherry enjoyed looting and fighting.*   Clements Library, University of Michigan.

army of 20,000 men. The increase occurred so rapidly that it is remarkable the troops were supplied and organized as well as they were. Yet many soldiers' first experiences with a large military organization were unfortunate.

Soldiers benefited from certain new products, such as canned condensed milk, but blankets, clothing, and arms were often of poor quality. Vermin abounded. Hospitals were badly managed at first. Rules of hygiene in large camps were badly written or unenforced; latrines were poorly made or carelessly used. One investigation turned up "an area of over three acres, encircling the camp as a broad belt, on which is deposited an almost perfect layer of human excrement." Water supplies were unsafe and typhoid epidemics common. About 57,000 army men died

424   Chapter 15   Transforming Fire: The Civil War, 1861–1865

from dysentery and diarrhea. The situation would have been much worse but for the United States Sanitary Commission. A voluntary civilian organization, the commission worked to improve conditions in camps and to aid sick and wounded soldiers. Even so, 224,000 Union troops died from disease or accidents, far more than the 140,000 who died as a result of battle. Confederate troops were less well supplied, especially in the latter part of the war, and they had no sanitary commission. Still, an extensive network of hospitals, aided by many female volunteers, sprang up to aid the sick and wounded.

On both sides troops quickly learned that soldiering was far from glorious. "The dirt of a camp life knocks all its poetry into a cocked hat," wrote a North Carolina volunteer in 1862. One year later he marveled at his earlier innocence. Fighting had taught him "the realities of a soldier's life. We had no tents after the 6th of August, but slept on the ground, in the woods or open fields, without regard to the weather. . . . I learned to eat fat bacon raw, and to like it. . . . Without time to wash our clothes or our persons, and sleeping on the ground all huddled together, the whole army became lousy more or less with body lice." Union troops "skirmished" against lice by boiling their clothes or holding them over a hot fire, but, reported one soldier, "I find some on me in spite of all I can do."

Realities of a Soldier's Life

Few had seen violent death before, but war soon exposed them to the blasted bodies of their friends and comrades. "Any one who goes over a battlefield after a battle," wrote one Confederate, "never cares to go over another. . . . It is a sad sight to see the dead and if possible more sad to see the wounded—shot in every possible way you can imagine." Many men died gallantly; there were innumerable striking displays of courage. But far more often soldiers gave up their lives in the mass, as part of a commonplace sacrifice. "They mowed us down like grass," recalled one survivor of a Union assault.

Advances in technology made the Civil War particularly deadly. By far the most important were the rifle and the "minie ball." Bullets fired from a smooth-bore musket tumbled and wobbled as they flew through the air and thus were not accurate at distances over eighty yards. Cutting spiraled grooves inside the barrel gave the projectile a spin and much greater accuracy, but rifles remained difficult to load and use until the Frenchman Claude Minie and the American James Burton developed a new kind of bullet.

Civil War bullets were sizable lead slugs with a cavity at the bottom that expanded upon firing so that the bullet "took" the rifling and flew accurately. With these bullets, rifles were accurate at four hundred yards and useful up to one thousand yards.

This meant, of course, that soldiers assaulting a position defended by riflemen were in greater peril than ever before. Even though Civil War rifles were cumbersome to load (relatively few of the new, untried, breech-loading and repeating rifles were ordered), the defense gained a significant advantage. While artillery now fired from a safe distance, there was no substitute for the infantry assault or the popular turning movements aimed at an enemy's flank. Thus advancing soldiers had to expose themselves repeatedly to accurate rifle fire. Large lead bullets shattered bones and destroyed flesh, and, because medical knowledge was rudimentary, even minor wounds often led to death through infection. Thus the toll from Civil War battles was very high. Never before in Europe or America had such massive forces pummeled each other with weapons of such destructive power. Yet the armies in the Civil War seemed virtually indestructible. Even in the bloodiest engagements, in which thousands of men died, the losing army was never destroyed. As losses mounted, many citizens wondered at what Union soldier (and future Supreme Court justice) Oliver Wendell Holmes called "the butcher's bill."

Impact of the Rifle

Still, Civil War soldiers developed deep commitments to each other and to their task. As campaigns dragged on, fighting and dying with their comrades became their reality, and most soldiers who did not desert grew determined to see the struggle through. "We now, like true Soldiers go determined not to yield one inch," wrote a New York corporal. When at last the war was over, "it seemed like breaking up a family to separate," one man observed. Another admitted, "We shook hands all around, and laughed and seemed to make merry, while our hearts were heavy and our eyes ready to shed tears."

The bonding may have been most dramatic among officers and men in the northern black regiments, for there white and black troops took their first steps toward bridging a deep racial divide. Racism in the Union Army was strong. Most white soldiers wanted nothing to do with black people and regarded them as inferior. "I never

Black Soldiers Fight for Acceptance

came out here for to free the black devils," wrote one soldier, and another objected to fighting beside African-Americans because, "We are a too superior race for that." For many, acceptance of black troops grew only because they could do heavy labor and "stop Bullets as well as white people." A popular song celebrated "Sambo's Right to Be Kilt" as the only justification for black enlistments.

But among some a change occurred. White officers who volunteered for black units only to gain promotion found that experience altered their opinions. After just one month with black troops, a white captain informed his wife, "I have a more elevated opinion of their abilities than I ever had before. I *know* that many of them are vastly the *superiors* of those (many of those) who would condemn them all to a life of brutal degradation." One general reported that his "colored regiments" possessed "remarkable apti-

tude for military training," and another observer said, "They fight like fiends."

Black troops created this change through their dedication. They had a mission to destroy slavery and demonstrate their equality. "When Rebellion is crushed," wrote a black volunteer from Connecticut, "who will be more proud than *I* to say, 'I was one of the first of the despised race to leave the free North with a rifle on my shoulder, and give the lie to the old story that the black man will not fight.'" Corporal James Henry Gooding of Massachusetts's black 54th Regiment explained that his unit intended "to live down all prejudice against its color, by a determination to do well in any position it is put." After an engagement he was proud that "a regiment of white men gave us three cheers as we were passing them," because "it shows that we did our duty as men should." Through such experience under fire the blacks and

Black enlistments were vital to the Union Army, and military service made a major impact on those who had been slaves. These photographs, taken by a photographer accompanying the Union troops, show Hubbard Pryor before and after he enlisted in 1864 in Tennessee. Pryor survived the war. He married a former slave, and he and his wife worked as farmers and raised four children.   National Archives.

whites of the 54th Massachusetts forged deep bonds. Just before the regiment launched its costly assault on Fort Wagner, in Charleston harbor, a black soldier called out to abolitionist Colonel Robert Gould Shaw, "Colonel, I will stay by you till I die." "And he kept his word," noted a survivor of the attack. "He has never been seen since."

Such valor emerged despite persistent discrimination. Off-duty black soldiers were sometimes attacked by northern mobs; on duty, they did most of the "fatigue duty," or heavy labor. The Union government, moreover, paid white privates $13 per month plus a clothing allowance of $3.50, whereas black privates earned only $10 per month less $3 deducted for clothing. Outraged by this injustice, the men of the 54th and 55th Massachusetts refused to accept any pay whatever, and Congress eventually remedied the inequity. In this instance, at least, the majority of legislators agreed with a white private that black troops had "proved their title to *manhood* on many a bloody field fighting freedom's battles."

 ## The Tide of Battle Begins to Turn

The fighting in the spring and summer of 1863 did not settle the war, but it began to place clear limits on the outcome. The campaigns began in a deceptively positive way for Confederates, as their Army of Northern Virginia performed brilliantly in the Battle of Chancellorsville. For once a large Civil War army was not slow and cumbersome but executed tactics with speed and precision. On May 2 and 3, some 130,000 members of the Union Army of the Potomac bore down on fewer than 60,000 Confederates (see map, page 427). Boldly, as if they enjoyed being outnumbered, Lee and Stonewall Jackson divided their forces, ordering 30,000 men under Jackson on a day-long march westward to gain position for a flank attack. This classic turning movement was boldly carried out in the face of great numerical disadvantage. Arriving at their position late in the afternoon, Jackson's seasoned "foot cavalry" found unprepared Union troops laughing, smoking, and playing cards. The Union soldiers had no idea they were under attack until frightened deer and rabbits bounded out of the forest, followed by gray-clad troops. The Confederate attack drove the entire right side of the Union Army back in confusion. Eager to press his advantage, Jackson rode forward with

Battle of Chancellorsville

a few officers to study the ground. As they returned, southern troops mistook them for federals in the fading light and fired, fatally wounding their commander. The next day Union forces left in defeat. Chancellorsville was a remarkable southern victory but costly because of the loss of Stonewall Jackson.

July brought crushing defeats for the Confederacy in two critical battles—Vicksburg and Gettysburg—that effectively circumscribed Confederate hopes for independence. Vicksburg was a vital western citadel, the last major fortification on the Mississippi River in southern hands (see map, page 409). After months of searching through swamps and bayous, General Ulysses S. Grant found an advantageous approach to the city. He laid siege to Vicksburg in May, bottling up the defending army of General John Pemberton. If Vicksburg fell, Union forces would control the river, cutting the Confederacy in half and gaining an open path into its interior. To stave off such a result, Jefferson Davis gave command of all other forces in the area to General Joseph E. Johnston and beseeched him to go to Pemberton's aid. Meanwhile, at a council of war in Richmond, General Robert E. Lee proposed a Confederate invasion of the North. Although such an offensive would not relieve Vicksburg directly, it could stun and dismay the North and, if successful, possibly even lead to peace.

Battle of Vicksburg

Lee's troops streamed through western Maryland and into Pennsylvania, threatening both Washington and Baltimore. As his superb army advanced, the possibility of a major victory near the Union capital became more and more likely. Confederate prospects along the Mississippi, however, darkened. Davis repeatedly wired General Johnston, urging him to concentrate his forces and attack Grant's army. Johnston, however, did nothing effective and telegraphed at one point, "I consider saving Vicksburg hopeless." Grant's men, meanwhile, were supplying themselves from the abundant crops of the Mississippi River valley and could continue their siege indefinitely. Their rich meat-and-vegetables diet became so tiresome, in fact, that one day, as Grant rode by, a private looked up and muttered, "Hardtack" (dry biscuits). Soon a line of soldiers was shouting "Hardtack! Hardtack!" demanding respite from turkey and sweet potatoes.

In such circumstances the fall of Vicksburg was inevitable, and on July 4, 1863, its commander surrendered. The same day a battle that had been rag-

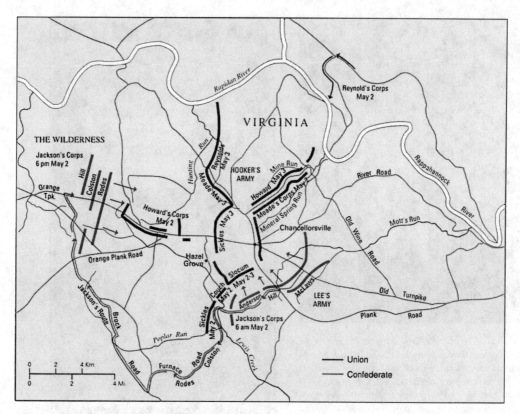

The Battle of Chancellorsville, May 2–3, 1863 *At Chancellorsville on the first day, Jackson and Lee successfully carried out a daring flanking movement to the west, around the Union forces' right. Although federal forces were driven back in confusion, the victory was costly to the Confederacy, for Jackson suffered a fatal wound.*

Battle of Gettysburg

ing for three days concluded at Gettysburg, Pennsylvania. On July 1 Confederate forces hunting for a supply of shoes had collided with part of the Union Army. Heavy fighting on the second day left federal forces in possession of high ground along Cemetery Ridge. There they enjoyed the protection of a stone wall and a clear view of their foe across almost a mile of open field. Undaunted, Lee believed his splendid troops could break the Union line, and on July 3 he ordered a direct assault. Full of foreboding, General James Longstreet warned Lee that "no 15,000 men ever arrayed for battle can take that position." But Lee stuck to his plan. Brave troops under General George E. Pickett methodically marched up the slope in a doomed assault known as Pickett's Charge. For a moment a hundred Confederates breached the enemy's line, but most fell in heavy slaughter. On

July 4 Lee had to withdraw, having suffered almost 4,000 dead and about 24,000 missing and wounded. The Confederate general reported to President Davis that "I am alone to blame" and offered to resign. Davis replied that to find a more capable commander was "an impossibility."

Southern troops displayed unforgettable courage and dedication at Gettysburg, but the results there and at Vicksburg were disastrous. The Confederacy was split in two; west of the Mississippi General E. Kirby Smith had to operate on his own, virtually independent of Richmond. Moreover, the heartland of the Confederacy lay exposed to invasion, and Lee's defeat spelled the end of major southern offensive actions. Too weak to prevail in attack, the Confederacy henceforth would have to conserve its limited resources and rely on a prolonged defense. By refusing to be beaten, the South might yet win, but its prospects were darker than ever before.

Who is He?—On the field of Gettysburg, after the battles, the dead body of a Union soldier was found, holding in his clasped hands an ambrotype picture of three children, a girl and two boys, aged apparently about nine, seven and five years. In the picture, the youngest child, a boy, is seated in a high chair, between his elder brother and his sister, while the dresses of the two latter are made of the same material. The soldier was buried on the field where he fell, and his grave is marked, but his name could not be ascertained. It is hoped, however, that he may yet be identified by means of the ambrotype of the children found in his hands when his body was discovered. The picture is now in possession of Dr. Bourns, 1104 Spring Garden street, Philadelphia, who can be called upon or addressed in reference to it.

These "children of the battlefield" aroused great interest in the North after a burial detail at Gettysburg found this ambrotype clutched in the hand of a fallen Union soldier. After thousands of copies of the picture were circulated, the wife of Sergeant Amos Humiston of the 154th New York Infantry (above) recognized her children and knew that she was a widow. The C. Craig Caba Gettysburg Collection, from *Gettysburg*. Larry Sherer © 1991 Time-Life Books, Inc.

The Disintegration of Confederate Unity

Both northern and southern governments waged the final two years of the war in the face of increasing opposition at home. Dissatisfactions that had surfaced earlier grew more intense and sometimes violent. The gigantic costs of a war that neither side seemed able to win fed the unrest. But protest also arose from fundamental stresses in the social structures of North and South.

The Confederacy's problems were both more serious and more deeply rooted than the North's. Vastly disadvantaged in industrial capacity, natural resources, and labor, southerners felt the cost of the war more quickly, more directly, and more painfully than northerners. But even more fundamental were the Confederacy's internal problems; crises that were integrally connected with the southern class system threatened the Confederate cause.

One ominous development was the planters' increasing opposition to their own government, whose actions often had a negative effect on them. Not only did the Richmond government impose new taxes and the tax-in-kind, but Confederate military authorities also impressed slaves to build fortifications. And when Union forces advanced on plantation areas, Confederate commanders burned stores of cotton that lay in the enemy's path. Such interference with plantation routines and financial interests was not what planters had expected of their government, and they complained bitterly.

Nor were the centralizing policies of the Davis administration popular. The increasing size and power of the Richmond administration startled and alarmed planters who had condemned federal usurpations. In fact, the Confederate constitution had granted substantial powers to the central government, especially in time of war. But many planters assumed with R. B. Rhett, editor of the *Charleston Mercury*, that the Confederate constitution "leaves the States untouched in their Sovereignty, and commits to the Confederate Government only a few simple objects, and a few simple powers to enforce them." Governor Joseph E.

Brown of Georgia took a similarly inflated view of the importance of the states. During the brief interval between Georgia's secession from the Union and its admission to the Confederacy, Brown sent an ambassador to Europe to seek recognition for the sovereign republic of Georgia from Queen Victoria, Napoleon III, and the king of Belgium.

Years of opposition to the federal government within the Union had frozen southerners in a defensive posture. Now they erected the barrier of states' rights as a defense against change, hiding behind it while their capacity for creative statesmanship atrophied. Planters sought, above all, a guarantee that their plantations and their lives would remain untouched; they were not deeply committed either to building a southern nation or to winning independence. If the Confederacy had been allowed to depart from the Union in peace and continue as a semideveloped cotton-growing region, they would have been content. When secession revolutionized their world, they could not or would not adjust.

Confused and embittered planters struck out at Jefferson Davis. Conscription, thundered Governor Brown, was "subversive of [Georgia's] sovereignty, and at war with all the principles for the support of which Georgia entered into this revolution." Searching for ways to frustrate the law, Brown bickered over draft exemptions and ordered local enrollment officials not to cooperate with the Confederacy. The *Charleston Mercury* told readers that "conscription . . . is . . . the very embodiment of Lincolnism, which our gallant armies are today fighting." In a gesture of stubborn selfishness, Robert Toombs of Georgia, a former United States senator, refused to switch from cotton to food crops, defying the wishes of the government, the newspapers, and his neighbors' petitions. His action bespoke the inflexibility and frustration of the southern elite at a crucial point in the Confederacy's struggle to survive.

The southern courts ultimately upheld Davis's power to conscript. He continued to provide strong leadership and steered through Congress measures that gave the Confederacy a fighting chance. Despite his cold formality and inability to disarm critics, Davis possessed two important virtues: iron determination and total dedication to independence. These qualities kept the Confederacy afloat, for he implemented his measures and enforced them. But his actions earned him the hatred of most influential and elite citizens.

Meanwhile, for ordinary southerners, the dire predictions of hunger and suffering were becoming a

The impoverishment of nonslaveholding white families was a critical problem for the Confederacy. The sale of this sheet music was intended not only to boost morale but also to raise money that could be used to aid the hungry and needy. This effort and larger government initiatives, however, failed to solve the problem. Chicago Historical Society.

reality. Food riots occurred in the spring of 1863 in Atlanta, Macon, Columbus, and Augusta, Georgia, and in Salisbury and High Point, North Carolina. On April 2, a crowd assembled in Richmond, the Confederate capital, to demand relief. A passerby, noticing the excitement, asked a young girl, "Is there some celebration?" "We celebrate our right to live," replied the girl. "We are starving. As soon as enough of us get together we are going to the bakeries and each of us will take a loaf of bread." Soon they did just that, sparking a riot that Davis himself had to quell at gunpoint. Later that year, another group of angry rioters looking for food ransacked a street in Mobile, Alabama.

Food Riots in Southern Cities

Throughout the rural South, ordinary people resisted more quietly—by refusing to cooperate with conscription, tax collection, and impressments of food. "In all the States impressments are evaded by every means which ingenuity can suggest, and in some openly resisted," wrote a high-ranking commissary officer. Farmers who did provide food for the army refused to accept payment in certificates of credit or

430   Chapter 15   Transforming Fire: The Civil War, 1861–1865

government bonds, as required by law. Conscription officers increasingly found no one to draft—men of draft age were hiding out in the forests. "The disposition to avoid military service is general," observed one of Georgia's senators in 1864. In some areas tax agents were killed in the line of duty.

Jefferson Davis was ill equipped to deal with such discontent. Austere and private by nature, he failed to communicate with the masses. Often he buried himself in military affairs or administrative details, until a crisis forced him to rush off on a speaking tour to revive the spirit of resistance. His class perspective also distanced him from the sufferings of the common people. While his social circle in Richmond dined on duck and oysters, ordinary southerners recovered salt from the drippings on their smokehouse floors and went hungry. State governors who responded to people's needs won the public's loyalty, but Davis failed to reach out to the plain folk and thus lost their support.

Such discontent was certain to affect the Confederate armies. "What man is there that would stay in the army and no that his family is sufring at home?" an angry citizen wrote

Desertions from the Confederate Army

anonymously to the secretary of war. Worried about their loved ones and resentful of what they saw as a rich man's war, large numbers of men did indeed leave the armies. Their friends and neighbors gave them support. Mary Boykin Chesnut observed a man being dragged back to the army as his wife looked on. "Desert agin, Jake!" she cried openly. "You desert agin, quick as you kin. Come back to your wife and children."

Desertion did not become a serious problem for the Confederacy until mid-1862, and stiffer policing solved the problem that year. But from 1863 on, the number of men on duty fell rapidly as desertions soared. By mid-1863, John A. Campbell, the South's assistant secretary of war, wondered whether "so general a habit" as desertion could be considered a crime. Campbell estimated that 40,000 to 50,000 troops were absent without leave and that 100,000 were evading duty in some way. Furloughs, amnesty proclamations, and appeals to return had little effect; by November 1863, Secretary of War James Seddon admitted that one-third of the army could not be accounted for. The situation was to worsen.

The defeats at Gettysburg and Vicksburg dealt a body blow to Confederate morale. When the news reached Josiah Gorgas, the genius of Confederate

ordnance operations, he confided to his diary, "Today absolute ruin seems our portion. The Confederacy totters to its destruction." In desperation President Davis and several state governors resorted to threats and racial scare tactics to drive southern whites to further sacrifice. Defeat, Davis warned, would mean "extermination of yourselves, your wives, and children." Governor Charles Clark of Mississippi predicted "elevation of the black race to a position of equality—aye, of superiority, that will make them your masters and rulers." Abroad, British officials held back the delivery of badly needed warships, and recognition of the Confederate state became even more unlikely (see page 433).

From this point on, the internal disintegration of the Confederacy quickened. A few newspapers began to call openly for peace. "We are for peace," admitted the *Raleigh* (North Carolina) *Daily Progress*, "because there has been enough of blood and carnage, enough of widows and orphans." A neighboring journal, the *North Carolina Standard*, tacitly admitted that defeat was inevitable and called for negotiations. Similar proposals were made in several state legislatures, though they were presented as plans for independence on honorable terms. Confederate leaders began to realize that they were losing the support of the common people. Governor Zebulon Vance of North Carolina wrote privately that independence would require more "blood and misery . . . and our people will not pay this price I am satisfied for their independence. . . . The great popular heart is not now & never has been in this war."

In North Carolina a peace movement grew under the leadership of William W. Holden, a popular Democratic politician and editor. Over one hundred public meetings took place in the summer of 1863 in support of

Southern Peace Movements

peace negotiations, and many seasoned political observers believed that Holden had the majority of the people behind him. In Georgia early in 1864, Governor Brown and Alexander H. Stephens, vice president of the Confederacy, led a similar effort. Ultimately, however, these movements came to naught. The lack of a two-party system threw into question the legitimacy of any criticism of the government; even Holden and Brown could not entirely escape the taint of dishonor and disloyalty. That the movement existed at all demonstrates deep disaffection.

The results of the 1863 congressional elections strengthened dissent in the Confederacy. Everywhere secessionists and supporters of the administration lost seats to men not identified with the government. Many of the new representatives were former Whigs who opposed the Davis administration or publicly favored peace. In the last years of the war, much of Davis's support in the Confederate Congress came from Union-occupied districts, whose people would share no burdens of the war effort until success was achieved.

Having previously secured the legislation he needed, Davis used the government bureaucracy and the army to enforce his unpopular policies. Ironically, as the Confederacy's prospects grew desperate, former critics such as the *Charleston Mercury* became supporters of the administration. They and a core of courageous, determined soldiers kept the Confederacy alive in spite of disintegrating popular support.

By 1864 much of the opposition to the war had moved entirely outside the political sphere. Southerners were simply giving up the struggle and withdrawing their cooperation from the government. Deserters dominated whole towns and counties. Secret societies favoring reunion, such as the Heroes of America and the Red Strings, sprang up. Active dissent spread everywhere and was particularly common in upland and mountain regions. "The condition of things in the mountain districts of North Carolina, South Carolina, Georgia, and Alabama," admitted Assistant Secretary of War John A. Campbell, "menaces the existence of the Confederacy as fatally as either of the armies of the United States." Confederate officials tried using the army to round up deserters and compel obedience, but this approach was only temporarily effective. The government was losing the support of its citizens.

 ## Antiwar Sentiment in the North

In the North opposition to the war was similar but less severe. Alarm intensified over the growing centralization of government, and war-weariness was widespread. Resentment of the draft sparked protest, especially among poor citizens, and the Union Army struggled with a desertion rate as high as the Confederates'. But the Union was so much richer than the South in human resources that none of these problems ever threatened the effectiveness of the government. Fresh recruits were always available, and there were no shortages of food and other necessities.

Also, Lincoln possessed a talent that Davis lacked: he knew how to stay in touch with the ordinary citizen. Through letters to newspapers and to soldiers'

families, he reached the common people and demonstrated that he had not forgotten them. The daily carnage, the tortuous political problems, and the ceaseless criticism weighed heavily on him. But this president—a self-educated man of humble origins—was able to communicate his suffering. His moving words helped to contain northern discontent, though they could not remove it.

Much of the wartime protest in the North was political in origin. The Democratic Party fought to regain power by blaming Lincoln for the war's carnage, the expansion of federal powers, inflation and the high tariff, and the emancipation of blacks. Appealing to tradition, its leaders called for an end to the war and reunion on the basis of "the Constitution as it is and the Union as it was." The Democrats denounced conscription and martial law and defended states' rights and the interests of agriculture. They charged repeatedly that Republican policies were designed to flood the North with blacks, depriving white males of their status, their jobs, and their women. These claims appealed to southerners who had settled north of the Ohio River, to conservatives, to many poor people, and to some eastern merchants who had lost profitable southern trade. In the 1862 congressional elections, the Democrats made a strong comeback, and peace Democrats—who would go much farther than others in their party to end the war—had influence in New York State and majorities in the legislatures of Illinois and Indiana.

Peace Democrats

Led by outspoken men like Representative Clement L. Vallandigham of Ohio, the peace Democrats made themselves highly visible. Vallandigham criticized Lincoln as a dictator who had suspended the writ of habeas corpus without congressional authority and had arrested thousands of innocent citizens. Like other Democrats, he condemned both conscription and emancipation and urged voters to use their power at the polling place to depose "King Abraham." Vallandigham stayed carefully within legal bounds, but his attacks seemed so damaging to the war effort that military authorities arrested him for treason after Lincoln suspended habeas corpus. Lincoln wisely decided against punishment—and martyr's status—for the senator and exiled him to the Confederacy, thus ridding himself of a troublesome critic and saddling puzzled Confederates with a man who insisted on talking about "our country." (Eventually Vallandigham returned to the North through Canada.)

Mobs in the New York City draft riots directed much of their anger at African-Americans. Rioters burned an orphanage for black children and killed scores of blacks. This wood engraving, which appeared in the Illustrated London News *on August 8, 1863, depicts a lynching in Clarkson Street.*   Chicago Historical Society.

Lincoln believed that antiwar Democrats were linked to secret organizations that harbored traitorous ideas, such as the Knights of the Golden Circle and the Order of American Knights. These societies, he feared, encouraged draft resistance, discouraged enlistment, sabotaged communications, and plotted to aid the Confederacy. Likening such groups to a poisonous snake, Republicans sometimes branded them—and by extension the peace Democrats—as Copperheads. Though Democrats were connected with these organizations, most engaged in politics rather than treason. And though some saboteurs and Confederate agents were active in the North, they never brought about any major demonstration of support for the Confederacy.

More violent opposition to the government arose from ordinary citizens facing the draft, which became law in 1863. The urban poor and immigrants in strongly Democratic areas were especially hostile to conscription. Federal enrolling officers made up the lists of eligibles, a procedure open to personal favoritism and prejudice. Many men, including some of modest means, managed to avoid the army by hiring a substitute or paying commutation, but the poor viewed the commutation fee as discriminatory, and many immigrants suspected (wrongly, on the whole) that they were called in disproportionate num-

bers. (Approximately 200,000 men born in Germany and 150,000 born in Ireland served in the Union Army.)

As a result, there were scores of disturbances and melees. Enrolling officers received rough treatment in many parts of the North, and riots occurred in New Jersey, Ohio, Indiana, Pennsylvania, Illinois, and Wisconsin. By far the most serious outbreak of violence occurred in New York City in July 1863. The war was unpopular in that Democratic stronghold, and racial, ethnic, and class tensions ran high. Shippers had recently broken a longshoremen's strike by hiring black strikebreakers to work under police protection. Working-class New Yorkers feared an inflow of black labor from the South and regarded blacks as the cause of the bloody war. Irish workers, many recently arrived and poor, resented being forced to serve in the place of others who could afford to avoid the draft.

New York City Draft Riot

Military police officers came under attack first; then mobs crying "Down with the rich" looted wealthy homes and stores. But blacks became the special target. Those who happened to be in the rioters' path were beaten; soon the mob rampaged through African-American neighborhoods, destroying an orphans' asylum. At least seventy-four people died in the violence, which raged out of control for three days. Only the dispatch of army units fresh from Gettysburg ended the episode.

Discouragement and war-weariness reached a peak in the summer of 1864, when the Democratic Party nominated the popular General George B. McClellan for president and inserted a peace plank into its platform. The plank, written by Vallandigham, condemned "four years of failure to restore the Union by the experiment of war," called clearly for an armistice, and spoke vaguely about preserving the Union. Lincoln, running with Tennessee's Andrew Johnson on a "National Union" ticket, concluded that it was "exceedingly probable that this Administration will not be reelected." During a publicized interchange with Confederate officials sent to Canada, Lincoln insisted that the terms for peace include reunion and "the abandonment of slavery." A wave of protest arose in the North from voters who were weary of war and dedicated only to reunion. Lincoln quickly backtracked, denying that his offer meant "that nothing *else* or *less* would be considered, if offered." He would insist on freedom only for those slaves (about 134,000) who had joined the Union Army under his promise of emancipation. Lincoln's action showed his political weakness, but the fortunes of war soon changed the electoral situation.

 ## Northern Pressure and Southern Will

Northern Diplomatic Strategy

The success of the North's long-term diplomatic strategy was sealed in 1864. From the outset, the North had pursued one paramount goal: to prevent recognition of the Confederacy by European nations. Foreign recognition would belie Lincoln's claim that the United States was fighting an illegal rebellion and would open the way to the financial and military aid that could ensure Confederate independence. The British elite, however, felt considerable sympathy for southern planters, whose aristocratic values were similar to their own. And both England and France stood to benefit from a divided and weakened America. Thus to achieve their goal, Lincoln and Secretary of State Seward needed to avoid both serious military defeats and unnecessary controversies with the European powers.

Aware that the textile industry employed one-fifth of the British population directly or indirectly,

southerners assumed that British leaders would have to recognize the Confederacy. But at the beginning of the war, British mills had a 50 percent surplus of cotton on hand; later on, new sources of supply in India, Egypt, and Brazil helped to meet Britain's needs; and throughout the war, some southern cotton continued to reach Europe, despite the Confederacy's recommendation that southerners plant and ship no cotton. Refusing to be stampeded into recognition of the Confederacy, the British government kept its eye on the battlefield. France, though sympathetic to the South, was unwilling to act independently of Britain. Confederate agents were able to purchase valuable arms and supplies in Europe and obtained loans from European financiers, but they never achieved a diplomatic breakthrough.

More than once the Union strategy nearly broke down. An acute crisis occurred in 1861 when the overzealous commander of an American frigate stopped the British steamer *Trent* and removed two Confederate ambassadors sailing to Britain. They were imprisoned after being brought ashore. This action was cheered in the North, but the British protested this violation of freedom of the seas and demanded the prisoners' release. Lincoln and Seward waited until northern public opinion cooled and then released the two southerners. Then the sale to the Confederacy of warships constructed in England sparked vigorous protest from United States ambassador Charles Francis Adams. A few English-built ships, notably the *Alabama*, reached open water to serve the South. Over a period of twenty-two months, without entering a southern port (because of the Union blockade), the *Alabama* destroyed or captured more than sixty northern ships. But the British government, as a neutral power, soon barred delivery of warships such as the Laird rams, formidable vessels whose pointed prows were designed to end the blockade by battering the Union ships.

On the battlefield, the northern victory was far from won in 1864. General Nathaniel Banks's Red River campaign, designed to capture more of Louisiana and Texas, quickly fell apart, and the capture of Mobile Bay in August did not cause the fall of Mobile. Union general William Tecumseh Sherman commented that the North had to "keep the war South until they are not only ruined, exhausted, but humbled in pride and spirit."

Military authorities throughout history have agreed that deep invasion is very risky: the farther an army penetrates enemy territory, the more vulnerable its own communications and support become.

434   Chapter 15   Transforming Fire: The Civil War, 1861–1865

Both General Grant (left) and General Lee (right) were West Point graduates and had served in the United States Army during the Mexican War. Their bloody battles against each other in 1864 stirred northern revulsion to the war even as they brought its end in sight.   National Archives.

Moreover, observed the Prussian expert Karl von Clausewitz, if the invader encountered a "truly national" resistance, his troops would be "everywhere exposed to attacks by an insurgent population." Thus if southerners were determined enough to mount a "truly national" resistance, their defiance and the South's vast size could make a northern victory virtually impossible.

General Grant, by now in command of all the federal armies, decided to test these conditions—and southern will—with a strategic innovation of his own: raids on a massive scale. Grant proposed to use whole armies, not just cavalry, to destroy Confederate railroads, thus ruining the enemy's transportation and damaging the South's economy. Abandoning their lines of support, Union troops would live off the land while laying to waste all resources useful to the military and to the civilian population of the Confederacy. After General George H. Thomas's troops won the Battle of Chattanooga in November 1863 by ignoring orders and charging up Missionary Ridge, the heartland of the South lay open. Moving to Virginia, Grant entrusted General Sherman with 100,000 men for a raid deep into the South, toward Atlanta.

Jefferson Davis countered by positioning the army of General Joseph E. Johnston in Sherman's path. Davis's entire political strategy for 1864 was based on demonstrating Confederate military strength and successfully defending Atlanta. The United States presidential election of 1864 was approaching, and Davis hoped that southern resolve would lead to the defeat of Lincoln and the election of a president who would sue for peace. When General Johnston slowly but steadily fell back toward Atlanta, Davis grew anxious and sought assurances that Atlanta would be held. From a purely military point of view, Johnston maneuvered skillfully, but the president of the Confederacy could not take a purely military point of view. When Johnston provided no information and continued to drop back, Davis replaced him with the one-legged General John Hood, who knew his job was to fight. "Our all depends on that army at Atlanta," wrote Mary Boykin Chesnut. "If that fails us, the game is up."

For southern morale, the game was up. Hood attacked but was beaten, and Sherman's army occupied Atlanta on September 2, 1864. The victory buoyed northern spirits and ensured Lincoln's re-election. "There is no hope," Mary Chesnut acknowledged, and a government clerk in Richmond wrote, "Our fondly-cherished visions of peace have vanished like a mirage of the desert." Davis exhorted southerners to fight on and win new victories before the federal elections, but he had to admit that "two-thirds of our men are absent . . . most of them absent without leave." Hood's army marched north to cut Sherman's supply lines and force him to retreat, but Sherman began to march sixty thousand of his men straight to the sea, planning to live off the land and destroying Confederate resources as he went (see map).

Sherman's army was an unusually formidable force, composed almost entirely of battle-tested veterans and officers who had risen through the ranks.

The March to the Sea

Before the march began, army doctors weeded out any men who were weak or sick. Tanned, bearded, tough, and unkempt, the remaining veterans were determined, as one put it, "to Conquer this Rebelien or Die." They believed "the South are to blame for this war" and were ready to make the South pay. Although many harbored racist attitudes, most had come to support emancipation because, as one said,

"Slavery stands in the way of putting down the rebellion." Confederate General Johnston later commented, "There has been no such army since the days of Julius Caesar."

As Sherman's men moved across Georgia, they cut a path 50 to 60 miles wide and more than 200 miles long. The totality of the destruction they caused was awesome. A Georgia woman described the "Burnt Country" this way: "The fields were trampled down and the road was lined with carcasses of horses, hogs, and cattle that the invaders, unable either to consume or to carry with them, had wantonly shot down to starve our people and prevent them from making their crops. The stench in some places was unbearable." Such devastation diminished the South's material resources and sapped its will to resist.

After reaching Savannah in December, Sherman marched his armies north into the Carolinas. To his soldiers, South Carolina was "the root of secession." They burned and destroyed as they moved through, encountering little resistance. The opposing army of General Johnston was small, but Sherman's men should have been prime targets for guerrilla raids and harassing attacks by local defense units. The absence

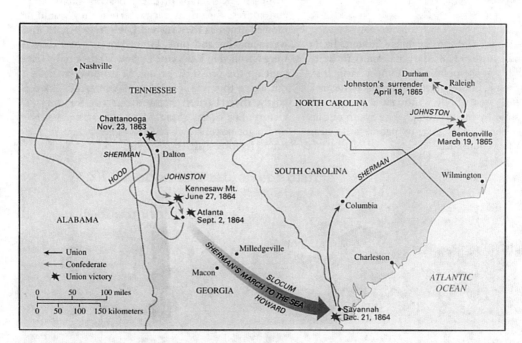

Sherman's March to the Sea   *The West proved a decisive theater at the end of the war. From Chattanooga, Union forces drove into Georgia, capturing Atlanta. Then General Sherman embarked on his march of destruction through Georgia to the coast and then northward through the Carolinas.*

436   Chapter 15   Transforming Fire: The Civil War, 1861–1865

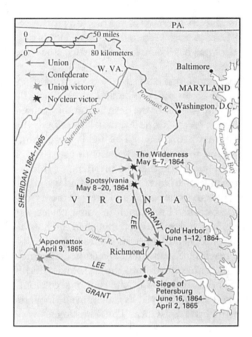

The War in Virginia, 1864–1865 *At great cost, Grant hammered away at Lee's army until the weakened southern forces finally surrendered at Appomattox Courthouse.*

of both led South Carolina's James Chesnut, Jr., (a politician and husband of Mary Chesnut) to write that his state "was shamefully and unnecessarily lost. . . . We had time, opportunity and means to destroy him. But there was wholly wanting the energy and ability required by the occasion." The South put up no "truly national" resistance; its people were near the end of their endurance.

Sherman's march drew additional human resources to the Union cause. In Georgia alone as many as nineteen thousand slaves gladly took the opportunity to escape bondage and join the Union troops as they passed through the countryside. Others remained on the plantations to await the end of the war, either from an ingrained wariness of whites or negative experiences with federal soldiers. The destruction of food harmed slaves as well as white rebels, and many blacks lost blankets, shoes, and other valuables to their liberators. In fact, the brutality of Sherman's troops shocked these veterans of the whip. "I've seen them cut the hams off of a live pig or ox and go off leavin' the animal groanin'," recalled one man. "The master had 'em kilt then, but it was awful."

It was awful, too, in Virginia, where the preliminaries to victory proved protracted and ghastly. Throughout the spring and summer of 1864, intent on capturing Richmond, Grant hurled his troops at Lee's army in Virginia and suffered appalling losses: almost 18,000 casualties in the Battle of the Wilderness, where skeletons poked out of the shallow graves dug one year before; more than 8,000 at Spotsylvania; and 12,000 in the space of a few hours at Cold Harbor (see map). Before the last battle, Union troops pinned scraps of paper bearing their names and addresses to their backs, certain they would be mowed down as they rushed Lee's trenches. In four weeks in May and June, Grant lost as many men as were enrolled in Lee's entire army. Undaunted, Grant kept up the pressure, saying, "I propose to fight it out along this line if it takes all summer." Though costly, these battles prepared the way for eventual victory: Lee's army shrank until offensive action was no longer possible, while Grant's army kept replenishing its forces with new recruits.

At the war's end, the United States flag flew over the state capitol in Richmond, Virginia, which bore many marks of destruction. National Archives.

The death of President Lincoln caused a vast outpouring of grief in the North. As this Currier and Ives print shows, on its way to Illinois, his funeral train stopped at several cities to allow local services to be held.   Anne S. K. Brown Military Collection, John Hay Library, Brown University.

The end finally came in the spring of 1865. Grant kept battering Lee, who tried but failed to break through the Union line. With the numerical superiority of Grant's army now greater than two to one, Confederate defeat was inevitable. On April 2 Lee abandoned Richmond and Petersburg. On April 9, hemmed in by Union troops, short of rations, and having fewer than thirty thousand men left, Lee surrendered at Appomattox Courthouse. Grant treated his rival with respect and paroled the defeated troops, allowing cavalrymen to keep their horses and take them home. Within weeks, Davis, who had wanted the war to continue, was captured in Georgia, and the remaining Confederate forces laid down their arms and surrendered. The war was over at last.

Heavy Losses Force Lee's Surrender

With Lee's surrender, Lincoln knew that the Union had been preserved, yet he did not live to see the war's end. On the evening of Good Friday, April 14, he accompanied his wife to Ford's Theatre in Washington to enjoy a popular comedy. There John Wilkes Booth, an embittered southern sympathizer, shot the president in the head at point-blank range. Lincoln died the next day. Twelve days later, troops tracked down and killed Booth. The Union had lost its wartime leader, and millions publicly mourned the martyred chief executive along the route of the funeral train that took his body home to Illinois. Relief at the war's end mingled uncomfortably with a renewed sense of loss and uncertainty about the future.

 ## Costs and Effects

The human costs of the Civil War were enormous (see figure, page 438). The total number of military casualties on both sides exceeded 1 million—a frightful toll for a nation of 31 million people. Approximately 360,000 Union soldiers died, 110,000 of them from wounds suffered in battle. Another 275,175 Union soldiers were wounded but survived. On the Confederate side, an estimated 260,000 lost their lives, and almost as many suffered wounds. More men died in the Civil War than in all other American wars combined until Vietnam. Fundamental disagreements that would continue to trouble the Reconstruction era had caused unprecedented loss of life.

Casualties

Although precise figures on enlistments are impossible to obtain, it appears that 700,000 to 800,000 men served in the Confederate armies. Far more, possibly 2.3 million, served in the Union armies. All

438 Chapter 15 Transforming Fire: The Civil War, 1861–1865

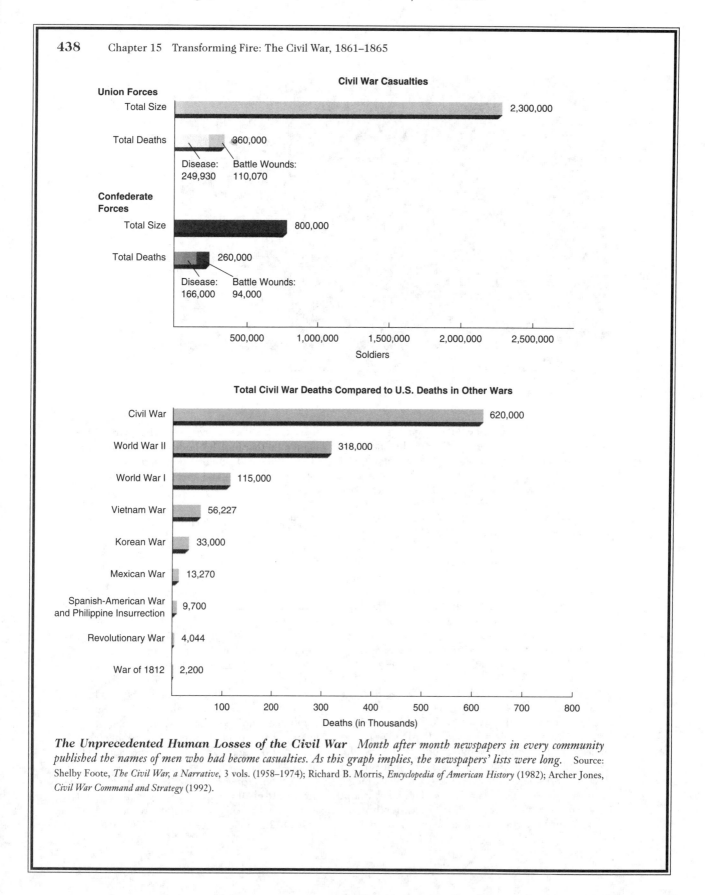

Civil War Casualties

Union Forces
- Total Size — 2,300,000
- Total Deaths — 360,000
  - Disease: 249,930
  - Battle Wounds: 110,070

Confederate Forces
- Total Size — 800,000
- Total Deaths — 260,000
  - Disease: 166,000
  - Battle Wounds: 94,000

Soldiers (500,000 · 1,000,000 · 1,500,000 · 2,000,000 · 2,500,000)

Total Civil War Deaths Compared to U.S. Deaths in Other Wars

- Civil War — 620,000
- World War II — 318,000
- World War I — 115,000
- Vietnam War — 56,227
- Korean War — 33,000
- Mexican War — 13,270
- Spanish-American War and Philippine Insurrection — 9,700
- Revolutionary War — 4,044
- War of 1812 — 2,200

Deaths (in Thousands) (100 · 200 · 300 · 400 · 500 · 600 · 700 · 800)

The Unprecedented Human Losses of the Civil War *Month after month newspapers in every community published the names of men who had become casualties. As this graph implies, the newspapers' lists were long.* Source: Shelby Foote, *The Civil War, a Narrative*, 3 vols. (1958–1974); Richard B. Morris, *Encyclopedia of American History* (1982); Archer Jones, *Civil War Command and Strategy* (1992).

these men were taken from home, family, and personal goals and had their lives disrupted in ways that were not easily repaired.

Property damage and financial costs were also enormous, though difficult to tally. United States loans and taxes during the conflict totaled almost $3 billion, and interest on the war debt was $2.8 billion. The Confederacy borrowed over $2 billion but lost far more in the destruction of homes, crops, livestock, and other property. As an example of the wreckage that attended four years of conflict on southern soil, the number of hogs in South Carolina plummeted from 965,000 in 1860 to approximately 150,000 in 1865, leaving many families without their primary source of meat. Scholars have noted that small farmers lost just as much, proportionally, as planters whose slaves were emancipated.

Financial Cost of the War

In southern war zones the landscape was desolated. Soldiers seeking fuel or shelter had cut down many large stands of trees, and artillery shells had blasted many others. Over wide regions fences and crops were destroyed, houses and bridges burned, and fields abandoned and left to erode. Union troops had looted factories and put two-thirds of the South's railroad system out of service. Levees and roads had deteriorated. Visitors to the countryside were struck by how empty and impoverished it looked. Nature would repair much of the damage in time, but large investments of human skill and energy were gone.

Estimates of the total cost of the war exceed $20 billion—five times the total expenditures of the federal government from its creation to 1861. The northern government increased its spending by 700 percent in the first full year of the war; by the last year its spending had soared to twenty times the prewar level. By 1865 the federal government accounted for over 26 percent of the gross national product.

Many of these changes were more or less permanent. In the 1880s, interest on the war debt still accounted for approximately 40 percent of the federal budget and Union soldiers' pensions for as much as 20 percent. The federal government had used its power to support manufacturing and business interests by means of tariffs, loans, and subsidies, and wartime measures left the federal government more deeply involved in the banking and transportation systems. Thus although many southerners had hoped to remove government from the economy, the war made such separation an impossibility. After the war,

federal expenditures shrank but stabilized at twice the prewar level, or at 4 percent of the gross national product.

 ## Conclusion

The Civil War altered American society in many ways. During the war, in both North and South, women had taken on new roles, which could grow or stagnate. Industrialization and large economic enterprises played a larger role than ever before. Ordinary citizens found that their futures were increasingly tied to great organizations. Politically, the defense of national unity brought far-reaching changes in government and policy. Under Republican leadership, the federal government had expanded its power not only to preserve the Union but also to extend freedom. In a sweeping expropriation of what had been considered property, the government emancipated the slaves, and Lincoln had called for "a new birth of freedom" in America. It was unclear, however, whether the nation would use its power to protect the rights of individuals. Would the government guarantee the rights of the former slaves, whose humanity was now recognized? Extreme forms of states' rights dogma clearly were dead, but would Americans continue to favor a state-centered federalism? How would white southerners, embittered and impoverished by the war, respond to efforts to reconstruct the nation?

Closely related to these issues was a question of central importance: what would be the place of black men and women in American life? The Union victory provided a partial answer: slavery as it had existed before the war could not persist. But whether full citizenship and equal rights would take slavery's place remained unclear. Black veterans and former slaves eagerly sought an answer. They would find it during Reconstruction.

Suggestions for Further Reading

The War and the South

Thomas B. Alexander and Richard E. Beringer, *The Anatomy of the Confederate Congress* (1972); Stephen Ash, *When the Yankees Came* (1995); Richard E. Beringer et al., *Why the South Lost the Civil War* (1986); Gabor S. Boritt, *Why the Confederacy Lost* (1992); Richard N. Current, *Lincoln's Loyalists* (1992); William C. Davis, *Jefferson Davis* (1991); Robert F. Durden, *The Gray and the Black: The Confederate Debate on Emancipation* (1972); Paul D. Escott, *Many Excellent People* (1985); Paul D. Escott, *After Secession: Jefferson Davis and the Failure of Confederate Nationalism* (1978); Eli N. Evans, *Judah P. Benjamin* (1987); Mark Grimsley, *The Hard Hand* of War (1995); J. B. Jones, *A Rebel War Clerk's Diary*, 2 vols., ed. Howard Swiggett (1935); Ella Lonn, *Desertion During the Civil War* (1928); Mary Elizabeth Massey, *Refugee Life in the Confederacy* (1964); Larry E. Nelson, *Bullets, Ballots, and Rhetoric: Confederate Policy for the United States Presidential Contest of 1864* (1980); Alan T. Nolan, *Lee Considered* (1991); Harry P. Owens and James J. Cooke, eds., *The Old South in the Crucible of War* (1983); James L. Roark, *Masters Without Slaves* (1977); Daniel Sutherland, *Seasons of War* (1995); Georgia Lee Tatum, *Disloyalty in the Confederacy* (1934); Emory M. Thomas, *The Confederate Nation* (1979); Emory M. Thomas, *The Confederacy as a Revolutionary Experience* (1971); William A. Tidwell, *April '65* (1995); Bell Irvin Wiley, *The Life of Johnny Reb* (1943); Bell Irvin Wiley, *The Plain People of the Confederacy* (1943); W. Buck Yearns, ed., *The Confederate Governors* (1985).

The War and the North

Ralph Andreano, ed., *The Economic Impact of the American Civil War* (1962); Robert Cruden, *The War That Never Ended* (1973); David Donald, ed., *Why the North Won the Civil War* (1960); James W. Geary, *We Need Men* (1991); Wood Gray, *The Hidden Civil War* (1942); Randall C. Jimerson, *The Private Civil War* (1988); Frank L. Klement, *The Copperheads in the Middle West* (1960); Susan Previant Lee and Peter Passell, *A New Economic View of American History* (1979); James M. McPherson, *Battle Cry of Freedom* (1988); James H. Moorhead, *American Apocalypse* (1978); Phillip S. Paludan, *"A People's Contest": The Union and the Civil War, 1861–1865* (1989); Robert Hunt Rhodes, ed., *All for the Union: The Civil War Diary and Letters of Elisha Hunt Rhodes* (1991); George Winston Smith and Charles Burnet Judah, *Life in the North During the Civil War* (1966); George Templeton Strong, *Diary*, 4 vols., ed. Allan Nevins and Milton Hasley Thomas (1952); Paul Studenski, *Financial History of the United States* (1952); Bell Irvin Wiley, *The Life of Billy Yank* (1952).

Women

John R. Brumgardt, ed., *Civil War Nurse: The Diary and Letters of Hannah Ropes* (1980); Beth Gilbert Crabtree and James W. Patton, eds., *"Journal of a Secesh Lady": The Diary of Catherine Ann Devereux Edmondston, 1860–1866* (1979); Jacqueline Jones, *Labor of Love, Labor of Sorrow* (1985); Mary Elizabeth Massey, *Bonnet Brigades* (1966); George C. Rable, *Civil Wars: Women and the Crisis of Southern Nationalism* (1989); Mary D. Robertson, ed., *Lucy Breckinridge of Grove Hill: The Journal of a Virginia Girl, 1862–1864* (1979); C. Vann Woodward and Elisabeth Muhlenfeld, eds., *Mary Chesnut's Civil War* (1981); Agatha Young, *Women and the Crisis* (1959).

African-Americans

Virginia M. Adams, ed., *On the Altar of Freedom: A Black Soldier's Civil War Letters from the Front* (1991); Ira Berlin, ed., *Freedom: A Documentary History of Emancipation, 1861–1867*, Series I, *The Destruction of Slavery* (1979), and Series II, *The Black Military Experience* (1982); David W. Blight, *Frederick Douglass' Civil War* (1989); Dudley Cornish, *The Sable Arm* (1956); Barbara Jeanne Fields, *Slavery and Freedom on the Middle Ground* (1985); Joseph T. Glatthaar, *Forged in Battle* (1990); Leon Litwack, *Been in the Storm So Long* (1979); James M. McPherson, *The Negro's Civil War* (1965); James M. McPherson, *The Struggle for Equality* (1964); Clarence L. Mohr, *On the Threshold of Freedom* (1986); Benjamin Quarles, *The Negro in the Civil War* (1953).

Military History

Nancy Scott Anderson and Dwight Anderson, *The Generals: Ulysses S. Grant and Robert E. Lee* (1987); Albert Castel, *Decision in the West* (1992); Bruce Catton, *Grant Takes Command* (1969); Bruce Catton, *Grant Moves South* (1960); Benjamin Franklin Cooling, *Forts Henry and Donelson* (1988); Peter Cozzens, *This Terrible Sound* (1992); William C. Davis, ed., *The Image of War*, multivolume (1983–1985); Michael Fellman, *Citizen Sherman* (1995); Shelby Foote, *The Civil War, a Narrative*, 3 vols. (1958–1974); Douglas Southall Freeman, *Lee's Lieutenants*, 3 vols. (1942–1944); Douglas Southall Freeman, *R. E. Lee*, 4 vols. (1934–1935); Joseph T. Glatthaar, *The March to the Sea and Beyond* (1985); Herman Hattaway and Archer Jones, *How the North Won* (1983); Laurence M. Hauptman, *Between Two Fires: American Indians in the Civil War* (1995); Archer Jones, *Civil War Command and Strategy* (1992); Alvin M. Josephy, Jr., *The Civil War in the American West* (1991); Gerald F. Linderman, *Embattled Courage* (1989); Thomas L. Livermore, *Numbers and Losses in the Civil War in America* (1957); Grady McWhiney and Perry D. Jamieson, *Attack and Die* (1982); J. B. Mitchell, *Decisive Battles of the Civil War* (1955); Reid Mitchell, *Civil War Soldiers* (1988); Roy Morris, Jr., *Sheridan* (1992); Charles Royster, *The Destructive War* (1991); Stephen W. Sears, *To the Gates of Richmond* (1992); Stephen W. Sears, *George B. McClellan* (1988); Emory M. Thomas, *Robert E. Lee* (1995); Emory M. Thomas, *Bold Dragoon: The Life of J. E. B. Stuart* (1987); Noah Andre Trudeau, *The Last Citadel* (1991); Steven E. Woodworth, *Jefferson Davis and His Generals* (1990).

Foreign Relations

Stuart L. Bernath, *Squall Across the Atlantic: American Civil War Prize Cases and Diplomacy* (1970); Kinley J. Brauer, "The Slavery Problem in the Diplomacy of the American Civil War," *Pacific Historical Review* 46, no. 3 (1977): 439–469; David P. Crook, *The North, the South, and the Powers, 1861–1865* (1974); Charles P. Cullop, *Confederate Propaganda in Europe* (1969); Norman B. Ferris, *The Trent Affair* (1977); Howard Jones, *Union in Peril* (1992); Frank J. Merli, *Great Britain and the Confederate Navy* (1970); Frank L. Owsley and Harriet Owsley, *King Cotton Diplomacy* (1959); Gordon H. Warren, *Fountain of Discontent: The Trent Affair and Freedom of the Seas* (1981).

Abraham Lincoln and the Union Government

Allan G. Bogue, *The Earnest Men: Republicans of the Civil War Senate* (1981); Gabor S. Borit, ed., *The Historian's Lincoln* (1989); Fawn Brodie, *Thaddeus Stevens* (1959); Richard N. Current, *The Lincoln Nobody Knows* (1958); Leonard P. Curry, *Blueprint for Modern America: Non-Military Legislation of the First Civil War Congress* (1968); Christopher Dell, *Lincoln and the War Democrats* (1975); David Donald, *Charles Sumner and the Rights of Man* (1970); Ludwell H. Johnson, "Lincoln's Solution to the Problem of Peace Terms, 1864–1865," *Journal of Southern History* 34 (November 1968): 441–447; Peyton McCrary, *Abraham Lincoln and Reconstruction: The Louisiana Experiment* (1978); James M. McPherson, *Abraham Lincoln and the Second American Revolution* (1990); Mark Neely, *The Fate of Liberty* (1991); Joel Silbey, *A Respectable Minority: The Democratic Party in the Civil War Era* (1977); Benjamin P. Thomas, *Abraham Lincoln* (1952); Hans L. Trefousse, *The Radical Republicans* (1969); Glyndon G. Van Deusen, *William Henry Seward* (1967); T. Harry Williams, *Lincoln and His Generals* (1952); T. Harry Williams, *Lincoln and the Radicals* (1941).

Textbook Features

Creating Your Own Study Guide

You might find that many textbooks do not include features such as lists of key words, outlines, and study questions. However, that doesn't mean readers have to make do without them. If the chapter content is challenging or wide in scope, consider creating your own study guide to help yourself master the material.

One feature of your study guide could be a list of what you believe to be the **key terms.** As you read, circle or highlight important words and phrases. Look for terms the author defines or explains. Then compile the words into a list (or create flash cards) and add their definitions. For example, the beginnings of a list of key terms for the "Transforming Fire" chapter might look like this:

Union: states that remained loyal to the United States of America during the Civil War

secession: formal withdrawal from an alliance

Confederacy: new government created by Southern states and territories, which functioned independently of the United States

Jefferson Davis: president of the Confederacy

Yankees: pro–Union Northerners

Battle of Bull Run: first battle of the Civil War on July 21, 1861; a Confederate victory

EXERCISE 1

In the space below (or on a separate sheet of paper), create a list of key terms and their definitions for the "War Transforms the South" section of the "Transforming Fire" chapter.

Another feature you could include in your study guide is a **visual summary** of information. You could compile timelines like the one in the "Transforming Fire" chapter entitled Important Events. You could create a chart that lists each Civil War battle with dates, numbers of casualties, and victor, or you could create a line graph of these results to help you get a visual picture of the struggle. You could create a diagram summary of all of the factors and characteristics that contributed to the Confederacy's defeat. The extra effort you put into creating such visuals will result in improved comprehension and retention of the information.

EXERCISE 2

In the space below (or on a separate sheet of paper), create a chart, line graph, or diagram described in the examples above, or create some other visual summary of information in the "Transforming Fire" chapter.

Your study guide might also include mnemonic devices to help you remember information. **Mnemonic devices** are systems that improve recall of information. They include rhymes, sayings, songs, and phrases. For example, if you need to remember all of the states that joined the Confederacy, you could list the first letter of each state:

Virginia   Tennessee
North Carolina   Alabama
South Carolina   Mississippi
Georgia   Arkansas
Florida   Louisiana
Texas   Indian Territory
                        New Mexico Territory

V N S G F T T A M A L I N

Now rearrange those letters to create a phrase or word group that you can remember more easily. For example:

FAINT MTV SLANG

You could also come up with a phrase instead of rearranging the letters into words. For example, let's say you need to remember the four slave states that did not join the Confederacy:

Missouri
Kentucky
Maryland
Delaware

You could form a phrase containing words that begin with those letters:

Don't Make Kentucky Mad!

EXERCISE 3

In the space below, create a mnemonic device to help you remember important Civil War battles of 1863:

Chancellorsville
Gettsyburg
Vicksburg
Chattanooga

Finally, you will probably want to include **questions** in your study guide. You can determine these questions by considering two things as you read:

1. Information or ideas that seem important to you
2. Information or ideas you think the instructor would call important

As you read a paragraph, pretend you are the instructor who is creating the test. What questions would you ask about the information in that paragraph? For example, for "The Tide of Battle Begins to Turn" section of the "Transforming Fire" chapter, you could create these questions:

What were three major Civil War battles in 1863?
Why was the Battle of Chancellorsville both good and bad for the Confederacy?
Why was Vicksburg important to the Confederacy?
What was Pickett's Charge?
How did the Battle of Gettysburg change the Confederate Army?

Of course, you'll be able to create questions more effectively after you actually take one of your instructor's tests. But even before the test, most instructors will go over the types of questions you can expect. They sometimes even tell you how to focus your studies. This information will help you devise good study questions for yourself.

After you create your study questions, set them aside for a few days. Then try to answer them to see what you recall and what you still need to learn. You could also partner with a classmate, create questions for each other, and then exchange them to check your understanding.

EXERCISE 4

In the space below, create at least five study questions for the "Emancipation Proclamations" section of the "Transforming Fire" chapter.

Tips and Techniques

Language and Learning

When you need to learn something new, use the power of language to do it. Language is an amazing tool for helping us understand what we know and for revealing what we don't know. Has anyone ever asked you to talk about a topic you'd thought about but never discussed before? As you searched for and said the words that expressed your thoughts or beliefs about that topic, you probably found that those thoughts and beliefs became clearer to you, too. As long as they stay only in our minds, ideas and opinions have a tendency to remain fuzzy, shadowy, and half-formed. When we communicate them to others—either orally or in writing—they assume more definite shape and form.

Therefore, when you read and study information in a textbook, you may not know for sure that you've grasped that information until you can talk about it or write about it.

Talking to Learn. Take advantage of opportunities to talk about what you're learning. Engage in the classroom discussions led by your instructor, and try to answer the questions he or she poses to the class. Form study groups with your classmates, and meet regularly to discuss the course material. Note the topics you aren't able to say much about, and spend more time reviewing those topics. You might even talk with friends and family about what you're learning. For example, if someone you know finds history interesting, talk to him or her about your Civil War studies.

EXERCISE 5

Form a study group with a few of your current classmates and talk about what you learned by reading the "Transforming Fire" chapter.

Writing to Learn.   Writing, too, requires you to find the language that helps solidify your knowledge about a subject. This writing does not have to be in the form of an assignment—such as an essay or a research paper—you submit for a grade. Informal types of writing can also be valuable learning tools. After reading a textbook section or chapter, put your book aside and try to write a summary of the information. Then reread that section to check for and fill-in any gaps in your knowledge.

Freewriting is another good way to explore and reinforce your understanding. For a set period of time, say 10 or 15 minutes, write as fast as you can about what you read, without stopping or pausing to correct or to censor anything. Don't worry about organization or grammar or spelling. Just concentrate on the topic itself and write down everything you can remember. This technique will reveal what you know and what you still need to learn.

EXERCISE 6

In the space below (or on a separate sheet of paper), freewrite for 10 minutes about the "Transforming Fire" chapter.

EXERCISE 7

What did this freewriting exercise reveal to you about what you learned? If you were going to be tested on the information in this chapter, what topics would you need to study more?

Answer Key

Part 1: Matter and Energy.
Answers to Exercise 3.

Chapter 3

5. (a) 2 (b) 5 (c) 3 (d) 4 (e) 1   **7.** (a) Physical (b) Chemical (c) Chemical (d) Physical (e) Chemical (f) Chemical
11. (a) Metal (b) Metalloid (c) Nonmetal (d) Metal (e) Metalloid (f) Metal (g) Metal   **13.** Co is the element cobalt, and CO is the compound carbon monoxide.   **15.** The percent H and O are the same for each experiment.   **17.** (a) 12 carbon atoms, 22 hydrogen atoms, 11 oxygen atoms (b) 2 potassium atoms, 1 chromium atom, 4 oxygen atoms (c) 8 hydrogen atoms, 2 nitrogen atoms, 3 oxygen atoms, 2 sulfur atoms (d) 1 zinc atom, 2 nitrogen atoms, 6 oxygen atoms   **21.** The atomic mass of sulfur would be 2 amu.   **23.** (a) 85.5 (b) 52.0 (c) 238.0 (d) 79.0 (e) 74.9
25. (a) 71.8 (b) 159.6 (c) 317.3 (d) 164.0 (e) 58.3 (f) 218.5 (g) 791.8 (h) 96.0   **27.** (a) 60.1 (b) 82.1 (c) 121.6 (d) 104.5 (e) 187.5 (f) 218.7 (g) 149.0 (h) 60.0   **35.** (a) Magnesium and chlorine (b) Nitrogen and oxygen (c) Nitrogen, hydrogen, sulfur, and oxygen (d) Hydrogen, phosphorus, and oxygen   **37.** (a) Element (b) Mixture (c) Compound (d) Mixture (e) Compound   **39.** (a) 254.2 (b) 63.0 (c) 89.8 (d) 601.9

Answers to Study Guide Questions for Part 4: "The Enlightenment in the United States" Chapter of *The Humanities*, Volume Two

1. True   **2.** emotion; people with little education   **3.** d   **4.** The unique American climate provided fertile ground for the development of the federal system. The early colonists' pioneer culture encouraged hard work and a flexible social structure, and the Great Awakening, a spiritual movement, also contributed to the republican environment. Founding fathers such as Thomas Jefferson and Benjamin Franklin, who both served as European diplomats, absorbed French and English philosophers' ideas about natural rights, freedom, and government and expressed these ideas on behalf of all Americans in the Declaration of Independence, which formally established the foundation of the rebellion. American leaders were also influenced by the republican ideals of ancient Rome. In their struggle to win independence from England, American patriots identified with Roman heroes and their causes, and they also adopted Roman words, symbols, and customs as they created the new federal system.   **5.** Palladian Villa Rotunda; portico and dome   **6.** Democratic principles: a. All men are created equal. b. All men are endowed with the unalienable rights of life, liberty, and the pursuit of happiness. c. Governments derive their powers from the governed. d. The governed can abolish an ineffective or destructive government and create a new one that better protects their safety and happiness. American grievances: King George's government was depriving people of their natural rights and failing to protect them or effect their happiness.   **7.** Classrooms, the library, and housing for both students and professors were arranged in a rectangular quadrangle that physically enclosed the academic community. The architecture of these buildings resembled ancient and Renaissance structures in order to reinforce classical ideals of learning and self-improvement. Gardens outside the main quadrangle encouraged scholars to pursue private reflection and study. To reinforce the ideal of free thought, the campus does not include a church or chapel.   **8.** True   **9.** *The activity of the spirit of God:* God actively inspires individuals to desire and to seek salvation, and His spirit is infectious. *Concern about the effect of evangelical preaching:* Edwards feared that people who were not affected by God's spirit would speak out against religion, pursue a hedonistic lifestyle, and/or become bitter or angry. *Spiritual awakening:* God inspires joy, love, and a desire to worship. People awakened to their own salvation are eager to attend church, to pray, and to discuss religious matters. *Spiritual matters versus worldly affairs:* People infused with God's spirit have a tendency to neglect their worldly affairs because they want only to worship, read the Bible, pray, and discuss religious matters. These people view worldly affairs as a duty rather than a pleasure. *Criticisms of the revival movement:* Skeptics compared the religious conversions to *distemper,* or disease. *Validity of these criticisms:* Edwards claims that many skeptics who visited towns filled with God's spirit were themselves affected and converted. He implies, therefore, that their criticisms were invalid. *Conversions:* Conversion awakened individuals to their salvation and inspired the emotions of love, joy, sorrow, distress, and concern for others.   **10.** They wanted to impose their own beliefs on others and interfere with freedom of thought and choice.   **11.** Give money to support a particular pastor.
12. False   **13.** a   **14.** Jefferson's beliefs led him to establish the Virginia Statute of Religious Liberty and omit a church or chapel from his design for the University of Virginia. Preferring rational thought and scholarship, he probably did not regularly attend worship services.

The Big Picture
Page 91 of Study Guide

Answers to these three questions will vary.

Answers to Questions Within "The Enlightenment in the United States" Chapter

Pages 265–266

1. An important cultural force in the American colonies, Christianity laid the foundation for rebellion by encouraging individual choice, voluntary church membership, and the decentralization of churches.   **2.** Enlightenment values included the acknowledgment of universal natural laws, emphasis on human rights, and belief in the power of human intellect to determine what is good and true.   **3.** No, it did not. The Declaration of Independence did not abolish slavery, so African Americans remained deprived of their liberty. The "pursuit of happiness" probably means the freedom to do the things you want to do; however, the Declaration cannot guarantee that a person will possess the talent or enjoy the circumstances required to achieve his or her goals. The phrase "all men are created equal" means that all possess natural rights; it does not mean that all people possess equal talents or abilities.
4. N/A   **5.** Answers will vary.

Page 267

1. Both Montesquieu and Jefferson believed in natural rights and in slavery's contradiction of that ideal. However, Jefferson could not apply these principles. He wanted to abolish slavery with the Declaration of Independence, but his proposal was rejected by other leaders, and Jefferson himself did not free his own slaves until his death.   **2.** No. He was not solely responsible.   **3.** Americans who benefited from the slave trade (including Jefferson himself) perpetuated it. Also, Jefferson ignores the fact that slavery existed before George III ruled England.

Answers to Questions Following "A Faithful Narrative of the Surprising Work of God"

Page 272

1. People cannot do anything to insure their salvation; instead, they must be saved through divine blessing.   **2.** Edwards explained the Great Awakening as God's spirit is contagious; people who interacted with the converted were themselves often awakened to God's presence.

Answers to Questions Following "The Virginia Statute of Religious Liberty"

Page 273

1. Jefferson's basis to establish religious tolerance was as follows: God created the human mind free to choose; therefore, coercion is impious.   **2.** Jefferson criticizes ecclesiastical leaders who presume to assert "dominion over the faith of others" and try to force people to pay money to pastors and churches.
3. *Truth* is an opinion or belief that can be defended as error-free through argument and debate.   **4.** Yes. Enlightenment Americans were optimistic about the potential of the human mind to discover the truth.   **5.** In his statute, Jefferson focuses on the right to hold individual religious opinions, the right to choose whether or not to worship or to support a religious institution, and the right to enjoy freedom from persecution or limitations, regardless of religious beliefs.

Photo Credits

Part 1

Page 15: Uranium single atoms and microcrystals. Credit: Courtesy of Albert V. Crewe.

Page 20: A mass spectrometer. Credit: Ed Degginger.

Part 2

Page 34: The Lear team. Credit: © 2000 Eric Haase.

Page 37: Peruvian jungle. Credit: Franz Lanting/Aurora and Quanta Productions.

Page 40: UCONN vs. Michigan State Warriors basketball game. Credit: *Sports Illustrated*.

Page 44: Earthquake victims. Credit: Israeli Army/SIPA PRESS.

Page 52: Italian tailors at work. Credit: Stefano Hunyady.

Page 53: IBM worker. Credit: Will McIntyre.

Part 3

Page 70: Drawing on memories. Credit: Paul Avis/LIAISON AGENCY.

Page 72: Learning by doing. Credit: Bob Daemmrich/STOCK BOSTON.

Page 73: Making implicit memories. Credit: J. Greenberg/THE IMAGE WORKS.

Page 75: Cartoon: How Not to Remember Names. Credit: © The New Yorker Collection 1994 Roz Chast, from cartoonbank.com. All Rights Reserved.

Page 80: Chunking in action, UN meeting. Credit: Reuters/Jon Levy/ARCHIVE PHOTOS.

Page 82: A photographic memory, drawing of Italian town. Credits: Franco Magnani (left), and Susan Schwartzenberg/THE EXPLORATORIUM (right).

Page 83: Context-dependent memories. Credit: Bob Daemmrich/THE IMAGE WORKS.

Page 86: A constructed memory. Credit: William F. Brewer, from *Cognitive Psychology*, 1981, 13, page 211. Published by Academic Press.

Page 86: Basketball players. Credit: ALLSPORT.

Page 89: Exploring memory processes. Credit: Paul Conklin.

Page 91: Cartoon. Credit: © The New Yorker Collection 1996 Arnie Levin, from cartoonbank.com. All Rights Reserved.

Page 91: Durable memories. Credit: David Strickler/THE IMAGE WORKS.

Page 98: A case of retrograde amnesia. Credit: Yves Forestier/CORBIS-SYGMA.

Page 100: Understand and remember. Credit: Robert Burke/LIAISON AGENCY.

Part 4

Page 116: Great seal of the U.S. Credit: Bureau of Engraving and Printing, U.S. Department of the Treasury.

Page 116: George Washington. Credit: Virginia State Library and Archives.

Page 117: Monticello. Credit: Thomas Jefferson Foundation, Inc.

Page 118: University of Virginia campus. Credit: University of Virginia Library.

Page 119: The Virginia State Capitol, Richmond. Credit: Virginia State Library and Archives.

Page 120: Massachusetts State House. Credit: Courtesy of the Trustees of the Public Library of the City of Boston.

Page 120: University of Virginia Pavilion. Credit: University of Virginia Library.

Page 120: University of Virginia Rotunda. Credit: University of Virginia Library.

Part 5

Page 136: Painting "Home Sweet Home," by Winslow Homer. Credit: Private
         collection, photograph courtesy of Hirschl and Adler Galleries, New York.
Page 141: "Departure of the Seventh Regiment." Credit: Museum of Fine Arts, Boston/
         M. and M. Karolik Collection.
Page 143: Irish regiment at worship. Credit: Library of Congress.
Page 146: Battle of Antietam (left). Credit: Library of Congress. Camera (right). Credit:
         Library of Congress.
Page 148: Confederate soldier with wife and brother. Credit: Collection of Larry
         Williford.
Page 150: Hudson Street. Credit: New-York Historical Society.
Page 158: Private Robert Sherry. Credit: Clements Library, University of Michigan,
         Ann Arbor.
Page 160: Black soldiers. Credit: National Archives.
Page 163: Soldier, his children, newspaper article. Credit: The C. Craig Caba Gettysburg
         Collection, from *Gettysburg*, Larry Sherer, © 1991 Time-Life Books, Inc.
Page 164: Music sheet. Credit: Chicago Historical Society.
Page 167: Lynching scene. Credit: Chicago Historical Society.
Page 169: Grant and Lee. Credit: National Archives.
Page 171: Ruins of Richmond. Credit: National Archives.
Page 172: Lincoln's funeral. Credit: Anne S.K. Brown Military Collection, John Hay
         Library, Brown University.